The Single-Neuron Theory

Steven Sevush

The Single-Neuron Theory

Closing in on the Neural Correlate of Consciousness

palgrave
macmillan

Steven Sevush
School of Medicine
University of Miami
Miami, Florida, USA

ISBN 978-3-319-33707-4 ISBN 978-3-319-33708-1 (eBook)
DOI 10.1007/978-3-319-33708-1

Library of Congress Control Number: 2016947045

Printed on acid-free paper

This Palgrave Macmillan imprint is published by Springer Nature
The registered company is Springer International Publishing AG Switzerland

Foreword

The question posed by this book is very simple yet very perplexing. When we look at a red rose, where exactly in our head are the mental events that give rise to that sense of redness? And if there were any doubt that this sensed redness is concocted inside the head, rather than outside, think of that viral smartphone snap of the blue and black—or was it white and gold?—dress. The colours we sense may track reflectance or transmission properties of patches of the outside world quite well, most of the time. But if the tracking can fail we know we must be getting an internal mock-up, not 'the outside world itself'. As Newton understood well, colours are 'phantasms' manufactured inside by brains and we want to know where. We want to know the neural correlates of consciousness.

It is sometimes suggested that thoughts and sensations have no particular position in space. What seems more likely, however, is that this is just a false inference based on the fact that we have no machinery for tracking where ideas are inside us in the way we do have for things we can see or pick up, like red roses. (We do seem to have internal time tracking.) In the same way, a police speed-trap camera can happily report to us the plate number of the car going past but cannot report where its hard drive is in relation to its light sensor because it has no device to sense that. That is no reason to think that the signals that indicate the plate number A675 RFT is passing by are in no particular place inside, even if, for other reasons, we may suspect that there is no sense of redness inside when it is a fire engine passing.

There are even those who claim that the redness is neither in the rose nor in our heads but in our 'active' interaction with the world. Suffice it to say that such theories have problems explaining quite what active interaction with the world is involved in hearing the doorbell ring unexpectedly, or dreams and afterimages, or why certain drugs in overdose make the world blue or yellow. Moreover, without specifying that any particular internal event is necessary for a particular sensation, they are almost certainly untestable and therefore outside science.

The redness must be in the brain, and to understand how it comes about we want to know where.

Strangely, although a lot has been written on this subject in the last 20 years, very few authors have grasped the nettle of how to produce a solution that makes physical sense. At least a proportion of people picking up this book will, like myself, already have a bookcase devoted to the topic of consciousness, sporting names like Crick, Penrose, Damasio, James, Edelman and Dennett. Whether you do or do not, it does not matter, because this book is different in one crucial respect. It asks the question 'how could that actually work?' And this goes beyond narrowly defined physics—it is the question we ask as children when faced with a conjuring trick. We have a basic sense of things having to join up. Strangely, apart from Steven Sevush, most neuroscientists in the field seem to have lost sight of that.

The recent resurgence of interest in studying how the 'mind' works owes a lot to a rather unlikely duo of champions, Stuart Hameroff and David Chalmers. Hameroff has pursued a detailed biophysical investigation into the fundamental physical events in brains that might constitute consciousness. Chalmers asked the question 'but why would that be conscious?' Another prominent figure, Christof Koch, has replied 'no idea, but don't worry, it will be obvious when we have the answer'. Sevush's approach seems to me to be much more powerful. Given the known structure of the brain and the fact that we can admire a red rose, he asks what sort of story could link the two that would actually work in terms of our basic understanding of cause and effect.

I should declare an interest here. Over much the same period as Sevush, I have, independently, come to a very similar conclusion about how the brain gives rise to experience. We have encountered the same issues and resolved them the same way. My approach, however, has focused on the more abstract questions about causality. Sevush can reasonably regard many of my arguments as 'filawsofy', as Richard Feynman called it. He is interested, as a neurobiologist, in how the link from brain cells to redness could work in practice. Moreover, he insists on seeing how it could work at all levels of structure and function. Very often, theorists of consciousness will work at one level or other—focusing on molecular physics or nerve networks or computational issues. Sevush wants a story that will make sense in practical terms all the way down from cortical lobes to fundamental physics. He may not have defined every step in full detail but he analyses each level closely enough to establish if it could actually work.

Sevush's approach has a long and venerable history, dating at least back to Hippocrates. It is amusing to reflect that the supposedly great and venerable Aristotle made a pig's ear of it in comparison, suggesting that the brain cooled the blood. William James perhaps most famously in modern times attacked the problem and concluded that there was simply no possible answer consistent with physics. He bottled out. That is not good enough for Sevush. There has to be an answer, even if common sense at first seems to suggest it is impossible.

From what I have said it might seem that this book has a rather dry agenda: more engine stripping than poetry. I hope not to give that impression. Sevush is motivated by the rose as much as any of us: the marvel of experience. It is just that he wants to know how the marvel works. After all, the rose itself, in all its splendour, grows effortlessly out of the possibilities laid down by the laws of nature we now understand quite well. Surely the redness should be the same sort of marvel? Leibniz had the idea that perfection was the generation of maximum richness from the simplest of reasons. The simpler the reasons, the more marvellous the result. It is very fashionable these days to think that mysterious things like experience 'emerge' from complexity. But all too often that seems to be a smoke screen for ignorance. Sevush would ask: 'but how could that work?'

The explanation for the redness of the rose given in this book will, I am pretty sure, prove puzzling and maybe inconceivable to many readers. As I have written in the past, it is the most difficult idea I have ever come across. It is difficult because it challenges our conception of our selves much in the way that Wallace and Darwin challenged the uniqueness of the human animal. If you might have thought the idea of having a monkey as an ancestor was an affront then you may be in for a tough time here. It is not so much that others have not produced similarly belittling theories. Daniel Dennett almost denies your very existence as a human subject or 'mind'. What is different here is that Sevush accepts that there are real human subjects, but places them, one each, inside a vast number of cells in a particular part of the brain. There is no single 'me', even if it seems that way. Again, this idea is not in itself new. Elizabeth Anscombe suggested long ago that each human being might contain multiple experiencing subjects. The difference is that Sevush gives reasons why this is the only reasonable interpretation of neurobiology and thereby confronts us with a practical possibility rather than a rhetorical philosophical question.

To build a theory of experience with this degree of depth and breadth in neurobiological terms is a pretty impressive achievement. The story is well worth reading.

London
15.3.2016

Jonathan C.W. Edwards

Introduction

One Friday in December

Every book has a story behind the story. The tale for this book begins on a Friday in December, three weeks before the millennium. It had been many years since I first embarked on my quest to understand consciousness and I was beginning to face up to the sad truth that my effort had grown cold, with little chance of rekindling. Then, a colleague at the University of Miami invited me to attend an informal discussion on consciousness that was to take place that afternoon in the philosophy department on the main campus. I usually avoided making the several mile trip to the main campus but I decided in this case to make an exception. Good decision. Not because of the discussion that took place at the meeting but for what happened after the meeting broke up.

The discussion focused on philosopher Charles Siewart's new book—an abstract philosophical work defending the position that consciousness is a significant construct, not just an epiphenomenon. In attendance were four or five philosophers, two neuroscientists, and me, a behavioral neurologist. I was both impressed and distressed by the interchange. I was impressed by Siewart's mental acumen—he was just flat-out smart. I was distressed by everyone's familiarity with terms and ideas that were unknown to me. Clearly, I had been out of the loop for a long time.

After the session ended, I meandered over to Charles Siewart's corner and initiated a conversation. Siewart was thoughtful and showed a genuine interest in my ideas but he laid bare their rough form with an incisive interrogation that rendered me uncharacteristically aphasic. I left the meeting unsettled and somewhat discouraged. Fortunately, my competitive nature caused me to rebound and for the next two weeks I immersed myself in a deep think and then a revelation occurred. It happened while I was jogging. I suddenly conceived of a way to get to the heart of the mind/brain relationship. My mind soared with a vivid "aha" experience. When the euphoria subsided, I looked around and could not recognize where I was. It took a few seconds for me to realize that, while deep in thought, I had jogged a half mile past the usual turn I make to get to my house.

I rushed home and pondered my new insight: that the secret to the mind/brain problem was to posit that all that existed were elementary sentient events, with each event being both a subject and an object, a subject with respect to past events and an object with respect to future events. Unfortunately for me, a little investigation revealed that approximately the same idea had already been proposed three hundred years ago by Leibniz, and that exactly the same idea had been explored by the philosopher Alfred North Whitehead in the first half of the twentieth century.

I then delved deeper into the literature and came upon what philosopher William Seager calls the "combination problem": if reality is composed of elementary sentient events, how do we account for the presence of macroscopic consciousness in systems composed of aggregates of these elementary events? It was nine months later, in September of 2000, when I came up with a presumptive answer to this question. Now, some 15 years later, I present this answer to you in the form of this book.

The Origin of a Theory

My interest in consciousness had developed when I was a teenager but my serious pursuit of the subject began in the winter of 1971–1972 while I was a first-year graduate student in physics at UC Berkeley in California.

I was holding my own in the program but it had become apparent that I was unlikely to achieve anything of importance in a field so infested with mathematical mutants. I decided on a change in course. My perspective, then as now, was that there were two fundamental enigmas that plagued science. One was explaining the origin and nature of the universe. The other was the mind/brain problem. I decided to leave the former to the mutants and to pursue the latter.

I figured that going to medical school was the right first move. I reasoned that studying human minds and human brains would give me the strongest background for pursuing the problem of sentience. After medical school I did a neurology residency and a few years later added a residency in psychiatry. During my neurology training I was exposed to the writings of Norman Geschwind, which introduced me to the constructs of multifocality and directed information flow that I discuss in Chap. 2. In due course I came to believe that conscious perception happens only when stimulus information reaches the frontal lobes, a notion that would later be championed by Francis Crick. I address this idea in Chap. 7.

In 1980 I went to Gainesville to do a fellowship with Geschwind's brilliant student Ken Heilman. There I chanced upon the notion that there are two different centers of conscious experience in the human brain, one in the left hemisphere and one in the right. Only afterwards did I learn that the philosopher Rolando Puccetti had already written about this in the 1970s and that the idea had in fact originally been proposed by Wigan in a book he published in 1825. I address this idea in Chap. 6.

For the next 20 years I worked intermittently on the mind/brain problem but made little progress. I gradually became disillusioned and turned my attention to practical research in Alzheimer's disease. By the end of 1999, I had all but given up any hope of making any significant contribution to consciousness research and had resigned myself to life as a prosaic clinical neuroscientist.

Then came the Friday meeting with the philosophers and the insights that led me to hypothesize what I have called the single-neuron theory. The crux of the theory came to me one evening in September 2000, when I was sitting on a couch in my living room re-reading Moshe Abeles' *Corticonics*. I was browsing his first chapter on the anatomy of the cerebral cortex (a subject that I felt I knew pretty well) when I came across his estimate that "in the human each cortical neuron generates about 40,000 synapses."

I was startled. There was obviously an embarrassing lacune in my anatomical fund of knowledge. I knew, of course, that dendritic trees were complex but I had unconsciously formed an intuition, based on the many simplified line drawings I had glanced at over the years, that neurons typically had hundreds of synaptic inputs, not tens of thousands. The larger number changed everything. Perhaps single neurons embodied a complexity sufficient to account individually for the complexity of conscious experience. And if individual neurons could account for the complexity of conscious experience, perhaps still smaller components within the neurons could account for this complexity equally well and, voilá, a connection between elementary sentient events and macroscopic behavior might be forged.

I envisioned a setup where conscious experience was a property of individual neurons whose outputs were coordinated by natural selection to give the appearance of a single macroscopic mind, when in actuality the conscious experiences remained separate and did not combine. Of course, there were issues to be worked out. Do dendritic trees offer a sufficient complexity to account for that of conscious experience? Do they receive the right kind of inputs? And how can single-neuron processing be integrated meaningfully into the enormous complexity of neuronal network activity? These and other questions would need to be addressed if the theory was to be worthwhile.

But the basic idea seemed straightforward. Consider the following analogy. A race of aliens on a scientific expedition aimed at seeking out sentient life in the universe has entered our solar system and has taken up orbit around the Earth. They turn their telescopes toward the planet and discover what appear to be living organisms scattered across the planetary land masses. They focus on one of the organisms, which they learn is named "New York City." They notice that the organism adheres to a circadian rhythm with tiny objects (that we call cars) moving into the city in the morning and out from the city in the evening. They hypothesize that these movements constitute some form of respiration. They notice further that the organism lights up at night and they speculate that this may be indicative of some sort of dream sleep. In all, they judge by the complexity of its behavior that this "New York City" organism is a sentient entity.

But then a rogue scientist aboard ship proposes that sentience is not associated with the organism as a whole but with little particles (that we call people) that he has observed to be populating the organism. And thus is born the "Single-Person Theory of Consciousness." What appears to be a single large focus of conscious experience is actually an aggregate of tiny, individually sentient people whose conscious experiences do not combine. The impression that the organism is sentient as a whole is an illusion created by the organized behavior of the constituent people. By analogy, the single-neuron theory of consciousness stipulates that individual neurons are sentient and the notion that the brain as a whole is sentient is an illusion created by the organized behavior of the constituent neurons.

Resistance

When I came upon the single-neuron concept, I thought simply, "Oh, that would work." No "aha," no jubilation. I searched the literature expecting to find many others who had arrived at the same conception but came up with nothing. I had apparently stumbled upon a notion that had been overlooked by others in the field (including the mutants I had left behind 30 years earlier in Berkeley).

I have spent the last 15 years developing the single-neuron concept into a coherent theory and working to get it a hearing. I thought initially that the idea would catch on readily. No such luck. To my dismay, many of my colleagues dismissed the theory out of hand, without making the effort to understand it. Fortunately, in 2004 I met up with Jonathan Edwards, a physician and philosopher at the University of London who had amazingly come up with the same single-neuron hypothesis. He came to visit me in Miami and we exchanged notes. Our ideas were quite similar and we both took delight in finding a soul mate with the same insight into the nature of conscious experience. We each published our work and anxiously awaited the response by the field. It was underwhelming by any measure.

And so I turned my attention to writing the book you are now reading. I have met with considerable resistance in getting the book published. The experience has been similar to that which I encountered in getting my journal article published a decade ago: a mix of reviewers who either love the theory or despise it. It took rejections by four journals before I was able to get the article published in the *Journal of Theoretical Biology*.

The effort, of course, must continue. It is not enough to come up with a novel idea. One must also persuade one's colleagues of its merit. As Charles Darwin's son, Sir Francis Darwin (1848–1925), wrote: "In science the credit goes to the man who convinces the world, not the man to whom the idea first occurs." Jo Edwards and I remain optimistic that the theory will soon catch on. Of course, we are aware that it may fall under Max Planck's dictum instead: "Truth never triumphs—its opponents just die out."

Which outcome applies is, dear reader, in your hands.

Acknowledgments

I wish to give thanks to my daughter, Jenn, and to my brother, Herb, for reviewing the manuscript and offering outstanding suggestions; to my brother Ralph for his help with both creative and contract matters; and to my son, Jeremy, for his often wry but always helpful comments. Thanks also to Jo Edwards for his help in developing some of the ideas in this book and for his moral support; to Cherelle Carrington for inspiration and keeping me on track; to Rick Mallia for his role as trusty amanuensis; to Nancy Tedone, Gloria Peruyera, and the University of Miami medical students for stimulating discussions that aided in the development of the theory; to Eleanor Christie and Sharla Plant at Palgrave MacMillan for their help in bringing the book to print.

Contents

1 The Mind/Brain Problem 1

2 Principles of Cortical Function 19

3 Perception 49

4 Memory 83

5 Feelings 109

6 The Split-Brain Paradigm 123

7 Frontal Convergence 151

8 Neuronal Networks 169

9 The Single Neuron 197

10 The Single-Neuron Theory 217

11 Quantum Consciousness 231

12 Reflections and Ramifications 251

Bibliography 261

Index 285

List of Figures

Fig. 1.1	Fechner's curve	14
Fig. 1.2	Alternative NCC models. (a) Macroscopic emergence model. (b) Microscopic single-neuron model	17
Fig. 2.1	Components of the central nervous system	20
Fig. 2.2	Alternative arrangements for cortical connectivity	32
Fig. 2.3	Wernicke's information processing model	35
Fig. 2.4	Progression of cortical maturation as proposed by Flechsig	36
Fig. 2.5	Behavioral conditioning models	40
Fig. 2.6	Directionality of cortical connectivity as proposed by Rockland and Pandya	42
Fig. 2.7	The directed modular pathway design	43
Fig. 2.8	Injection of spontaneous frontal activity renders cortical information flow best modeled by a Skinnerian design	47
Fig. 3.1	The perception pathway	50
Fig. 3.2	Early visual processing pathways. Abbreviations: LGN, lateral geniculate nucleus	51
Fig. 3.3	Dual stream arrangement of visual processing. Abbreviations: F, frontal; O, occipital; P, parietal; T, temporal	53
Fig. 3.4	Dual route model of reading. Abbreviation: VWFA, visual word-form area	54
Fig. 3.5	The ventral stream for visual processing	56

Fig. 3.6 Hierarchical visual processing as proposed by Hubel and Wiesel. Output from neurons in the lateral geniculate nucleus (left) that are activated by adjacent points in the visual field project onto a neuron in V1 (right) whose receptive field consists of an oriented line 59

Fig. 3.7 Modular pathway for form perception. Abbreviation: MTL, medial temporal lobe 63

Fig. 3.8 Modular pathway for color perception. Abbreviation: LGN, lateral geniculate nucleus 73

Fig. 3.9 Kanizsa triangle illusion 80

Fig. 3.10 Demonstration of the blind spot. If you cover your right eye and look at the middle of the row of numbers with your left eye with the page held about 10 inches away, the "X" on the left disappears! 80

Fig. 4.1 Anatomy of working memory 88

Fig. 4.2 Working memory, which is composed of posterior slave modules interacting with a frontal central executive, is incorporated within the perceptual pathway 89

Fig. 4.3 The MTL loop is grafted onto the perception pathway as a directed modular loop that receives information from the working memory slave modules, processes the information in feedforward modular fashion, and returns the processed signals back to the working memory slave modules. Abbreviation: MTL, medial temporal lobe 91

Fig. 4.4 Mirror-reflected words 108

Fig. 5.1 The modular pathway for interoception runs from sensory input through the brainstem and thalamus, then through three hierarchical stages within the insula, and then on to the orbitofrontal cortex and other portions of the frontal lobes 113

Fig. 6.1a Response of a split-brain patient to a pencil seen in the right visual field: says "pencil" while pointing to the pencil with the right hand 129

Fig. 6.1b Response of a split-brain patient to a key seen in the left visual field: says "nothing" while pointing to the key with the left hand 130

Fig. 6.1c Response of a split-brain patient to the simultaneous presentation of a key in the left visual field and a pencil in the right visual field: says "pencil" but points to the key with the left hand 131

Fig. 6.2	Brain mechanisms underlying the split-brain effect	132
Fig. 7.1	For any continuously distributed NCC, a corresponding focal NCC is also possible, whether the information flow is unidirectional, as in (a), or omnidirectional, as in (b)	152
Fig. 7.2	Frontal lobe subdivisions. Abbreviations: ACC, anterior cingulate cortex; DL, dorsolateral; DM, dorsomedial; M, motor; OFC, orbitofrontal cortex; PM, premotor; PO, polar; VL, ventrolateral	154
Fig. 7.3	A directed modular pathway model of perception, memory, and feelings is shown. The NCC is assumed to be localized within the VL-PFC, which receives perceptual input from the ventral stream (both directly and via the amygdala, OFC and ACC), and input leading to feelings from the insula (via the OFC and ACC). Short-term memory is mediated by the same pathways as those that mediate perception, while long-term memory is mediated by an auxiliary loop passing through the MTL. Abbreviations: ACC, anterior cingulate cortex; MTL, medial temporal lobe; OFC, orbitofrontal cortex; VL-PFC, ventrolateral prefrontal cortex	157
Fig. 8.1	The neuron	172
Fig. 8.2	Point neuron model	172
Fig. 8.3	A simple feedforward PDP neuronal network. Abbreviation: PDP, parallel distributed processing	173
Fig. 8.4	Hebb's postulate	177
Fig. 8.5	The retinal/tectum structural topographic mapping	187
Fig. 8.6	Retinal/cortical structural topographic map is described by a complex logarithmic function	190
Fig. 8.7	Feedforward progression through the cortical layers	194
Fig. 9.1	Cajal's law of dynamic polarization: information processing runs from dendrites to axon in feedforward fashion	200
Fig. 9.2	The Hodgkin-Huxley model starts with the establishment and maintenance of an intra-axonal resting potential	206
Fig. 9.3	Voltage-gated ion channels	207
Fig. 9.4	Action potential propagation	208
Fig. 9.5	Pyramidal neuron	211
Fig. 9.6	Generation of the BAP and non-propagating Ca^{++} action potentials. Abbreviations: BAP, back-propagating action potential	212

Fig. 10.1 Information content for a vr-conscious experience is expressed in the spatial activation patterns at the neuronal network level and again at dendritic synaptic level 219
Fig. 10.2 Holographic projection from network to dendrite levels: the entire vr-conscious content is received by each of a pool of recipient dendrites in reduplicative fashion 220
Fig. 10.3 Information encoded in the spatial patterns formed by synchronously activated cortical neurons at the L2/3 network level maps onto spatial synaptic activation patterns on distal dendritic branches of individual L5 pyramidal neurons, and these then map back up to the L5 neuronal network level 223
Fig. 11.1 Whitehead's subject/object framework 235
Fig. 11.2 Whitehead/Heisenberg framework 241
Fig. 11.3 High energy transverse vibratory modes and low energy longitudinal vibratory modes in the dendritic bilipid membrane 244

1

The Mind/Brain Problem

Where Is the Red?

For all its successes, science at present falls short in one vital regard: it fails to account for our existence as conscious, experiencing subjects. This is not a trivial deficiency, since it is precisely through our conscious experience that we know anything at all. Yet, when looked at logically, there seems to be no place in a stark, material universe for the pleasures, pains, and sensations that so personally color our lives.

Imagine that you are walking in a garden and chance upon a red rose. You gaze at the rose and take in its rich redness. The critical question is, "Where in the world does this redness reside?" Let's briefly step through the physical processes involved. To begin with, does the redness reside in the rose itself? This is where naive intuition places it, but of course science says something else. The only reason we call a red rose "red" is that it reflects light within a certain wavelength band (roughly 625–740 nm) while absorbing light of all other wavelengths. It is the reflected light that signals the color of the rose. The rose itself is not red.

Does the redness reside in the reflected light, then? This, too, is an intuitive choice but one that cannot be correct. In fact, light of a given

S. Sevush, *The Single-Neuron Theory*,
DOI 10.1007/978-3-319-33708-1_1

wavelength cannot even be assigned a unique color. For example, while light with a wavelength of, say, 680 nm will usually be perceived as red by a human observer, that same observer may also perceive it as scarlet, crimson, pink, gray, or even black, depending on the makeup of the surrounding environment and other factors.

Furthermore, there are "non-spectral colors" that are formed only by combinations of wavelengths. Magenta, for example, cannot be signaled by any one wavelength of light. It takes a combination of "red" and "blue" wavelengths of light to give magenta. But the "red" and "blue" light waves do not combine out in space. The combining occurs only after the light has been received by a perceiving eye.

Does the color experience occur, then, when the light enters the eye and strikes the retina? Again, this cannot be. In the retina, while there are specialized photoreceptors for "red" and "green" light, there are no photoreceptors for "magenta" light. Nor is there a mechanism in the retina by which "red" and "blue" photoreceptors can merge their activity. Such merging happens only later, after the segregated signals have passed into the brain proper. We thus arrive at the conclusion reached by most modern purveyors of the subject: it is only when signals reach the brain that conscious perception happens, although it is a matter of considerable dispute as to which particular brain structures are doing the "seeing" and by what mechanism this is accomplished.

Whatever the structures and mechanisms might be, a problem will always remain. The structures and mechanisms will invariably offer only a *correlate* for the experience of red, not an explanation for the experience itself. Chemicals may churn and electricity may flow, but nowhere will the redness itself be found. If we accept that the brain is the site at which the conscious experience of red arises, we are led to the awkward conclusion that two different phenomena are associated with the redness of the rose: one, physical and objectively observable, consisting of brain processes that correspond to red; the other, mental and subjectively experienced, consisting of the conscious experience of red itself.

Now, to make it clear that all this is not just a matter of word play, consider the same exercise but with a computer rather than a brain reacting to the red rose. With current technology, a computer can easily be equipped to optically identify a red rose and produce appropriate verbal output, such as,

"I am now experiencing a red rose in my mind." If we were to examine the inner workings of such a computer at the moment it was focusing on the rose, we would find, as we do with brains, complex electrical and other physical events that correspond to the processing of the optical input. And, as with brains, we would fail to find redness itself anywhere in the chain of events. However, and herein lies the crucial difference, with a computer we wouldn't find ourselves asking where the red is. We would be satisfied that the electrical and other physical processing is all there is. In contrast to the situation with a brain, the computer would be considered "empty" inside, incapable of attaching experience to the processing.

It appears, then, that two types of arrangements are possible for matter and energy, one that is associated with conscious experience and another that is not. For computers, thermostats, and rocks, there is no conscious experience; the physical arrangement is all there is. But for brains, or at least for human brains, the physical description is incomplete. An additional ingredient, conscious experience, is somehow included in the mix, an ingredient that is, for all we can tell, unobservable through logical, objective means.

The Mind/Brain Problem

The difficulty in accounting for conscious experience in an ostensibly physical world is known as the *mind/brain* (or *mind/body*) *problem*. The crux of the problem is the duality entailed by the insertion of a subjective element into an otherwise objective universe. It is a peculiar duality, one that brings together odd bedfellows of vastly disparate natures. On the one hand, there are objectively observable physical objects such as brains. On the other, there are subjectively experienced mental impressions. The two domains are clearly linked but we can't say how or why. Accounting for this duality within a scientific framework presents a conundrum that, according to some, has no prospects for a resolution anytime soon. In 1879, the renowned Irish physicist John Tyndall (1820–1893) famously summarized the predicament:

> The passage from the physics of the brain to the corresponding facts of consciousness is unthinkable. Granted that a definite thought and a definite molecular action in the brain occur simultaneously; we do not possess the

intellectual organ, nor apparently any rudiment of the organ, which would enable us to pass, by a process of reasoning, from one to the other.[1]

More than a century later, Tyndall's assessment was echoed by the philosopher Colin McGinn:

> How is it possible for conscious states to depend upon brain states? How can technicolour phenomenology arise from soggy grey matter? ...We have been trying for a long time to solve the mind-body problem. It has stubbornly resisted our best efforts. The mystery persists. I think the time has come to admit candidly that we cannot resolve the mystery.[2]

Particularly vexing is the subjective, experiential side of the duality. In the 1990s the Australian philosopher David Chalmers underscored this point when he coined the phrase, the "hard problem" of consciousness, in reference to subjective experience. According to Chalmers, the "easy" problems of consciousness are those pertaining to brain functions such as focusing attention, integrating and discriminating sensory stimuli, controlling behavior, and executing higher cognitive processes. These, he argues, offer their own challenges but there is every expectation that they will eventually succumb to the usual investigative methods used by science. In contrast, the "hard problem" of consciousness is the problem of explaining subjective experience. It is a problem that, according to Chalmers, challenges the reach of routine scientific inquiry.

Additionally enigmatic is the fact that every subjective experience is tied to its own particular point of view. This peculiarity formed the theme of philosopher Thomas Nagel's classic essay entitled, "What is it like to be a Bat?"[3] Imagine that you woke up one Kafkaesque morning and found that you were a bat. How would you experience the world? Bats, unlike humans, use sonar and echolocation to navigate through a darkened environment. That is, they use sound and their auditory brain areas, rather than vision and their visual brain areas, to construct three-dimensional images of their unlit surroundings. If you were a bat, how

---

[1] Tyndall 1871.

[2] McGinn 1989.

[3] Nagel 1974.

would the inside of a darkened cave look to you? Would it appear as a visual image, just as it does for humans? If so, then you would be using your auditory brain components to construct visual images, something that humans cannot generally do. Or would the world appear as some sort of acoustic image peculiar to bats? Because of the subjective nature of conscious experience, there is no way to tell. Even if the bat were caught in the very act of echolocating and its brain immediately examined, all attempts to know what it was experiencing would fail.

The point is, if you want to know what a bat experiences, you cannot do so merely by observing the bat's brain. You can only know what it is like to be a bat by actually being a bat and experiencing the world from the bat's point of view. For Nagel, the presence of a point of view is the defining aspect of conscious experience. For a given arrangement of matter and energy to be regarded as a consciously experiencing subject, there must be "something it is like to be" that physical arrangement.

Because of its tie to a particular point of view, conscious experience is deeply private. Its contents cannot be conveyed from its owner to others, a property referred to as *ineffability*. The Australian philosopher Frank Jackson illustrated the ineffability of conscious experience with his famous thought experiment involving Mary, a hypothetical expert in the neurobiology of color vision. Through her studies Mary has learned everything there is to know about the physical nature of light, about how the brain identifies and discriminates different wavelengths of light, and about how the brain produces verbal reports pertaining to these wavelengths of light. Unfortunately, Mary is herself completely colorblind. Since birth, all she has experienced has been white, black, and shades of gray and, as a result, she lacks the knowledge of what it is like to experience color. Due to the ineffability of subjective experience, Mary will forever remain with this deficiency. No amount of interaction with her color-seeing friends will be able to change this fact.

The ineffability of conscious experience also blocks any attempt to compare one's conscious experiences to that of others. Suppose two people are observing the same red rose. Do they experience the rose in the same way? Because of the ineffability of conscious experience, it is impossible for them to tell. They may both call the rose "red," and they may make the same mental associations with the rose's color and have the same emotional reactions to it, but whether or not they have the same conscious experience of the rose is beyond their ken. It may even be that a given individual has no conscious experience at all. That is, perhaps the individual is a "zombie," a creature that acts in every way as if it has conscious experience but is actually empty inside. How can we tell?

In sum, the mind/brain problem poses a formidable obstacle to logical explication. The combined presence of duality, subjectivity, privacy, and ineffability renders conscious experience profoundly enigmatic. I would argue, however, that an effective mind/brain theory compatible with modern science may yet be attainable. Over the course of this book, I will offer what I believe is a significant step toward developing such a theory. Before proceeding, however, there is a matter of terminology that we need to discuss.

A Word on Terminology

Throughout this book, my intended focus is on the "hard" problem of *conscious experience*, not the "easy" problems of consciousness more generally. The latter have in fact begun to succumb to the investigative work of prominent researchers such as Christof Koch, Francis Crick, Gulio Tononi, Gerald Edelman, Bernard Baars, Stanislas Dehaene; Antonio Damasio, and many, many others past and present.[4] Gains have been made by these investigators in explaining attention, memory, language, perception, and emotion, with proposed theories usually based on a *systems level* approach to cerebral functioning involving brain-wide networks of interconnected nerve cells (*neurons*).

It is the particular problem of conscious experience, in contrast, that leads uniquely to the philosophical puzzles I have previously described, and it is to this specific problem that the current work is directed. To emphasize this point, I will throughout the book use the explicit terms "conscious experience," "conscious awareness," "sentience," "mind," "mental," or "mentality" whenever it is consciousness in the "hard problem" sense that is being denoted.

---

[4] Baars 2005; Tononi 2008; Koch 2004; Dehaene 2001; Damasio 1989; Edelman 1989.

With this emphasis in mind, we can now turn to the approaches philosophers have taken to solve the mind/brain problem, the problem of conscious experience. Getting the philosophy of the mind/brain problem right is a crucial first step in tackling the mind/brain problem. The review will be brief, just enough to establish a basic framework while omitting the many philosophical niceties that would fill a book by themselves.

Substance Dualism

Shared by every normal human being, from early childhood through adulthood, is a compelling intuition that the mind and the body are two distinct entities. While we think of ourselves as physical bodies in a physical world, we are also aware of our dreams, we picture things in our minds, and we experience feelings and sensations. These experiences seem to be different in nature from the physical world around us. The natural outgrowth of this intuition is the oldest of all mind/brain theories, namely *substance dualism.* Substance dualism stipulates that every conscious being is composed of two distinct but interacting substances, one physical, the other ethereal, with each residing in its own separate realm: the body in the material world, the mind in a non-material domain. Causation flows not only within the physical world from one event to the next but also between events in the physical and mental worlds.

Since with substance dualism the mind and the body are deemed separate and distinct, the way is opened for the existence of disembodied minds. Hence the commonplace belief in the existence of "souls" that can continue to exist even after the demise of the body.

To casual inspection, the substance dualistic thesis is not problematic. To the contrary, most humans, both past and present, have viewed substance dualism as a natural and sensible way to account for what is a compelling commonplace observation. Add to this the promise of an afterlife and it becomes understandable that substance dualism has been the predominant belief of human beings since prehistoric times and remains by far the most widely held belief by the world's population today.

Despite its vast following and apparent plausibility, substance dualism suffers from a major drawback: it clashes irreconcilably with modern science. This first became evident in the mid-seventeenth century when the great French philosopher and mathematician Rene Descartes (1596–1650) presented a substance dualistic theory forged in the spirit of the nascent science of his day. Descartes began by taking the two substances to be *res cogitans* ("thinking thing") and *res extensa* ("spatially extended thing"), the former being experiential and present only in humans, the latter being physical and making up the whole observable universe. In keeping with a substance dualism framework, he deemed the two substances independent but mutually interactive, the action of the physical on the mental producing conscious perception and the action of the mental on the physical producing acts of free will. He then went on to pave new ground, offering a specific neurological model of mind/brain interaction centered on the pineal gland, a tiny structure located deep within the brain.

Alas, Descartes' theory quickly became a target of scientific attack and was soon discredited. The most damaging criticism was one that applies equally well to all substance dualistic formulations: the theory failed to adequately account for mind/brain interaction. The deficiency was twofold. First, on a practical level, his pineal gland mechanism of mind/brain interaction could not stand up to scientific scrutiny and appears positively foolish when looked at through modern eyes. Nor have alternative mechanisms come to light in the centuries following Descartes that could explain just how mental and physical substances might interact.

Second, and on a deeper level, the very notion of causal mental/physical interaction conflicted with the newly emerging Newtonian worldview. Newtonian physics is ruled by two conservation laws that hold for any closed system: conservation of energy and conservation of momentum. These conservation laws are anathema to substance dualism. This is so because for substance dualistic theories to thrive, it is necessary that they posit that the mind act on the brain to produce physical effects. But that would entail an introduction of new energy and momentum into the system not accountable by physical laws. The result would be a violation of energy and momentum conservation, violations that have never been observed (except in the context of quantum mechanics, which we will consider in a later chapter).

Ultimately, this incompatibility of substance dualism with the basic structure of physics sounded its death knell, and scientists and philosophers from the eighteenth century onward have generally looked elsewhere for solutions to the mind/brain problem.

Idealism

A radical alternative was essayed at the beginning of the eighteenth century by the Irish philosopher, Bishop George Berkeley (1685–1753). Berkeley averted the interaction difficulties of Descartes' substance dualism with the simple but jarring proposal that only the mind exists and that the physical world is no more than an illusion. According to this view, called *idealism*, only thoughts and perceptions are assumed to be real, providing the basis for Berkeley's famous dictum, "esse est percipi" ("to be is to be perceived"). With his one bold maneuver, Berkeley solved the problem of mind/brain interaction by denying the existence of one of the offending components.

Although successfully avoiding the difficulties of mind/brain interaction, idealism clashed with native intuition and common sense. This was the point made by the English author Samuel Johnson (1709–1784) who, in critiquing Berkeley's idealism, famously kicked a stone and declared "I refute it thus." But unintuitive ideas are not necessarily wrong ones. Indeed, quantum mechanics and general relativity, the pillars of post-nineteenth-century physics, are theories that are downright bizarre. Hence the retort to Johnson by an anonymous poet: "Kick the rock Sam Johnson, Break your bones, But cloudy, cloudy is the stuff of stones."

Ultimately, however, Berkeley's idealism is inadequate as a solution to the mind/brain problem. The critical shortcoming of Berkeley's thesis is that, having eliminated the physical world, it begs the question: From where do our ideas originate if not from an external reality? Berkeley responded by proposing that God provided for the ideas that fill our minds. If you perceive a red rose, it is God who puts that perception in your mind. And so on for all the thoughts and perceptions that make up your conscious experience. But this does no more than rename the problem. By what rules does God put perceptions in one's mind? If this is not specified, then the theory lacks substance.

In the end, then, idealism's undoing is that it offers no explanation for the content of conscious experience. It operates entirely under the auspices of a supervisory agent, divine or otherwise, that resides outside the system, functioning according to rules that we know nothing about. This outcome falls short of scientific aspirations. While Berkeley's idealism has been advocated by occasional philosophers over the years and has a few adherents even today, its failure to offer an explanation for the content of experience denies it a place in mainstream thinking.

Eliminative Materialism

An equally radical method for eradicating mind/brain dualism is to assume that it is the mind that does not exist. According to this view, which philosophers call *eliminative materialism*, once all the physical processes are accounted for, there is nothing left to explain. The mental component is removed from the equation and the need for mind/brain interaction evaporates.

Eliminative materialists acknowledge that there is something special happening in conscious systems but believe that this "special happening" is accounted for entirely by the organization and behavior of the physical system. A common version of this view, called *functionalism*, equates the mind of an organism with its function, regardless of how it is physically constructed. If there is any duality to be identified, it is that between function and structure, not between mentality and physicality.

We encounter forms of eliminative materialism in the writings of the ancient Greeks, such as in those of Democritus (460–370 BC) who conjectured that everything in the world, including the mind, is composed of atoms: "Sweet exists by convention, bitter by convention, in truth only atoms and the void." Much later, in the seventeenth century, Thomas Hobbes was the figure most associated with eliminative materialism: "Sense…in the sentient can be nothing else but motion in some of the internal parts of the sentient."

Unlike idealism, eliminative materialism has a substantial following among modern scientists and philosophers. Its most visible proponent is the philosopher Daniel Dennett who, in his well-known book

"Consciousness Explained," makes his position clear: "The sort of difference people imagine there to be between any machine and any human experience…is one I am firmly denying: There is no such sort of difference. There just seems to be."[5] According to Dennett, subjective experience simply does not exist. There is no "ghost in the machine."[6]

The eliminative materialist supposes that only things that are observable can be said to exist. Since subjective experiences are private and ineffable, they are not observable. Subjective experience cannot therefore be said to exist. In support of this contention, experiments are cited that indicate that we are far from being infallible experts with regard to our own conscious experiences. Take for example the well-studied phenomenon of "change blindness," in which a scene is briefly flashed to an observer and then, a moment later, it is flashed again with one of the objects from the original scene removed. The observer is asked to report whether the two scenes were the same or different. Observers often fail to detect any differences, being "blind" to the removal of one of the objects. Yet, they maintain that they consciously perceived the entire scene in both instances. There is clearly a discrepancy between what they think they saw and what they actually saw. Dennett extrapolates from this and other similar examples to arrive at the conclusion that the notion of conscious experience must be a fantasy produced by a fallible brain.

But it is a long way from fallibility in judging the content of one's own conscious experience to the denial of the existence of conscious experience altogether. Suppose you were to enter a completely blue room. Everything in the room is blue: the walls, the ceiling, the floor, the furniture. When asked what you are experiencing you respond unequivocally that you are experiencing the color blue. Here, change blindness doesn't apply. The experience of blueness, whether obtained directly or from immediate memory, is simple and unchanging. Is it really plausible that nothing at all is actually being experienced?

On this point, Descartes' "First Meditation," which takes the reader through progressive stages of doubt, remains as good now as when first

[5] Dennett 1991, p. 375.

[6] Ryle 1949, p. 15.

written. You can doubt the existence of the world around you, you can doubt the existence of your own body, and you can even doubt the reliability of your introspections. But you cannot doubt experience itself. To do so would be empirically incoherent.

David Chalmers homes in on the essential point:

> Some say that consciousness is an "illusion," but I have little idea what this could even mean. It seems to me that we are surer of the existence of conscious experience than we are of anything else in the world. I have tried hard at times to convince myself that there is really nothing there, that conscious experience is empty, an illusion. There is something seductive about this notion, which philosophers throughout the ages have exploited, but in the end it is utterly unsatisfying. I find myself absorbed in an orange sensation, and *something is going on*. There is something that needs explaining, even after we have explained the processes of discrimination and action: there is the *experience*.[7]

An anonymous limerick puts it more succinctly:

There was a faith-healer of Deal
Who said "Although pain isn't real
If I sit on a pin
And it punctures my skin
I dislike what I *fancy* I feel"

In my view, and that of many others, eliminative materialism is ultimately inadequate as a solution to the hard problem. Its main deficiency is that it denies primary data, which is the lifeblood of science. Its advocates may succeed in assuaging their philosophical angst by banishing conscious experience from the universe, but only at the cost of giving up on trying to explain the full extent of reality. Conscious experience cannot be disposed of so lightly. To paraphrase philosopher John Heil, conscious experience is a fact one investigates, not a fact one seeks to establish.[8]

---

[7] Chalmers 1996, p. xii.

[8] Heil 1979, p. 554.

Aspect Dualism

If we reject idealism and eliminative materialism, insisting that some form of mental/physical duality is in fact present and must be accounted for, but at the same time reject substance dualism as incompatible with the laws of physics, we are left with *aspect dualism*, the thesis that the mental and the physical are different aspects of a single source. The idea here is that by having the mental and physical events derive from the same source, they are automatically kept in correspondence without the imposition of the troublesome mental/physical causal interactions that plague substance dualism.

Aspect dualism is generally considered to have originated with the Jewish/Dutch philosopher Benedict de Spinoza (1632–1677). For Spinoza, the originating source giving rise to the mental and physical aspects was God, which, once again, ran counter to the spirit of science. Subsequent to Spinoza, however, aspect dualism began to take on a more naturalistic flavor. In the nineteenth century it took the form of *psychophysical parallelism*, which focused on the lawful relationship between the mental and physical spheres that was evident in psychophysical experiments. In the twentieth century it was refashioned variously as the *identity thesis* and as *neutral monism*, both of which emphasized the unitary origin of the dual aspects. With each of these subsequent formulations, the originating source of the mental/physical duality was nature herself, without any imposition by a supreme deity.

At present, some form of aspect dualism is the approach of choice for most of those who accept the presence of mental/physical duality but insist on a theory consistent with science. It has been particularly popular among physicists, including Albert Einstein, who gave it his endorsement:

> To guard against the collision of the various sorts of "realities" with which physics and psychology deal, Spinoza and Fechner invented the doctrine of psychophysical parallelism, which, to be frank, satisfies me entirely.

While all aspect dualistic theories share the assumption that the mental and the physical are two different manifestations of a single natural source, they differ in what they assume is the single source and what they assume are the two aspects. Chalmers, for one, has suggested that "information" is the unitary source, with physical and mental aspects deriving from a single informational thread. I believe Chalmers is on the right track, a point upon which I will expand in later chapters.

Object-Object Versus Subject-Object Dualities

In constructing an aspect dualistic mind/brain theory, we note that not just any aspect duality will do. Nature is rife with aspect dualities that have nothing to do with conscious experience. C-sharp is also D-flat, Superman is also Clark Kent, fathers are also sons, and so on, but these dualities are object-object dualities entirely unrelated to sentience.

In the early nineteenth century, the physicist, psychologist, and philosopher Gustav Theodor Fechner (1801–1877) proposed that mind/brain duality might be one of perspective. His suggestion was that the mind and the brain might be the same thing, only viewed from different vantage points. He gave as an analogy the curved line shown in Fig. 1.1. Is the curve convex or concave? How it is perceived depends on one's vantage point: viewed from the left it is concave, viewed from the right it is convex. Or consider the duality of the planet Venus, which is either the "morning star" or the "evening star" depending on the perspective of the viewer: in the morning and to the east it is the "morning star"; in the evening and to the west it is the "evening star." The analogy still falls short, however, in that it is again an object-object duality and is again unrelated to sentience.

An aspect duality that has been given particular attention in the contemporary literature is that between the whole of a system and the system's constituent parts. Invoked here is the notion of *emergence*, where whole systems take on new properties not present in the component elements. Take water, for example. At the molecular level, water

Fig. 1.1 Fechner's curve

is just H_2O molecules. But at the systems level, the H_2O molecules in aggregate form a liquid with properties quite different from those of the individual molecules. We say that liquidity is an emergent property of water at the systems level. Similarly, forests emerge from the aggregation of trees, nations emerge from the aggregation of citizens, and galaxies emerge from the aggregations of stars. Perhaps, say emergentists, sentience emerges in a similar manner from the aggregation of brain cells.

Again, however, the emergent duality is of the object-object variety. What typifies the mind/brain relationship, in contrast, is that it is a "subject-object" duality. This in fact gives us a working definition of conscious experience: *if and only if an entity is both a subject and an object is it conscious in the hard-problem sense.* For emergence to be relevant to the mind/brain problem, it would have to be a type of emergence that features subject-object duality at its core. But developing such a theory must overcome what the Canadian philosopher William Seager[9] calls the *generation problem*, which is the challenge of explaining how subjectivity could arise from non-subjective elements. No theory has yet been proposed that yields a satisfactory solution to the generation problem. Many in the field hang their hopes on brain complexity as an answer,[10] suggesting that complexity might somehow lead to sentience. If complexity were the basis for the emergence of conscious experience, however, then why isn't China a consciously experiencing subject? The number of people in China is comparable to the number of nerve cells in the higher areas of the human brain, and both are characterized by an unimaginably complex interconnectivity. Yet, there is nothing that "it is like to be" the population of China. Similarly, the Internet and the global economy are complex but they are not conscious experiencing subjects. On the other hand, creatures with simple brains, such as the roundworm *C. elegans*, exhibit behaviors that leave the question of their having conscious experience unresolved.

[9] Seager 1995.
[10] Tononi 2015.

The Neural Correlate of Consciousness (NCC)

Stymied by the generation problem, investigators have, for the time being, set their sights on an intermediate goal, that of merely identifying the specific brain components that give rise to conscious experience while temporarily ignoring the mechanism by which this happens. Contemporary mind/brain researchers call the sought after physical substrate the *neural correlate of consciousness* (*NCC*), which is defined as *the minimal set of brain elements whose activity correlates directly with conscious experience.*[11] The NCC is the "bridge locus," the conjectural site where the physical maps directly onto the experiential. The hope is that if the NCC can be discovered, then the solution to the generation problem may become evident as well. Caltech neuroscientist Christof Koch rates discovering the NCC as "one of the ultimate scientific challenges of our times."

The search for the NCC has so far been unsuccessful. In my view, the principal impediment to its discovery has been the near-universal dogged assumption that it must be macroscopic and spatially dispersed. This assumption leads inexorably to what is called the *binding problem*, which is the difficulty of explaining how a macroscopically spatially disparate physical substrate could congeal into a single experiential flow. Some have suggested that 40 cycle/second electrical oscillations, called gamma waves, which have the property of being widespread, synchronous, and in phase during episodes of conscious experience, might provide a mechanism for binding. But attempts to convert this suggestion, or any other like suggestion, into a satisfying explanation for mental unity have not yet proved adequate.

In light of this obstacle, I wish to put forth the thesis that the search for the NCC might be facilitated by a shift in focus from the macroscopic level of interacting brain regions to the microscopic level of individual neurons. Specifically, my proposal is that information processing in the brain ultimately converges upon individual nerve cells where it yields single neuron NCCs. What the proposal buys is a reduction in the size of the NCCs, a feature that might mitigate the binding problem. Additionally, microscopic NCCs have the potential of bringing unique

[11] Chalmers 2013; Crick 2003; Koch 2004; Tononi 2008.

physical mechanisms into play that could possibly help in tackling the generation problem.

According to my single-neuron proposal, sentience is a property confined to individual neurons. While the collected output of populations of sentient neurons may yield behavior that gives the impression of whole brain conscious experience, this impression is illusory. Conscious experiences are entirely tied to individual neurons and no combining of these conscious experiences into some higher order sentience is deemed possible. It is the organization of the individual experiences, rather than their combining, that gives the appearance of whole brain sentience. Fig. 1.2 illustrates the point. In Fig. 1.2a we have the macroscopic emergence approach in which populations of neurons join together to produce one emergent conscious experience. In Fig. 1.2b we have the single-neuron view, where neurons individually sustain the entire conscious experience and do so redundantly across a population of neurons. With the single neuron view, the "you" who is reading this sentence is not, as you might have thought, the experiential aspect of your brain as a whole. You are, rather, the experiential aspect of a single neuron in your brain. All around you are other neurons having similar experiences to yours and with whom you cooperate in order to influence whole brain behavior. In no way, however, does your conscious experience merge with those of any of the other neurons.

The arrangement can be likened to a crowd watching fireworks. With every pyrotechnic explosion, each person in the crowd takes in the entire spectacle independently and verbalizes his or her own personal reaction

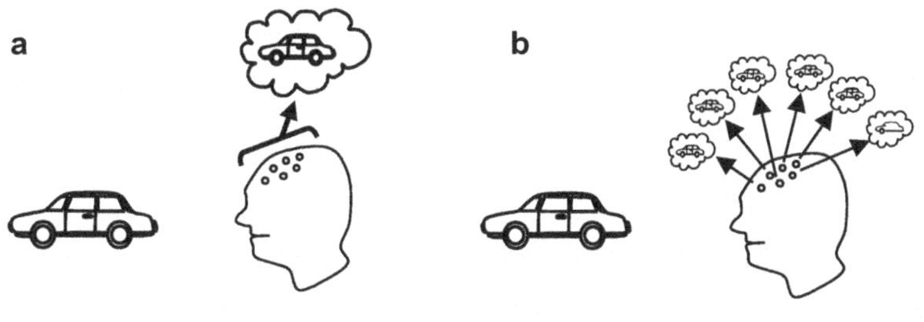

Fig. 1.2 Alternative NCC models. **(a)** Macroscopic emergence model. **(b)** Microscopic single-neuron model

with a muffled "ooh" or "aah." What is heard from a distance, however, is the collective stentorious vocalization of all the members of the crowd. As with individual neurons in the brain, the individual people in the crowd are responding separately to the stimulus but the group appears to be responding as one.

Or take fans in a football stadium. Just by listening to their collective vocalizations one can draw inferences about what is happening on the field, a roar signaling a score, a groan indicating a penalty. Again, the fans are individually and separately reacting to what they see on the field but the group effectively responds to the stimuli as a whole.

These scenarios illustrate that agents that are individually sentient can coordinate their outputs to produce the appearance of macroscopic sentience without any combining actually taking place. Defining how such an arrangement might apply to individual neurons in the brain will be the objective of this book. In the chapters that follow, I will attempt to make the case that single neuron sentience is both a coherent and a plausible notion, and that it has the potential to move us forward on the generation problem itself.

2

Principles of Cortical Function

The Search for the NCC in Antiquity

To assess the plausibility of single neuron sentience we need to start by considering the brain's anatomy. From knowledge of anatomy comes insight into function. Nobel laureate Francis Crick (1916–2004) made this point when he offered this sage advice: "If you do not make headway studying a complex system, study its structure and knowledge of its function will follow automatically."[1] Nobel laureate Gerald Edelman (1929–) waxed dramatic on the issue: "If someone held a gun to my head and threatened oblivion if I did not identify the single word most significant for understanding the brain, I would say 'neuroanatomy'."[2]

We begin with an inspection of the general structure of the central nervous system. Broadly speaking, the central nervous system can be divided into cerebrum, diencephalon, brainstem, cerebellum, and spinal cord (Fig. 2.1). These components are arranged phylogenetically, that is, in the order in which they first appeared in evolution. The phylogenetic trend runs caudal to rostral ("tail" to "crown"), the spinal cord being the

[1] Martin 2002, p. 418.

[2] Edelman 1999, p. 68.

S. Sevush, *The Single-Neuron Theory*,
DOI 10.1007/978-3-319-33708-1_2

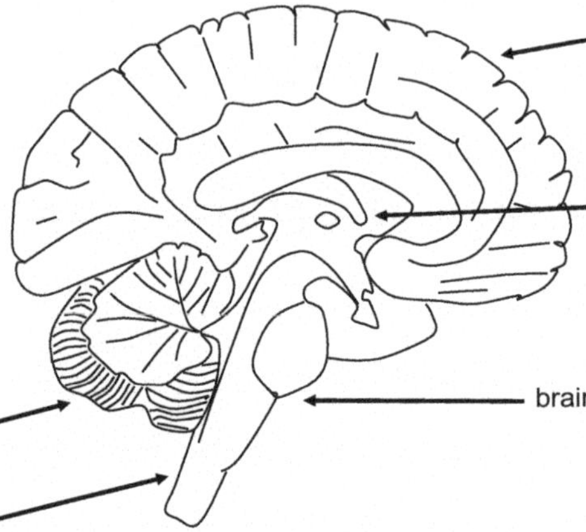

Fig. 2.1 Components of the central nervous system

first to develop and the cerebrum the last. The caudal to rostral trend is also present ontogenetically, that is, according to the order in which the structures first appear during fetal development. The match between the phylogeny and ontogeny is in keeping with the old adage, "ontogeny recapitulates phylogeny."

The cerebral cortex is the thin (~4 mm thick) outer covering of the cerebrum. It is composed of gray matter, which is brain tissue containing nerve cell bodies and short-range connecting fibers. The cortical sheet is extensively folded into alternating furrows (sulci) and ridges (gyri) that give the cortex its characteristic corrugated appearance and that serve to increase its surface area, thereby increasing the number of neurons it can contain. Deep to the cerebral cortex is white matter, which consists of long range connecting fibers.

The cerebral cortex will command much of our attention as we search for the NCC. The cerebral cortex is responsible for higher cognitive functions such as memory, language, perception, reasoning, and the execution of complex motor tasks, and its destruction leaves one in a vegetative state. It is the cerebral cortex that has been proposed as the site of the NCC in most contemporary mind/brain theories.

The connection between the cerebral cortex, or the brain more generally, and conscious experience has not always been evident.

For thousands of years the ancient Egyptians, like others before them, linked the mind with the body as a whole rather than with any particular organ. They believed that the spiritual "Ka," which they held was the repository for memory and personality, was a "body double" that assumed the shape of the whole person. As for the brain, the ancient Egyptians thought so little of it that they routinely scooped it out through the nose and discarded it ignominiously when preparing mummies for the afterlife.

It wasn't until the ascendance of the Greeks, and most notably Hippocrates of Eos (of "Hippocratic Oath" fame), that a mind/brain connection was first proposed. In the early fifth century BC Hippocrates perceptively wrote:

> One ought to know that on the one hand pleasure, joy, laughter, and games, and on the other, grief, sorrow, discontent, and dissatisfaction arise only from the brain. It is especially by it that we think, comprehend, see, and hear, that we distinguish the ugly from the beautiful, the bad from the good, the agreeable from the disagreeable.

Aristotle famously opposed Hippocrates' choice of organ, suggesting instead that the heart was the site of mental function and that the brain's sole purpose was to cool the blood. He offered as evidence for this the fact that some primitive animals lacking brains were capable of movement, which the ancients took as indicative of the presence of a mind.

Five centuries later, the great Greek physician Galen (130–200 AD) endorsed Hippocrates' view over that of Aristotle. He based his preference on his observation that pressure on the brain caused stupor and that head injuries produced changes in sensation and cognition. Additionally, he demonstrated that the nerves carrying motor messages to the muscles originated from the brain rather than from the heart. He did this by showing that a struggling pig would stop squealing as soon as what is now known as the recurrent laryngeal nerve, which connects the brain to the larynx or "voice box," was severed. He repeated this experiment before incredulous onlookers using bleating goats, barking dogs, and even roaring lions from Rome's Coliseum.

Galen mockingly dismissed Aristotle's assertion that the brain's only purpose was to cool the blood:

> What is this language? I blush even today to cite this statement…Indeed, to imagine that the brain was created because of the natural heat of the heart, to refresh it and moderate its temperature, is wholly absurd…In my opinion it is just as sensible to say that the heel was created for the heart. Do not believe that I speak thus in jest, since an attentive examination will show you that refrigeration reaches the heart more promptly from the heel than from the brain.

Galen's case for the brain as the substrate for the mind was persuasive and has dominated thinking on the matter ever since. To modern eyes, the specific connection between the mind and the brain seems self-evident. Why, then, did it take so long for the ancients to eschew the old Egyptian view that the mind is coextensive with the whole body and replace it with a more localized view? I would suggest that the explanation resides in a universal illusion that the conscious perception of sensory stimuli happens at the site of stimulation rather than at some distant location in the brain. If you prick your finger with a pin, the pain seems to be localized to your finger at the site of the pinprick, not to your head. It requires a degree of abstraction to hypothesize that the pain is actually experienced in the distantly located brain.

The difficulty the ancients faced illustrates how hard it is for one to change one's intuitions regarding the localization of conscious experience. The theory I am presenting will require most readers to make such a change. Indeed, single-neuron sentience will strike many as ridiculous and their first instinct will be to dismiss it out of hand. As Chalmers points out, however, "If the mind-body problem has taught us anything, it is that nothing about consciousness is obvious, and that one person's obvious truth is another person's absurdity."[3] I would suggest that an open mind may be our most important tool in our quest to identify the NCC.

---

[3] Chalmers 1997, p. 1.

Localizing the Mind to the Cerebral Cortex

For fifteen hundred years following Galen, there was little further in the way of attempts to localize the mind, other than the ill-conceived suggestion made by the early Christian writers that the mind was associated with the cavitations, now known as the cerebral ventricles, that reside deep within the substance of the brain. These writers were drawn to their conclusion by their invalid assumption that the cerebral ventricles were filled with air, which, they suggested, offered an ideal diffuse correlate for what they saw as an ethereal mind. We know now that the cerebral ventricles are filled with water, not air, and that they play no role in mental functioning whatsoever.

The long stagnation in mind/brain theorizing was broken in seventeenth-century Europe, the highlight being the publication of the influential Cerebri Anatome by the English anatomist, Thomas Willis, in 1664. In this work, Willis placed mental function in the brain substance itself rather than in the cerebral ventricles. He proposed, specifically, that the cerebral cortex was the site at which memories and conscious perceptions arose and it was from this structure that voluntary movement was initiated. He based his supposition on dissections he performed on humans and animals, work made possible by the lifting of the age-old ban on human autopsies in the previous century. Willis drew his inference from his observation that the complexity of the cerebral cortex increased in step with the level of intelligence of the species examined.[4]

In the eighteenth century, a fresh debate erupted that centered on which type of brain tissue served as the correlate to the mind, the gray matter or the white matter. The anatomical distinction between these two types of brain tissue, easily observable with the naked eye, was well known in the eighteenth century. What was not known was what their respective functions were.

Willis supposed that it was the gray matter that was responsible for the highest mental functions. Contesting this view was the prominent eighteenth-century Swiss physiologist and anatomist Albrecht von Haller (1708–1777). Haller noted that the gray matter was segregated into disconnected regions while the white matter formed one continuous mass

---

[4] Gross 1997.

that infiltrated every part of the brain and spinal cord. Motivated in part by this observation, Haller, in what led to a century-long regression in neurological thinking, rejected Willis' assertion that mental function was mediated by the cerebral cortex, proposing instead that it was the ubiquitous white matter that gave rise to the mind and that it did so in a diffuse manner.[5] Haller formalized his idea with his "doctrine of equipotentiality" according to which all portions of the white matter were equivalent and if one portion were damaged the remaining mass could take over the lost function.

Haller's proposal did not persist for long once he passed from the scene. By the beginning of the nineteenth century the consensus had shifted back to the view that it was the gray matter, specifically the gray matter of the cerebral cortex, that was the basis for the mind. This consensus continues today.

From the nineteenth century onward the debate over localization would be directed to the question of how the cortical gray matter mediated mental function. At issue would be two putative principles of cortical functioning: the *localization principle*, which asserts that cognitive functions are mediated by the cerebral cortex in a multifocal rather than diffuse manner, and the *reflex principle*, which states that the cerebral cortex can be described as a complex reflex apparatus that connects stimulus to response by dedicated input-output pathways. Opinions on the validity and relevance of these two principles have oscillated back and forth over the centuries, and the controversy has not yet ended. Since the dispute bears crucially on our mind/brain agenda, we will need to become familiar with the arguments that have driven it and with the contemporary stance that now holds sway.

The Great Cortical Localization Debate

Gall

At the beginning of the nineteenth century, the Austrian neuroanatomist Franz Joseph Gall (1758–1828) hypothesized for the first time that the cerebral cortex mediated cognitive functions in focal fashion. His vision

[5] Gross 1997.

was of a cortex divided into a patchwork of localized regions, each associated with a specific cognitive ability.

Gall was drawn to his theory by an observation he made as a boy that highly intelligent people seemed to be endowed with protuberant eyes, which he took as evidence of underlying enlargement of the frontal part of their brains. Generalizing on this association, Gall hypothesized that the cerebral cortex might consist of a mosaic of localized "organs," each subserving a different cognitive function, with the strength of each function correlating with the size of the protuberance in the overlying region of the skull. Gall called his new theory "organology" (later renamed "phrenology") and suggested the presence of 27 different specialized cortical regions, each dedicated to its own particular behavioral function.

Gall's theory offered a cookbook method for analyzing an individual's cognitive abilities through simple skull palpation. The method had popular appeal, with phrenology becoming for a brief period a sensation throughout Europe and America. Ultimately, however, Gall's theory failed to stand up to scientific scrutiny and was rejected by the scientific community as pseudoscience, and Gall himself became cast as somewhat of a charlatan.

This negative assessment has been revised in recent years and Gall's historical standing has been resurrected. Although his "phrenology" turned out to be inaccurate in its detail, his idea that the cortex consisted of an amalgam of localized functional regions has proven both prescient and seminal.

Flourens

The most vociferous attack on Gall's localizationist theory came from Jean Pierre Flourens (1794–1867), a prominent French neuroscientist who insisted that the cortex did its job in a diffuse rather than a parcellated manner. Flourens was actually a supporter of Gall's theory initially, but later came to be its harshest critic. His opposition derived from a series of experiments he conducted in which he removed portions of the cerebral cortex from birds, rabbits, dogs, and other animals. He observed that the behavioral impairments following partial destruction of the cortex spanned all cognitive faculties independent of which portion of the cortex was damaged. Furthermore, he found that if one function subsequently recovered, so did all the rest. Flourens concluded that the cerebral cortex mediated cognitive functions in a diffuse, holistic manner and not, as Gall had supposed, in a parcellated fashion.

Flourens' view dominated the scientific world through the first half of the nineteenth century. But his methods were necessarily crude and his conjectures were based on the erroneous assumption that one could extrapolate from animal studies to pronouncements about human brain anatomy and function.

Broca

The defects in Flourens' analysis became evident when, in 1861, the French anatomist/neurologist Paul Broca reported his autopsy findings on a language impaired patient, "Tan," so nicknamed because "tan" was the only word he could utter following his brain injury. Broca discovered that a localized cystic cavitation was present in the left frontal portion of Tan's cerebral cortex, indicating a special role for this region in expressive language function.

Broca's discovery was followed in ensuing decades by reports of other instances of specific behavioral defects resulting from localized cortical damage. These included isolated impairments in the ability to read, to write, to comprehend spoken language, and to engage in skilled motor acts. In each case, the behavioral impairments were found on autopsy to be associated with focal damage to a specific cortical region.

In 1870, Hitzig and Fritsch cemented the locationist perspective by complementing the studies of brain-damaged humans with electrical stimulation studies in animals. They demonstrated that focally administered electrical stimulation to a dog's frontal lobes caused movement of the dog's limbs, while electrical stimulation of other areas had no effect. This thrust the proverbial dagger into Flourens' delocalizationist vision.

Lashley

While the work of the late nineteenth-century investigators held center stage during their day, by the start of the twentieth century the profusion of localizationist findings had mostly played itself out. Without fresh reports of new focal syndromes, interest in cortical localization began to wane, and the cortical localization thesis again came under question. Flourens' old argument that cognitive functions were mediated by the cortex in a diffuse manner resurfaced in a new form. While the cortex might contain some focality, it was argued, it remained fundamentally an undifferentiated and infinitely pliable neuronal sheet.

The most outspoken proponent of the renewed nonlocalizationist initiative during this period was the experimental psychologist Karl Lashley (1890–1958) who doggedly searched the brains of his laboratory animals for localized areas devoted to memory function. His search was unfruitful, leading him to contend that memories were stored and managed diffusely, with no focal areas of specialized memory function.

Lashley revived Flourens' and Haller's non-localizationist doctrines. He expounded his own theories of "mass action" and "equipotentiality," asserting that, while some focality was present, the intrinsic nature of the cortex was defined by its plasticity and adaptability. Lashley's nonlocalizationist view of cortical function came to dominate neuroscientific thinking during the first half of the twentieth century, in step with the anti-anatomical behaviorist movement in psychology that had reached its zenith at the same time.

Neuroimaging

The pendulum swung back again, this time for good, in the second half of the twentieth century when Lashley's nonlocalizationist thesis was confronted by new localized findings. Most trenchant was the discovery in the 1950s that a profound loss of memory in humans could result from the surgical removal of a localized portion of the temporal lobes. This observation directly refuted Lashley's assertion that memory was entirely unlocalizable. In the decades that followed, a renewed fascination with the classical focal syndromes arose, and a new round of focal syndromes were discovered.

The pace of discovery of focal syndromes quickened in the 1970s and onward due to a technical advance in x-ray technology. Until the 1970s, the mainstay of experimental investigation of cortical localization was the clinico/anatomical case study, which required luck and tenacity to achieve success. Patients found to be suffering from well-defined cognitive impairments following strokes, brain tumors, or other causes of focal brain damage would be carefully evaluated while they were alive and then, often years later, their brains would be examined post-mortem and a clinico/anatomical correlation established. This was the method used by Paul Broca and the other nineteenth-century investigators to explore cortical function in the 1800s and it continued to be the method used by researchers for much of the twentieth century. Progress with this method was agonizingly slow. Investigators had to depend on the serendipitous occurrence of unusual clinical events and then had to wait for the opportunity to study the brain after the patient died.

The situation changed abruptly in the 1970s with the invention of the computer assisted tomographic (CAT) scan, followed in the 1980s by the development of the higher resolution magnetic resonance imaging (MRI) scan. These new brain scans used computer reconstruction to produce cross-sectional views of the brain that matched the cross-sectional views provided by brain slices at autopsy. The technique allowed investigators to quickly identify the precise location of cortical damage from strokes, tumors, and trauma, allowing for clinical/anatomical correlations to be made within hours of the clinical examination. As a neurology resident in training at the time, I was able to use the new technology to easily replicate in just a few months the classical clinical/anatomical correlations that had previously taken a century of autopsy studies to unearth.

In the 1990s functional MRI (fMRI) scans became available. These scans produced high-resolution cross-sectional images of function rather than of structure. A dynamic experimental paradigm became possible, one in which activity patterns could be imaged at high resolution while subjects were engaged in specific cognitive tasks. A wave of fMRI studies ensued that provided further evidence for the focality of cortical function.

The Modern View: The Modular Cortex

In the wake of these and other experimental findings, the case for localization of function in the cerebral cortex has now become overwhelming. Many functionally localized areas have been identified and extensively studied, including a number of language areas, more than twenty visual areas, and dozens of other specialized areas. Lashley's contention that the cerebral cortex operates in an entirely homogeneous and diffuse manner may be respectfully laid to rest.

The modern view is not, however, a mere reinstatement of Gall's phrenology. With phrenology, the link between cognitive functions and focal cortical regions was one-to-one, each function being mediated by a single cortical region and each cortical region mediating only a single cognitive function. With the modern view, the correlations between cognitive functions and focal cortical regions are rarely one-to-one. Instead, each cognitive function is typically mediated by the combined activity of multiple focal regions, and each focal region is typically associated with multiple cognitive functions. Additionally, there are some psychological constructs, like intelligence and personality, that are hardly localizable at all. The functional arrangement of the cortex is therefore a hybrid that combines both focal and distributed themes. Neuroscientists commonly refer to this arrangement as *modular*.[6]

Brodmann's Map

The modular arrangement was featured in a number of cortical anatomical maps that were published early in the twentieth century. The most widely used of these maps was that published in 1909 by the German neuroanatomist Korbinian Brodmann (1868–1918). Brodmann distinguished cortical regions on the basis of variations in the types of cells inhabiting each region and on the way these cells were distributed throughout the depth of the cortical sheet. Brodmann's original map identified about 50 anatomically distinct cortical regions. Over the years, suggestions for further subdividing Brodmann's regions have been offered, with some maps distinguishing as many as 100 separate cortical fields.

At the time the cortical maps first appeared, they were strictly anatomical. Whether or not the maps had functional significance was entirely a matter of speculation. Now, a century later, we know that many of

[6] Gazzaniga 2013.

the Brodmann regions do have functional correlates, with commonality of function within regions and sharp differences in function between adjacent regions. The Brodmann arrangement can be likened to that of the world's ethnogeography, where ethnicity and language tend to be relatively homogeneous within national borders but heterogeneous when borders are crossed.

Within some Brodmann regions there is further localization. For example, functional subregions have been identified for face recognition in Brodmann area 37 and a subregion for thirst has been identified in Brodmann area 32, to name just two. Localization is also present within most Brodmann areas at a finer, microscopic scale, with stunning spatial patterns of neuronal activation being observed in many regions. We will examine these spatial patterns and consider their implications for the mind/brain problem in Chap. 8.

Why the Modular Arrangement?

Why is it that the cortex is organized in modular fashion? After all, one could, as Lashley did, imagine a cortex consisting of an undifferentiated expanse of interconnected neurons without anatomical demarcation or functional localization. Such is, in fact, the case with the hydra, a primitive animal featuring a diffuse, distributed nerve net, without nerve clusters or functional modules. The hydra is small and simple, however, so a diffuse nerve net serves it well. For the cerebral cortex, which is large and complex, the effects of *wire length* (the total length of inter-neuronal connecting fibers) come into play.[7] Wire length is energetically costly, with signal transmission over connecting fibers accounting for a third of the total energy consumed by the cerebral cortex. Wire length is also space consuming, with long-range connecting fibers accounting for more than 40 percent of total cortical volume in humans. Additionally, long wire lengths slow down the speed of computation.

These features make wire length a ready target for evolutionary pressure. The cortex has responded to this pressure by minimizing wire length as much as possible. There is, however, also evolutionary pressure

[7] Laughlin 2003.

to maximize the total interconnectivity of the network. The greater the interconnectivity, the more complex are the computations that can be supported. But increased interconnectivity requires increased wire length, and with it a greater energy expenditure.

It is at this point that the modular arrangement becomes relevant. Theoretical arguments and computer simulations show that a modular spatial arrangement is precisely that which best balances the opposing tendencies of wire length minimization and interconnectivity maximization.[8] Accordingly, natural selection has favored a modular over a diffuse arrangement as the dominant functional cortical design.

The Reflex Principle

Introduction

Given its modular structure, what can we say about how the cortex operates? How do the various cortical modules interact to produce coherent cortical function? Here is where the reflex principle enters into the discussion. According to the reflex principle, the cortex can be regarded as a complex reflex machine, with external stimuli initiating a sequence of cortical activations running from input to output along unidirectional, parallel pathways (Fig. 2.2a). The alternative is that cortical connectivity is omnidirectional with no preferred input-output pathways (Fig. 2.2b).

The omnidirectional arrangement, which is favored by many contemporary investigators, recalls the *sympathy model* of body function subscribed to by the ancients.[9] According to the sympathy model, the constant goal of an organism is to maintain harmony among its components. It was this perspective that propelled Hippocrates to expound his humoral theory of medicine: illness results from a disturbance in the balance of the four humors (black bile, yellow bile, phlegm, and blood) and treatments are designed to restore the balance.

[8] Meunier 2010.

[9] Clarke 1987.

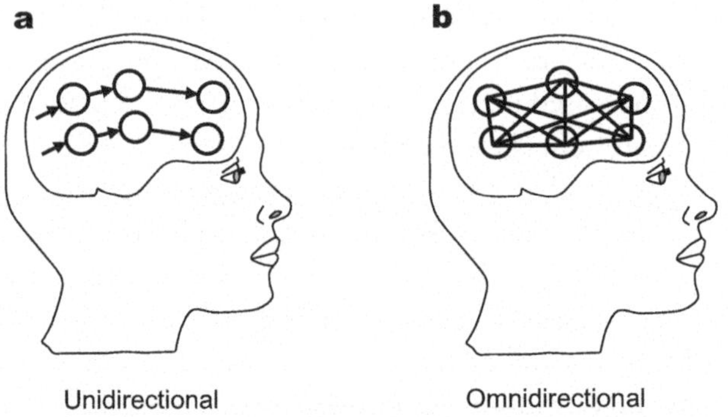

Fig. 2.2 Alternative arrangements for cortical connectivity

The sympathy mechanism is evident in much of the chemistry and physiology of all living things. Hormonal systems certainly work this way, as do acid/base and electrolyte balancing mechanisms. Brain neurochemistry offers an additional example, with clinical depression and other psychiatric disorders being usefully modeled as chemical imbalances that move the emotional control system away from the normal steady state.

As applied specifically to cortical function, the sympathy model portrays the cerebral cortex as a network of reciprocally interconnected modules striving to maintain steady-state balance. Activity deriving from incoming stimuli acts to disturb the balance and the response of the organism is to initiate behavior designed to reinstate the balance, the overall design being devoid of directional preference.

The contention that omnidirectional processing dominates cortical functioning is currently fashionable. There is, however, a long line of evidence favoring unidirectional reflex processing that has accrued over the last three and a half centuries. A review of this evidence will provide a needed context for a proper evaluation of the issues.

Descartes' "Doctrine of Reflex Action"

The idea that the nervous system could be modeled in terms of reflex action was first put forth by Rene Descartes in the seventeenth century. Descartes proposed a model of brain function built on the premise that brains are for the most part no more than complex reflex machines that receive sensory signals from the external world via inbound sensory nerves and issue motor commands to the muscles via outbound motor nerves. He famously likened the reflex apparatus to the automated royal gardens in Saint-Germain outside Paris that utilized water pressure channeled through an assembly of conduits to move figures and play musical instruments. He suggested that the reflex apparatus accounted for all behavior in animals and all non-sentient behavior in humans. Sentience in humans, he contended, was non-reflexive, a product of the non-physical res cogitans.

Descartes' reflex model, and especially its exclusion of human consciousness from the reflex scheme, was controversial when it was first proposed and remains a subject of debate and conjecture today. Much has been written on it. According to the neuroscience historians Clarke and Jacyna, "The evolution of the concept of reflex activity…has received more attention from writers than any other topic in the history of the neurosciences."[10]

Proposed solely on conceptual grounds by Descartes, the reflex model gained an empirical footing in the early nineteenth century when the British anatomist Charles Bell (1774–1842) and the French physiologist Francois Magendie (1783–1855) uncovered a remarkable rule pertaining to peripheral nerve pathways: sensory nerves enter the spinal cord via the dorsal (toward the back) roots; motor nerves exit the spinal cord via the ventral (toward the belly) roots. It would subsequently be found that this dorsal/ventral dissociation applied as well to the brainstem, with sensory components positioned dorsally and motor components positioned ventrally, and to the thalamus and cerebral cortex, where sensory components are positioned posteriorly and motor components are positioned anteriorly. The discovery of the Bell–Magendie law was of fundamental significance and had lasting impact. Early twentieth-century writers would rate it as second only to William Harvey's discovery of the circulation of the blood as the most important advance in the history of physiology.[11] It upended the prevailing opinion that sensory and motor

[10] Clarke 1987, p. 101.

[11] Carmichael 1926.

nerves were jumbled and intertwined. The implication was that a simple reflex arc was present at the level of the spinal cord that, independent of the brain, linked sensory input to motor output via dedicated input-output pathways.

The Bell–Magendie law laid the foundation for the broader thesis that input-output reflex action is the modus operandi of the nervous system in general. This broader tenet was given structure by the venerable English neurologist, John Hughlings Jackson (1832–1911) who proposed that the nervous system could be modeled as a phylogenetically arranged hierarchy of reflex arcs. His idea was that there was a caudal to rostral progression of the reflexes, with the more rostral reflexes being built upon and subjugating the more caudal reflexes. Thus, brainstem reflexes supervene over spinal reflexes, diencephalic reflexes supervene over brainstem reflexes, and reflex activity in the cerebrum, perched atop the reflex hierarchy, supervenes over diencephalic reflexes.

Extending the Doctrine of Reflex Action to the Cortex

What about higher mentation in humans? Was Descartes correct when he excluded human mentation from his reflex model? Or was even the human mind reducible to reflex action? The prevalent view in the nineteenth century was that Descartes was right, that humans were in fact immune to the determinate laws that guided the behavior of nonhuman animals, that the higher brain regions of humans were uniquely able to generate ideas and actions de novo, outside of a reflex framework.

Contesting Descartes' view were those who denied the cortex any unique status, regarding it as just the next higher level in the reflex hierarchy. The "principle of continuity" was invoked: since the cortex is anatomically and functionally analogous to the brainstem and spinal cord, it should exhibit a similar input-output reflex design. For William James, the principle of continuity was decisive:

> To Descartes belongs the credit of having first been bold enough to conceive of a completely self-sufficing nervous mechanism which should be able to perform complicated and apparently intelligent acts. By a singularly

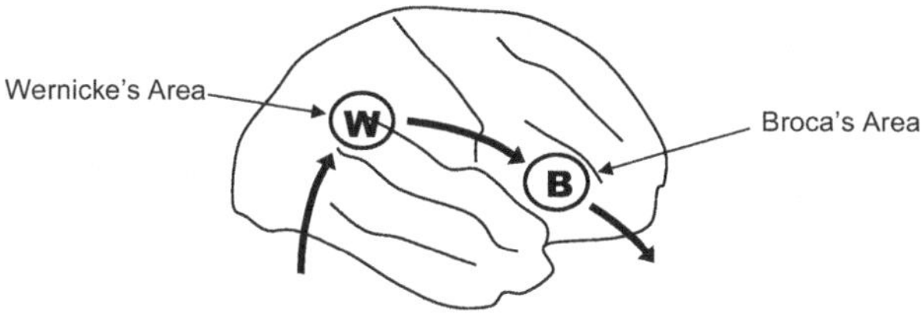

Fig. 2.3 Wernicke's information processing model

arbitrary restriction, however, Descartes stopped short at man, and while contending that in beasts the nervous machinery was all, he held that the higher acts of man were the result of the agency of his rational soul…The conception of reflex action is surely one of the best conquests of physiological theory; why not be radical with it? Why not say that just as the spinal cord is a machine with few reflexes, so the hemispheres are a machine with many, and that that is all the difference? The principle of continuity would press us to accept this view.[12]

In 1874, the 26-year-old German neurologist Carl Wernicke (1848–1905) was the first to provide explicit evidence of reflex activity in the cortex. He reported his observations of a patient who had lost his ability to comprehend speech following damage to his posterior temporal cortex. Wernicke hypothesized that the damaged cortical region, now known as "Wernicke's area," served as a second language center to complement the one identified by Broca a decade earlier. Wernicke proposed that the two areas joined to form a language reflex arc (Fig. 2.3). On the input side, incoming auditory signals were delivered to Wernicke's area, where words were recognized and meanings were attached to them. The results were then passed to Broca's area, where speech output programs were activated and commands were issued to the mouth and tongue muscles to produce speech.

Wernicke's conception of directional cortical pathways was seized upon by other neurological investigators who generated like-minded models to explain reading, writing, and the execution of skilled motor

[12] James 1890, p. 129.

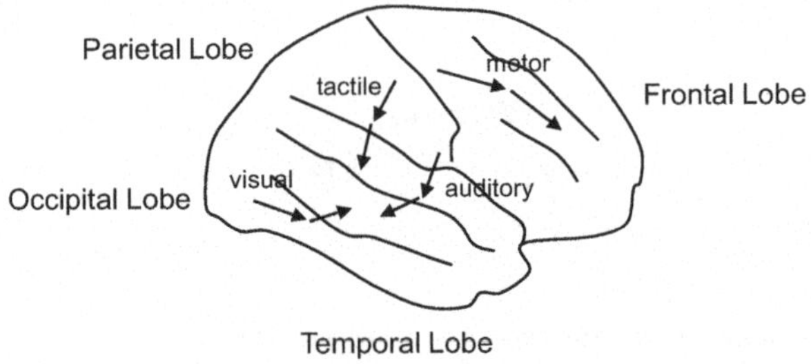

Fig. 2.4 Progression of cortical maturation as proposed by Flechsig

tasks. These elaborate schemes earned the researchers the pejorative nickname of "diagram makers," alluding to the apparent cookbook naiveté of their models. In fact, as we will see, these diagrams would turn out to have enduring relevance.[13]

A Hierarchy of Cortical Reflexes

At the turn of the twentieth century, the German neuroanatomist Paul Emil Flechsig (1847–1929) made observations that further supported the idea of a hierarchy of reflexive pathways in the cerebral cortex.[14] Analyzing the maturity of connecting nerve fibers as a function of brain development in the human fetus and infant, Flechsig found that the order in which cortical regions matured followed a patterned progression (Fig. 2.4).

The first connections to mature were those involving the primary cortices, which on the sensory side included the primary visual (occipital), auditory (temporal), and tactile (parietal) cortices, and which on the motor side consisted of the primary motor (frontal) cortex. The next connections to mature were those involving the secondary sensory cortices and the secondary motor cortex (or "premotor cortex"), which were the cortical regions immediately adjacent to the primary cortices. The last of the connections to mature were those involving what Flechsig called the "association cortices," which in the posterior cortex were regions of

[13] Heilman 2006, pp. 149–150.

[14] Finger 2000; Flechsig 1920.

confluence in the temporal and parietal lobes that were positioned adjacent to the secondary cortices, and which in the frontal lobes was the region anterior to the premotor cortex.

Flechsig speculated that in the posterior cortices the anatomical progression was mirrored by a corresponding progression in functional complexity.[15] His view was that the primary sensory cortices were devoted to simple sensory processing, while the association cortices were responsible for the complex multimodal processing underlying intelligent thought. He proposed an analogous progression for the frontal cortices, with the primary motor cortices being devoted to simple motor commands and the frontal association cortex being responsible for abstract behavioral plans.

Since the posterior and frontal cortices were themselves amply interconnected by white matter tracts, Flechsig's observations allowed for an extension of Jackson's hierarchical reflex model to the cerebral cortex.

The Rise of Behaviorism

By the early twentieth century, theorizing about cortical reflexes began to outstrip empirical observation and consequently stalled. In the wake of this lull came the ascendance of behaviorism, a school of psychology that was to dominate the field for half a century. With behaviorism, theories about mind and brain were looked upon as beside the point. All that mattered were the stimuli received by the organism and the behaviors emitted in response to them. Despite its ostensibly anti-biological stance, behaviorism produced important insights of relevance to brain function, and will therefore be worth a brief look.

At the start was the work of the great Russian physiologist, Ivan Petrovich Pavlov (1849–1936), who pioneered the study of behavioral reflexes in higher animals. Amazingly, Pavlov's work on reflexes did not come until he was in his fifties and had already won the 1904 Nobel Prize for his work on the circulatory system and on gastric secretions. It was his exploration of reflex behavior, however, that gained him enduring fame. With his

[15] Flechsig 1920.

renowned classical conditioning paradigm, a reflex normally initiated by an innate "unconditioned" stimulus (such as the smell of food inducing the secretion of gastric enzymes) is made to come under the control of a neutral stimulus, such as the ringing of a bell, by simply pairing the neutral stimulus with the unconditioned stimulus repeatedly during conditioning trials. Eventually, control passes to the neutral stimulus, which becomes a "conditioned" stimulus that can initiate the reflex unaided.

Although Pavlov's conditioning experiments were limited to elementary behaviors, they raised the possibility that higher-level behaviors might also be explained in terms of conditioned reflexes. If a dog could be taught to associate a ringing bell with an aromatic slab of meat, then perhaps more subtle and complex associations could be established as well. Expanding on this theme, the American biologist John Broadus Watson (1878–1958) pressed for extending Pavlov's stimulus-response relationship to its natural limit by hypothesizing that all behavior, including that of humans, could be explained entirely in terms of Pavlovian conditioning. In 1913, he expressed his newly formed behaviorist view in a now classic paper entitled, "Psychology as the Behaviorist Sees It." This essay, which came to be known as the "Behaviorist Manifesto," launched the behaviorist school of psychology. Watson summarized its central tenet as follows:

> Psychology as the behaviorist views it is a purely objective experimental branch of natural science. Its theoretical goal is the prediction and control of behavior. Introspection forms no essential part of its methods, nor is the scientific value of its data dependent on the readiness with which they lend themselves to interpretation in terms of consciousness. The behaviorist, in his efforts to get a unitary scheme of animal response, recognizes no dividing line between man and brute. The behavior of man, with all of its refinement and complexity, forms only a part of the behaviorist's total scheme of investigation.[16]

He maintained that the potential to mold human behavior by Pavlovian conditioning methods was boundless. In 1925 he boasted:

---

[16] Watson 1913.

> Give me a dozen healthy infants, well formed, and my own specified world to bring them up in, and I'll guarantee to take any one at random and train him to become any type of specialist I might select—doctor, lawyer, artist, merchant-chief and, yes, even beggar-man and thief—regardless of his talents, penchants, tendencies, abilities, vocations, and race of his ancestors.[17]

Skinner and Operant Conditioning

Watson's behaviorism had a significant shortcoming. Despite its usefulness in explaining behaviors in a controlled laboratory setting, it was too rigid to account for the broader ability of animals to flexibly meet the shifting contingencies they routinely encounter in their natural habitats. In the 1930s, the American psychologist Burrhus Frederick Skinner (1904–1990) responded to this deficiency by offering a different approach to behavioral learning, one that featured what he called "operant conditioning." In his "The Behavior of Organisms," published in May 1938,[18] Skinner laid out more than 400 pages of experimental findings on the behavioral conditioning of the male white rat. His investigations showed that behaviors that were at first produced randomly could be brought under operant control through a mechanism of selective reinforcement by the environment.

Skinner's incursion into experimental psychology was met initially by a largely negative response from the psychological community. With time, however, his ideas began to gain acceptance. Ultimately, he succeeded in achieving a popularity that, at its peak, is said to have exceeded even that of Sigmund Freud, at least in the United States.[19]

Operant conditioning imputes a more subtle relationship between stimuli and behavior than that offered by simple Pavlovian stimulus-response conditioning. While the environment is still the shaper of behavior, it plays this role only after the fact. Behavior always comes first, environmental molding always comes after. As Skinner put it, "operant conditioning shapes behavior as a sculptor shapes a lump of clay."[20]

---

[17] Watson 1925.

[18] Skinner 1938.

[19] Staddon 2014.

[20] Skinner 1965.

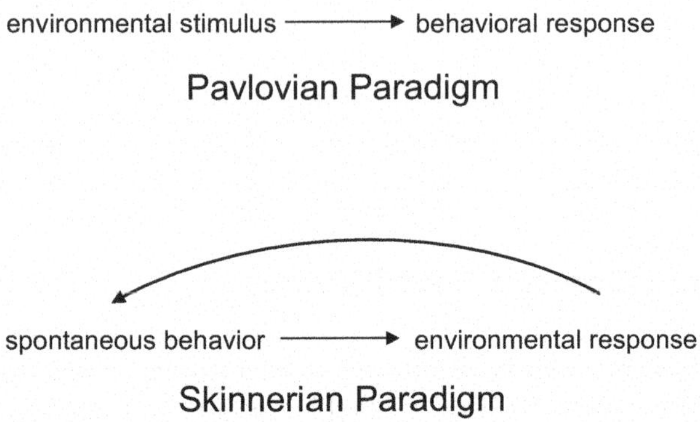

Fig. 2.5 Behavioral conditioning models

Since it does not deal with stimulus-response reflexes, operant conditioning is outside the purview of the reflex principle, at least in the Pavlovian sense. Instead, operant conditioning brings a new element into the stimulus-response relationship, one based on the shaping of spontaneously emitted random behavior.

Fig. 2.5 illustrates the difference between Pavlovian classical conditioning and Skinnerian operant conditioning. The key distinction is in their starting points. With Pavlovian conditioning the starting point is the environmental stimulus, which drives behavior; while with Skinnerian conditioning the starting point is spontaneously emitted behavior, which evokes feedback from the environment. Skinner likened the selection of behaviors by operant conditioning to the selection of genes by Darwinian natural selection: in both cases, spontaneous activity occurs first, environmental shaping comes after.

Both Pavlovian and Skinnerian conditioning have plausible brain correlates. We will encounter the Skinnerian correlate a little later in this chapter and the Pavlovian correlate in Chap. 4.

Geschwind and the Return of the Diagram Makers

By mid-twentieth century, behaviorism had become the dominant school of psychology but its reign was soon to end. Beginning in the 1950s, a renewed interest in intervening cognitive variables spawned a "cognitive revolution" in psychology, and advancing technology revitalized research into the brain correlates of learning and behavior. Before long, the nineteenth-century theories of directional cortical pathways began to resurface. Most influential in this development was the publication in 1965 of the monumental "Disconnexion Syndromes in Animals and Man"[21] by the Brooklyn-born neurologist, Norman Geschwind (1926–1984). Geschwind revisited the pathway theories of Wernicke and the "diagram makers" and highlighted the anatomical analyses performed by Flechsig. He went on to make the case that a modular pathway model of cortical function best explained the clinical syndromes that he and his predecessors had observed. The influence of Geschwind's paper was enormous.[22] Its publication sparked a return to the nineteenth-century cortical pathway perspective, bringing terms like "Broca's aphasia" and "Wernicke's aphasia" to the level of textbook teaching.

Rockland and Pandya

In 1979, neuroanatomists Kathleen Rockland and Deepak Pandya at Boston University reported a startling finding regarding cortical connectivity that considerably strengthened the argument for directional pathways in the cerebral cortex. Rockland and Pandya's work capitalized on the multilayer nature of the cortical sheet, a feature known since the mid-nineteenth century, when anatomists found that most well-developed parts of the cortex consisted of six layers oriented parallel to the cortical surface. The layers could be distinguished by the types and densities of nerve cells and processes present at various cortical depths. Rockland and Pandya asked whether the interconnectivity between adjacent cortical regions depended in any way on the cortical layer in which the connecting neurons resided. They chose for their study the first three regions in Flechsig's visual cortical processing hierarchy, commonly referred to as V1, V2, and V4. Using the then recently developed retrograde tracer, horseradish peroxidase, they examined the interconnectivity between these cortical regions as a function of cortical layer.

[21] Geschwind 1965a,b.

[22] Absher 1993.

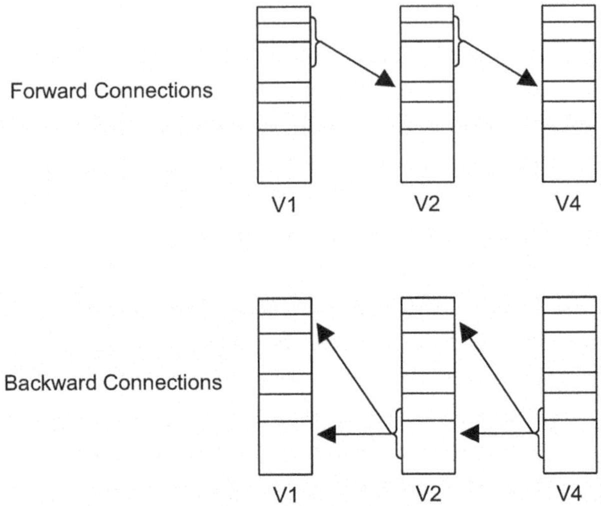

Fig. 2.6 Directionality of cortical connectivity as proposed by Rockland and Pandya

They uncovered a dramatically asymmetric pattern in the connections between adjacent regions (Fig. 2.6). They found that in the V1 to V4 direction (Fig. 2.6, top row), the connecting fibers originated in the upper layers and targeted layer 4, while in the V4 to V1 direction (Fig. 2.6, bottom row), the connecting fibers originated in the lower layers and targeted every layer except layer 4. Their results were subsequently extended to other visual areas, where as many as 10 sequential levels were identified, and to other sensory modalities as well.

Rockland and Pandya interpreted their observations as evidence of the presence of directional pathways in the cortex. They suggested that the connections running from V1 to V4 were *feedforward* in nature and those running in the reverse order were of a *feedback* variety. In support of their proposed distinction, they noted that the degree of divergence of the connections was different for the two directions, with connections in the backward direction being more divergent than those in the forward direction.[23] This, they suggested, was as would be expected for feedback versus feedforward connectivity.

---

[23] Rockland 2002.

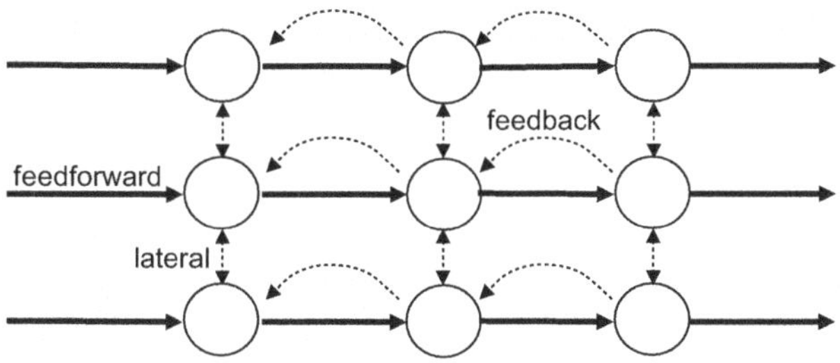

Fig. 2.7 The directed modular pathway design

A word on terminology is needed here. Rockland and Pandya's use of the term "feedback" places the reverse flow in a subordinate position, as merely a modifier of the feedforward flow. There are, however, other types of reverse flow with prominent roles in brain function. For example, there is *reentrant* flow, in which the results of computations are cycled back into the processing sequence, creating a feedback loop that introduces certain emergent properties into cortical function. In addition, there are *top-down* effects, which are of two varieties: the top-down action of a system on its constituent elements, and the top-down action of the frontal lobes on the posterior cortices. Reentrant flow and top-down actions have effects that in some circumstances supersede those introduced by the feedforward flow. We will need to keep the varied nature of reverse flow mechanisms in mind as we go along.

Over the decades since Rockland and Pandya's report, the case for directional cortical pathways has been supported in other ways, including by the observation that neuronal responses in successive modules of a pathway are tuned to increasingly complex stimuli and come after progressively longer time delays.[24] The directional theme has also been expanded to include multiple pathways running in parallel. I will refer to the resulting arrangement, which combines directionality with modularity as a *directed modular pathway* design, depicted schematically in Fig. 2.7. Shown are the feedforward and feedback connections identified by Rockland and Pandya, as well as lateral connections that provide for communication between parallel directed pathways.

[24] Lamme 2000; Felleman 1991.

The Information Processing Model of Cortical Function

The directed modular arrangement features sequential processing along successive modules in parallel pathways. What, we might ask, is being processed along these pathways? An important advance was the proposal that *information* played this role. The burgeoning field of information theory could then be brought to bear on the study of cortical processing, and with it the ability to cast cortical processing in mathematical terms.

The idea of modeling brain function in terms of information processing arose in concert with the cognitive revolution of the 1950s and in particular with the 1958 publication of "Perception and Communication" by the British psychologist, Donald Broadbent (1926–1993).[25] According to Broadbent's scheme, information is processed sequentially from one cognitive module to the next, the processed information "flowing" along directed pathways. Within each module the information coming in from the module just before it in the pathway is filtered and undergoes computational transformation. The result is then relayed to the next module in the pathway where a further round of information processing takes place, and so on for each of the modules in the pathway. The resulting sequence of information processing and transmission forms an *information processing pathway*, which in turn serves as the basis for an *information processing model* of cortical function.

Is the Cerebral Cortex a Reflex Machine?

Given the foregoing, can we conclude that a more or less complete description of cortical function can be provided in terms of information processing along input-output modular pathways? That is, can we regard the cortex as no more than a complex reflex device, one that receives signals from the environment, modifies them in a predictable fashion, and then uses the results to control the organism's behavior? To some degree we can. When Pavlov's dogs drooled reflexively at the sight of meat, or when humans reflexively recoil at the sight of a snake, cortical reflexes

---

[25] Broadbent 1958.

are clearly invoked. The visual recognition of the meat or snake requires sensory analysis at the cortical level, and the automatic and stereotyped nature of the response indicates that the information is being processed in a simple reflexive manner.

The question of interest, however, is not whether there is reflex action present in the cerebral cortex but whether such action is the guiding principle for cortical function in general. Accumulating evidence suggests that there are, in fact, at least two factors that complicate the response to this question. First, there are the relative roles of feedforward, feedback, and lateral directionality in the processing of information. Proponents of the directed modular pathway design contend that connectivity is predominantly feedforward, with feedback and lateral connections playing only an ancillary role. Proponents of omnidirectional connectivity, on the other hand, tend to emphasize the impact of the feedback and lateral connections in cortical processing. While the issue is still under debate, the perspective that places feedforward connections as the "driving" connections, with feedback and lateral connections playing the role of modifiers of the feedforward flow, would seem to be the most widely held view at this time.

The second complicating factor, which is difficult to explain away, is the presence of spontaneous activity arising from within the cortex itself. For the cortex to be regarded as a reflex machine it would need to be established that intrusions of any spontaneously arising cortical activity have only a minor effect on the ongoing information processing, serving as no more than perturbations of the feedforward reflex activity. Experiments have shown, however, that the cortex is rife with spontaneously generated intrinsic activity that in fact accounts for most of the total activity present in the cortex. Direct measurements show that in a subject at rest with eyes closed, cortical neurons fire spontaneously every 10 seconds or so on average, implying the presence of a resting energy expenditure dwarfing that associated with incoming stimuli.[26] Only a small portion of cortical activity, often less than 5 percent of the total, is stimulus-induced.[27]

In addition to the quantity of spontaneous activity generation, there is also a matter of its organization. Until recently, the tendency was to

[26] Kerr 2005.

[27] Raichle 2010.

consider spontaneous cortical activity as mere noise, a nuisance to be subdued and eliminated. It has become evident, however, that this "noise," although appearing to be haphazard on casual inspection, is actually organized in its own right. The quantity and organization of intrinsically generated cortical activity have prompted some investigators to go so far as to regard the intrinsic activity as the dominant variable in cortical function, with sensory input playing only the ancillary role of moving the intrinsic activity from state to state.[28]

Spontaneous Activity Generated in the Frontal Lobes

Nowhere is the impact of spontaneously generated cortical activity more manifest than in the frontal lobes. Clinical observation of patients with extensive frontal lobe damage makes this clear. Patients with severe frontal lobe damage lose all spontaneity, their attention becoming glued to objects immediately in front of them and their actions being reduced to stereotyped, reflexive grasping movements. Additionally, behavior becomes repetitive and inflexible. This is evident even in patients with only modest frontal lobe dysfunction. For such patients, the Wisconsin Card Sort test may be used to expose the inflexibility of their thinking and behavior. The testing procedure begins with subjects receiving a pack of stimulus cards with symbols printed on each card that vary in shape, color, and number. Subjects are required to place the cards in piles according to either the shape, color, or number of symbols printed on them. They are not told which criterion to use, however. This they must discover by trial and error based on feedback they are given as they place cards on the piles one by one. Once a subject discovers the rule, the test takes a devious turn. Unbeknownst to the subject, the sorting criterion is suddenly changed, requiring the subject to detect the alteration and to deduce the new rule by trial and error. The number of trials it takes for the rule change to be detected and for the new rule to be learned is noted. Normal individuals discover the rule change quickly and adapt their responses within a few trials. Frontally damaged patients,

[28] Raichle 2010.

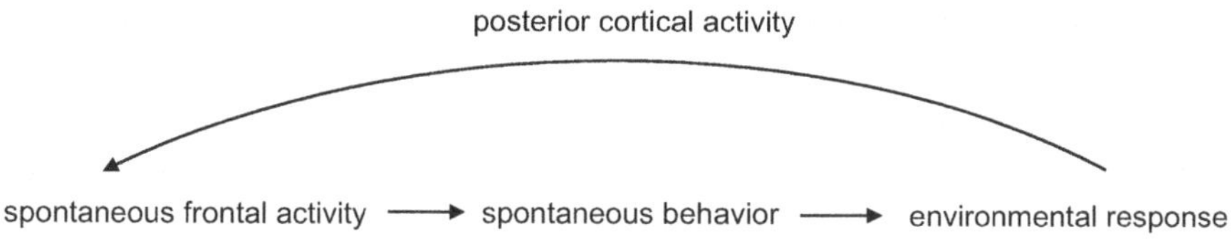

Fig. 2.8 Injection of spontaneous frontal activity renders cortical information flow best modeled by a Skinnerian design

in contrast, are slow to pick up on the rule change and frequently fail to readapt their behavior at all.

Abundant evidence has accrued in support of the thesis that the frontal lobes are a preeminent source of behavioral spontaneity. The frontal lobes can be thought of as injecting spontaneity into what might otherwise be a Pavlovian reflex machine. Indeed, the insertion of frontal lobe spontaneity renders the cortex better modeled by Skinner's operant conditioning paradigm than by Pavlov's reflex paradigm (Fig. 2.8).

In keeping with the Skinnerian paradigm, spontaneous frontal activity can be regarded as the driver of spontaneous non-reflexive behavior, the role of the posterior cortices being reduced to bringing environmental feedback to bear on the decisions being made by the frontal lobes. Analysis of frontal lobe connectivity corroborates this perspective. The connections between the posterior cortices and the frontal lobes are not merely a continuation of the feedforward flow exhibited within the posterior cortices but are bidirectionally symmetric, with no clear feedforward and feedback distinction.

In all, then, the reflex principle cannot adequately explain cortical processing. Although there is a directional component to cortical information flow, the influx of spontaneous activity renders a reflexive view of cortical processing problematic.

Cortical Processing and Conscious Experience

Our extended review of the long debate over cortical localization and information flow has therefore led us to a description of cortical processing not in terms of reflex pathways but of directed modular pathways that admit spontaneous activity into the information processing scheme. We may now ask where this leaves us with respect to our search for the NCC. Current dogma dictates that an architecture that emphasizes directed pathways cannot support conscious experience, it being assumed that only a collection of fully interacting modules with no preferred direction of information flow can provide for the emergence of sentience. In the coming chapters I will attempt to counter this bias by presenting evidence in support of a predominant role of directed modular pathways in cortical function and by presenting a mechanism by which such pathways can serve as a neural substrate for conscious experience. The effort will begin with an examination of the brain basis for three principal categories of conscious experience: perception, memory, and feelings.

3

Perception

Introduction

The Contents of Conscious Experience

To determine whether a directed modular pathway model provides an appropriate framework for a cortically based NCC, I will for convenience divide conscious experience into three categories: *perceptions*, *memories*, and *feelings*, devoting one chapter to each. I am not suggesting that this partition is in any way fundamental. In fact, I will ultimately argue that conscious experiences of all types share the same basic brain mechanisms.

Perception and the Directed Modular Pathway Model

We start in this chapter with *perception*, the process by which the brain learns of the outside world. Figure 3.1 shows the proposed directed modular pathway arrangement, with perception defined as *a neurobiological process that starts with stimuli impinging on sensory*

S. Sevush, *The Single-Neuron Theory*,
DOI 10.1007/978-3-319-33708-1_3

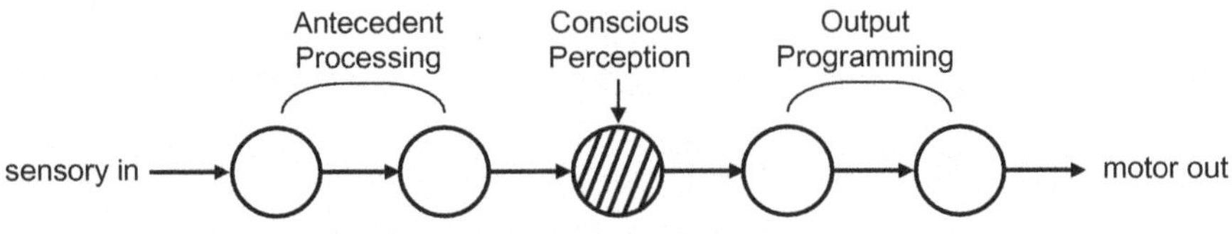

Fig. 3.1 The perception pathway

receptors, continues with processing along directed modular pathways, and culminates in the generation of conscious experiences and behavioral output. Note that in this example only one of the modules corresponds to conscious experience, the remainder being linked to antecedent or subsequent unconscious processing.[1] I will use the term *conscious perception* to connote the limited portion of the perceptual pathway that is directly linked to conscious experience.

The sequence of modules portrayed in Fig. 3.1 is presumed to play out in space as well as time. That is, each module is assumed to be in a separate location on the cortical sheet, the sequence representing an actual spatial succession that moves from posterior to anterior along the cortical surface. This is quite different from the situation that would accompany an omnidirectional information processing arrangement. In the omnidirectional case, the information processing sequence would play out over time but not over space, with successive stages representing a progression of states in a widely distributed modular network that evolves over time but remains spatially stationary. It is crucial, if we are to make progress in our search for the NCC, that we determine whether in fact the directed modular pathway model applies to information processing as it occurs in the cortex. With this in mind, we turn now to an analysis of visual perception, which is the best studied of the perceptual modalities. We will attempt to determine for this modality how well a directed modular pathway model can account for the empirical evidence that has accrued over the years.

[1] Miller 2014.

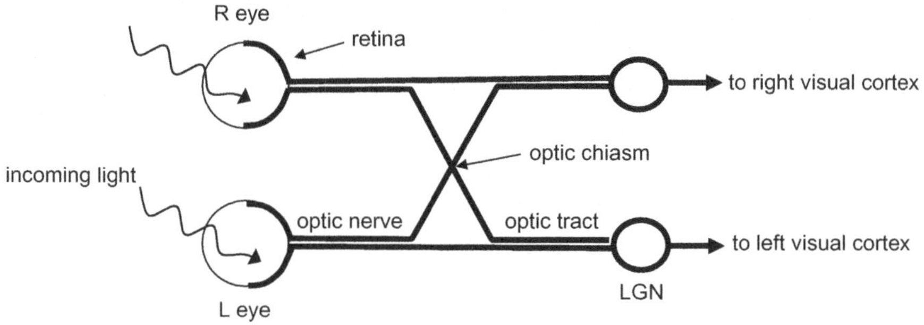

Fig. 3.2 Early visual processing pathways. Abbreviations: LGN, lateral geniculate nucleus

Visual Perception Starts in the Retina

We begin with an overview of the early stages of visual processing, where the applicability of a directed modular pathway model is generally agreed upon. All visual perception starts in the retina, which is situated in the back of the eye. The retina is populated by a variety of cell types arranged in layers. Processing begins when the light entering the eye impinges on the *photoreceptors* in the rearmost layer of the retina and then proceeds in a strongly feedforward manner by successively engaging bipolar, horizontal, and amacrine cells, and ultimately reaching the *ganglion cell* layer, which is the output layer of the retina.

In the next step, the outgoing signals from the retina are carried to the brain by the *axons* (emitting fibers) of the ganglion cells, which bundle together to form the optic nerve. The information flow is entirely feedforward; there are no signals transmitted from the higher centers back onto the retina.[2] On their way to the brain, the fibers of the optic nerves rearrange themselves at the *optic chiasm* to form the right and left *optic tracts*. As a result of the rearrangement, each tract transmits information referable to the opposite side of space only (Fig. 3.2).

The optic tracts transmit the retinal signals to the *lateral geniculate nuclei* (LGN) in the thalamus. Here, both feedforward and feedback

[2] Westheimer 2004.

transmission come into play. Although the feedforward connections account for only 10–20 percent of the input the LGN receives, they are nevertheless the principal determinants of LGN responses to visual stimuli.[3]

In the next step, the LGNs project their output to the primary visual cortex in the occipital lobes, which is the starting point for all cortical processing. Evaluation of visual stimuli is a high-priority item, with a full 20 percent of the cortex, comprising some five billion neurons, being devoted to visual analysis.[4] This number represents an immense expansion from the three million axons that are present in the optic nerves and reflects an insertion of abundant new information into the processing flow. As with the projection from the retina to the geniculate nuclei, the projection from the geniculate nuclei to the primary visual cortex is dominated numerically by feedback connectivity. The feedforward connections are, however, individually much stronger than the feedback connections and, despite their smaller number, remain the significant driving force in primary visual cortical processing.[5]

Ventral and Dorsal Streams

The processing in the visual cortex proceeds separately in the two cerebral hemispheres. Within each hemisphere, there is a further segregation of processing into what has come to be known as the *dorsal* and *ventral streams* (Fig. 3.3).[6] The discovery of the dual stream arrangement was made in the 1980s and has turned out to have widespread applicability throughout the cerebral cortex. Both streams are well modeled by directed modular pathways that run from the occipital to the frontal cortices, with the dorsal stream passing through the parietal cortex and the ventral stream passing through the temporal cortex.

The two streams differ in how they process visual information. The ventral stream is devoted to figuring out the identity of an object being looked

[3] Sherman 1998.

[4] Wandell 2007.

[5] Ferster 2000.

[6] Milner 1995.

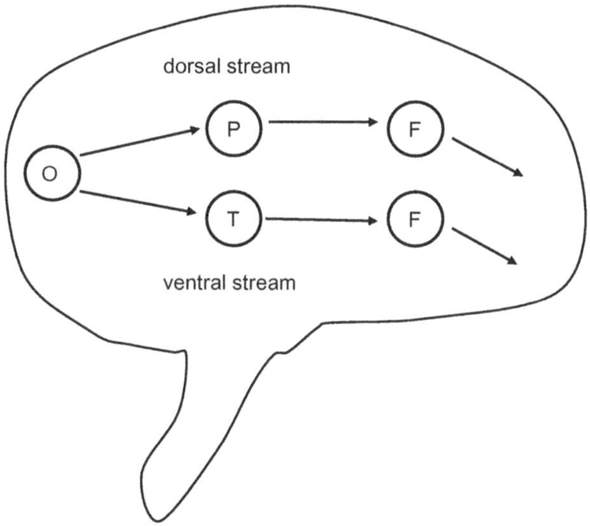

Fig. 3.3 Dual stream arrangement of visual processing. Abbreviations: F, frontal; O, occipital; P, parietal; T, temporal

at and is accordingly referred to as the "what" stream. The focus in this stream is on the form, texture, and color of objects, and on associating them with meaning, memory, emotion, and reward value. Separate parallel ventral stream pathways have been identified that are specialized for faces, colors, written and spoken words, and a number of other categories.

The dorsal stream is concerned with the visual guidance of motor responses. When the motor responses take place in three-dimensional space, such as with head and eye movements, reaching hand movements, and movements of attention, the dorsal stream is referred to as the "where" stream. The dorsal stream also includes motor responses that are not spatial, such as the lip and tongue movements involved in speaking. It may therefore be more appropriate to label the dorsal stream a "how" stream rather than a "where" stream.

Both streams, and others as well, are engaged simultaneously in real-life visual perception. The identity of an object, for example, can be discerned independently by shape, color, texture, or motion. The multiple avenues lend the perceptual process a robust flexibility in facing the wide range of stimuli encountered in the naturally occurring environment.

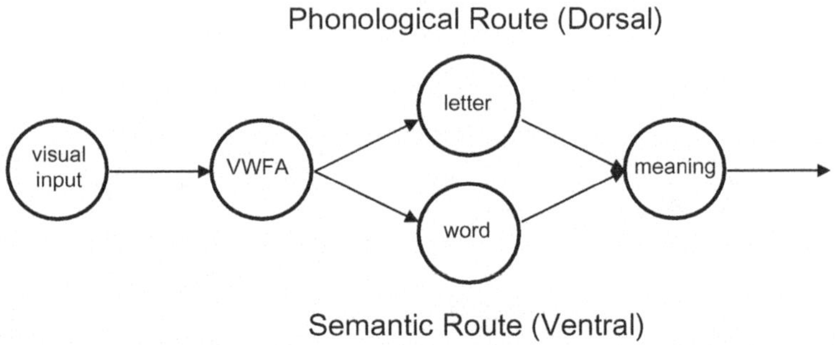

Fig. 3.4 Dual route model of reading. Abbreviation: VWFA, visual word-form area

Ventral and Dorsal Routes for Reading

The cortical mechanisms of reading illustrate the workings of the dual-stream architecture (Fig. 3.4). Reading begins with processing of visually presented letter strings, first by the retina and primary visual cortex and then by a *visual word-form area* (VWFA) in the occipito-temporal cortex.[7] At this point, processing diverges into two parallel routes. One, a dorsally positioned *phonological route*, proceeds by a strategy of "sounding out" written words letter by letter (grapheme-to-phoneme conversion) and then attaching meaning to the words on the basis of their pronunciation. In keeping with its dorsal location, the phonological route associates visual stimuli directly with motor responses. The other, a ventrally positioned *semantic route*, proceeds by a strategy of "reading by sight," where words are recognized visually as a whole and linked directly to meaning without any phonological intermediary.

The phonological route is the one we use when we first learn to read during childhood. The semantic route dominates when we become fluent readers. With the semantic route, written words are assessed as a whole, the exact placement of the letters within the words being of minimal importance. To experience the semantic route in action, try reading this:

> I cdnuolt blveiee that I cluod aulaclty uesdnatnrd waht I was rdanieg. Bceuase of hte phaonmneal pweor of the hmaun mnid, it dseno't mtaetr in

[7] Warrington 1980.

waht oerdr the ltteres in a wrod are, the olny iproamtnt tihng is that the frsit and lsat ltteers be in the rghit pclae. The rset can be a taotl mses and you can sitll raed it whotuit a pboerlm. Tihs is bcuseae the huamn mnid deos not raed ervey lteter by istlef, but the wrod as a wlohe. Azanmig huh? Yaeh and I awlyas tghuhot slpeling was ipmornatt!

The two reading routes are anatomically separable, the phonological route proceeding by a more dorsal pathway, the semantic route by a more ventral pathway. The anatomical separation makes it possible for brain damage to selectively impair one or the other route. In the 1980s, Ken Heilman and I reported a case in which a patient's phonological route was selectively damaged as a consequence of a stroke.[8] The patient was a 61-year-old man who suffered a left occipito-parietal infarction that left him able to read words but unable to identify their constituent letters. Amazingly, he was able to read the word "pea" but could not identify or say the letter "p." A similar distinction was evident for "eye" vs "I," "bee" vs "b," and "tea" vs "t."

An analogous disability occurs in children suffering from "developmental phonological dyslexia." These children have difficulty reading by sounding out letters and instead attack words as a whole via the semantic route. Not surprisingly, they make mistakes involving letter omissions and letter inversions both when reading and when writing.

The opposite syndrome, in which reading letters is intact but whole word reading is impaired, is also seen.[9] In such cases, which result from selective damage to the ventrally situated semantic route, patients may resort to a strategy of naming the individual letters aloud and deciphering words through their spelling.

It is hypothesized that the ventral stream is the one most closely linked to conscious perception.[10] It will therefore be the focus of our attention as we continue our analysis of cortical processing. As a matter of terminology, the cortical modules in the ventral stream are usually labeled successively as V1, V2, and V4 in the occipital lobe, and as TEO and TE in the inferior temporal lobe (Fig. 3.5).

---

[8] Sevush 1984.

[9] Warrington 1980.

[10] Milner 1995.

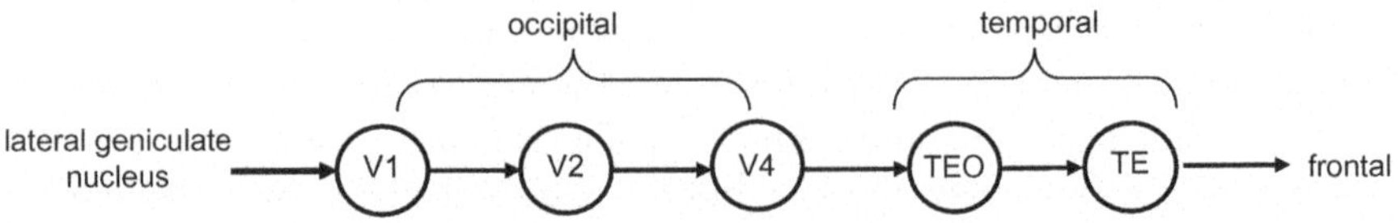

Fig. 3.5 The ventral stream for visual processing

In all, then, we see that information processing can, at least for early visual functions, be plausibly viewed in terms of directed modular pathways. We turn now to a detailed analysis of two of the ventral stream's most salient functions, *form* perception and *color* perception. We ask whether the information processing pertaining to these two functions can be convincingly viewed as proceeding along a succession of modular stages arranged in a spatially directed fashion. We start with form perception.

Visual Perception of Form

Form Perception Begins in the Retina

Perception of the visual form of an object is perception of its shape as it would be captured in a line drawing. Its brain basis provides a clear example of directed modular processing in the cortex. The sequence begins in the retina where the incoming light generates a two-dimensional activation pattern of the photoreceptors on the retinal surface. The processing then traverses the successive retinal layers, ultimately reaching the ganglion cell output layer. The activation patterns of the ganglion cells in this layer represent the final result of all the retinal computations performed on the incoming light.

The activation of ganglion cells in response to visual stimuli was first studied in the 1930s by the American physiologist and Nobel laureate Keffer Hartline (1903–1983). In work on frogs, Hartline discovered that each ganglion cell responds to changes in illumination of a small disc-shaped area on the retinal surface. He used the term *receptive field* to designate the region of the retina to which a ganglion cell was most responsive.[11] The term has became a staple in brain research, its meaning now generalized to connote the preferential responsivity of a neuron within any stimulus space, be it the visual field, the retina, the body surface, the set of all speech sounds, the set of all smells, and so on. Receptive fields are the link between neuronal activity and the happenings in the outside world.

In the 1950s, the Hungarian-American neurophysiologist Stephen Kuffler, working on cats and using more refined visual stimuli, mapped out the ganglion cell receptive fields in greater detail. He determined that they consisted of two separate concentric regions within which changes in illumination had opposite effects: a central excitatory region within which an increase in illumination causes an increase in cell firing, and a peripheral inhibitory region within which an increase in illumination causes a decrease in cell firing.[12] The effect of this *center-surround* arrangement was that a given ganglion cell had its strongest response when a stimulus consisted of a spot of increased illumination surrounded by a ring of decreased illumination. The cell was therefore excited not merely by the presence or absence of light but by a change in illumination across a circular boundary.

Subsequent work has shown that the center-surround arrangement is widespread in the cortex, with variations on the theme being observed in all stages of the visual information processing sequences and in other sensory processing sequences as well. Kuffler suggested that the center-surround arrangement response pattern might serve to enhance contrast detection. Contrast enhancement would, in turn, facilitate the categorization of visual stimuli in terms of their spatial makeup.

V1 Line/Orientation Detectors

Signals from the retinal ganglion cells are sent to the *lateral geniculate nucleus* (LGN) of the thalamus, where neurons continue to have concentric receptive fields, and are then relayed to the primary visual cortex,

---

[11] Hartline 1938.

[12] Kuffler 1953.

V1. Here the receptive fields undergo a significant change. In landmark studies beginning in 1959 at Johns Hopkins and continuing through the 1960s at Harvard, David Hubel and Torsten Wiesel established the nature of this change.

Their key discovery came inadvertently while they were assessing the electrical responses of visual cortical cells in anesthetized cats.[13] They were exploring the receptive fields of the cells using disc-shaped stimuli on glass slides, in line with what Hartline and Kuffler had done with the ganglion cells. Their objective was to determine if any of the disc-shaped stimuli could elicit a response in a cell from which they were recording.

During one of the sessions, following hours of futile efforts in their search for a suitable stimulus, a breakthrough occurred. On one of the trials, they noticed that a neuron from which they were recording began firing vigorously as the slide was being inserted into the projector, well before the disc-shaped stimulus had moved into view. With some effort they were able to determine that the effective stimulus had nothing to do with what was on the glass slide but consisted instead of the edge of the slide itself as it passed through the visual field. They had serendipitously discovered that neurons in the visual cortex were sensitive not to circular patches of light but to edges or lines. They were awarded the Nobel Prize for their discovery in 1981.

The finding that primary visual cortical neurons respond to edges led Hubel and Wiesel to hypothesize that when exploring the visual environment the brain only takes note of boundaries and ignores the spaces in between. They suggested that the brain fills in the missing information, such that our conscious perceptions are of complete images. The brain apparently assumes that if no edge is detected in a particular region, then nothing new is happening in that region, and therefore it must consist of the same color and texture as that present at the boundary. Reflecting on the discovery, Hubel wrote:

> Many people, including myself, still have trouble accepting the idea that the interior of a form … does not itself excite cells in our brain—that our awareness of the interior as black or white or colored … depends only on

[13] Hubel 1998; Hubel 1962.

Fig. 3.6 Hierarchical visual processing as proposed by Hubel and Wiesel. Output from neurons in the lateral geniculate nucleus (left) that are activated by adjacent points in the visual field project onto a neuron in V1 (right) whose receptive field consists of an oriented line

> cells sensitive to the borders. The intellectual argument is that perception of an evenly lit interior depends on the activation of cells having fields at the borders and on the absence of activation of cells whose fields are within the borders, since such activation would indicate that the interior is not evenly lit. So our perception of the interior as black, white, gray or green has nothing to do with cells whose fields are in the interior—hard as that may be to swallow. But if an engineer were designing a machine to encode such a form, I think this is exactly what he would do. What happens at the borders is the only information you need to know: the interior is boring. Who could imagine that the brain would not evolve in such a way as to handle the information with the least number of cells?[14]

With further experimentation, Hubel and Wiesel found that not only was the presence of an edge important in evoking a neuronal response, but the spatial orientation of the edge was important as well. That is, neurons in V1 responded best to the presence of edges with particular spatial orientations.

In their classic 1962 paper, Hubel and Wiesel speculated on the mechanism by which the receptive fields of visual cortical cells were generated. They suggested that convergent input from oriented linear arrays of lateral geniculate cells onto V1 neurons might account for the V1 visual fields taking the form of oriented edges (Fig. 3.6). They went on to speculate that this might be a general theme of cortical function, with convergent connections from one cortical level to the next yielding receptive fields

[14] Hubel 1995.

of ever-increasing abstraction and complexity as the modular pathway is traversed.

As it pertains to conscious experience, we can say that the receptive fields of neurons in successive modules become ever more *explicit*.[15] That is, the receptive fields of the neurons become increasingly removed from the raw stimuli and progressively closer to what we consciously perceive. The directed modular pathways can therefore be regarded as not only directional but hierarchical as well. We note also that when the receptive fields have become fully explicit we will have arrived at the NCC.

Hand Detectors, Face Detectors

Following the processing in the retina and in V1, information processing relating to form perception passes to V2, then to V4, and then to TEO, the neuronal receptive fields becoming progressively more sophisticated as the hierarchy is ascended. With processing subsequent to V1, oriented lines give way to oriented line segments and then to angles and curves that may serve as an "alphabet" for constructing more complex percepts.[16] In V2, neurons respond to the texture of a visual stimulus.[17] In V4, object boundaries and figure-ground relationships are established.[18] At each stage, the receptive fields edge ever closer to what we experience consciously.

When processing reaches TE, representations become quite explicit, with neurons being found that have preferential responsivity to recognizable objects. The first experimental evidence of this came with the work of Charles Gross and his colleagues at MIT beginning in the late 1960s.[19] Gross recalls that he and his colleagues were examining neurons in the inferior temporal cortex in macaque monkeys using the same single-cell recording techniques that Hubel and Wiesel had used so successfully in the primary visual cortex. They had set their focus on the inferior temporal cortex because damage to this area had been known

---

[15] Koch 2004.

[16] Ungerleider 2011.

[17] Freeman 2013.

[18] Roe 2012.

[19] Gross 1969.

to result in clinical syndromes in which patients are unable to visually identify objects placed in front of them despite having otherwise normal vision.

Their choice turned out to be a good one. Like Hubel and Wiesel, Gross and colleagues made their key discovery accidentally. They were in the process of testing the responses of a particular neuron in a monkey's inferior temporal cortex to various standard stimuli (bars, circles, rectangles, and so forth) and had so far been unable to find a stimulus that could drive the cell. Then, in a moment of exasperation, or might we say inspiration, they simply waved a hand in front of the apparatus. The neuron responded vigorously! They spent the next 12 hours trying to determine whether it was the waving hand or some other aspect of the stimulus that had triggered the cell. Try as they might, they could find no stimulus that excited the cell as much as did a hand or something resembling a hand. The cell responded better to a realistic model of a hand than to just an outline, and it responded best of all to a real hand.

Because of the then prevailing bias against conceptions of hierarchal cortical pathways and explicit receptive fields, the researchers were reluctant to use the term "hand cells" for the hand-reactive neurons. Although the initial report, and subsequent ones as well, were published in the most highly regarded journals and the research was conducted at an esteemed university, the findings were ignored in the scientific literature for nearly a decade.

In the early 1980s, cells in the temporal lobe were discovered that were specifically responsive to faces.[20] This did catch the attention of the field. The responsive neurons increased their firing rate in response to human and monkey faces but not to bars, spots, edges, gratings, hands, or other objects.

That some sort of "face cells" might be found in the inferior temporal lobe was plausible, given the established connection between the temporal lobes and facial recognition. What was striking, however, was that each neuron was individually responsive to the entire face, countering the prevailing bias against receptive fields with such a high degree of explicitness.

---

[20] Richmond 1983; Bruce 1981.

Face Identity Detectors

The discovery of face cells provided clear evidence of hierarchical processing in the ventral stream and raised the question of whether the hierarchical progression went still further. The answer came in 2005 when neuroscientist Rodrigo Quian Quiroga and his colleagues at Caltech reported their findings on single neuron activity in patients undergoing surgery for refractory epilepsy. The surgical procedure, performed on awake patients, consisted of removing parts of the patients' temporal lobes to eliminate suspected seizure foci. Prior to the surgical removal, electrical readings from neurons in various locations had to be taken in order to localize the region of dysfunctional tissue. Quiroga and his group took advantage of the opportunity this afforded to measure the responsivity of individual neurons in awake humans to various stimuli.

Their observations were spectacular. The researchers identified medial temporal lobe neurons that could be characterized as "face identity cells," cells that were selectively responsive to the image of the face of a particular individual but to no other faces. It didn't matter from what perspective the face was observed or how the face was adorned, the neuron would still respond. In one case, a cell was activated selectively by different images of former president Bill Clinton.[21] The neuron responded to a drawing of Clinton's face, a picture of Clinton alongside two other people, and other images of Clinton. On the other hand, it failed to respond to fifty other items, including pictures of three other presidents.

Other single neurons were found that responded selectively to pictures of The Beatles, Michael Jordan, Oprah Winfrey, Tom Cruise, and Saddam Hussein. One neuron was activated by pictures of the actress Jennifer Aniston alone but not to pictures of her together with the actor Brad Pitt and not to other famous faces, nor to landmarks, animals, or objects. Neurons would respond even when the target face was just imagined with eyes closed.[22]

Neurons selectively responsive to the actor Steve Carell would, when activated, fire up to 20 times per second, compared to almost total silence

[21] Quian Quiroga 2005.

[22] Crick 2004.

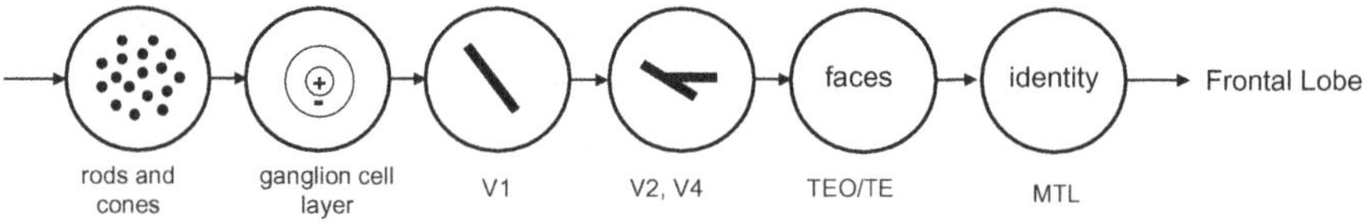

Fig. 3.7 Modular pathway for form perception. Abbreviation: MTL, medial temporal lobe

at baseline. Neurons selectively responsive to items other than faces were also observed. Over the course of the investigations, selective responsivity was found for landmark buildings, animals, and food items.[23]

In one instance, an individual neuron was activated not only by pictures and drawings of the actress Halle Berry, but also by the letter string H-a-l-l-e-B-e-r-r-y. Other neurons that responded to both the name and picture of a face or object were also observed.[24] This suggested that not only are there individual neurons present in the brain that recognize familiar faces, but there are neurons present that are tuned to more abstract notions of an individual's identity.

The significance of all these findings is that individual neurons could be identified whose responsivity was stunningly explicit, indicating a degree of hierarchical processing scarcely imagined a half century ago. The hierarchical process apparently extended across three stages, yielding first an analysis of sensory features, then a recognition of object class, and lastly a recognition of specific identity.

Summary of Form Perception

In summary, for the category of form perception, a compelling case can be made for the presence of a hierarchical modular progression along the ventral stream (Fig. 3.7). First, photoreceptors in the retina encode the incoming light. Retinal ganglion cells then integrate the photoreceptor responses to identify points of contrast in the visual field. Neurons in V1 and V2 then integrate the ganglion cell responses to identify the presence

[23] Quian Quiroga 2005.

[24] Quian Quiroga 2005.

of edges in the visual field. V4 then integrates the input from V1 and V2 to detect object boundaries and figure-ground relationships. Areas TEO and TE then integrate the input from V4 to detect objects. Finally, further processing in the medial temporal cortex, and likely in the frontal lobes, leads to neurons that respond preferentially to the unique identity of faces and other objects.

Visual Perception of Color

Color Perception Begins in the Retina

We now turn to color perception, which, like form perception, is effectively described in terms of hierarchical modular processing. We start by noting that light itself is colorless, a fact intuited by Isaac Newton three hundred years ago:

> The rays, to speak properly, are not colored. In them there is nothing else than a certain power to stir up a sensation of this or that color … to determine by what modes or actions light produceth in our minds the phantasm of colour is not so easie.[25]

The great nineteenth-century Scottish physicist James Clark Maxwell drew the same conclusion:

> If the sensation which we call colour has any laws it must be something in our own nature that determines the nature of these laws … The science of colour must therefore be regarded as essentially a mental science.[26]

We cannot even attach a specific color to a given wavelength of light. Contextual effects that determine the colors we experience are actively created by the brain, not by the outside world. Again, the light itself is properly described in terms of wavelengths, not color.

---

[25] Newton 1730.

[26] Maxwell 1872.

Color Processing by the Cones

So how does the brain convert colorless wavelengths of light into conscious color perceptions? The process begins in the retina, where there are two types of photoreceptors, *rods* and *cones*, that translate the wavelength information contained in the incoming light into electrical signals that can be interpreted by the brain. The rods, which account for 95 percent of all photoreceptors, are specialized for rapid black and white peripheral vision. They are exquisitely sensitive to light, being able to detect even single photons, making them ideal for night (*scotopic*) vision. The less numerous cones, which account for only 5 percent of all photoreceptors, are used for daytime (*photopic*) perception of the color, shape, and texture of objects. They are located preferentially in the center of the retina, have high spatial resolution, and are differentially responsive to the wavelengths of incoming light.

The retina's first objective in color vision is to determine the wavelength composition of the incoming light. This is done by the cones, which assess the wavelength composition by sampling intensity at various wavelengths and sending corresponding electrical output to cells in the successive retinal layers. In primates, including humans, the sampling is carried out by three types of cones, each with responsivity centered on a different wavelength. There are short wavelength cones (*S-cones*) that react best to wavelengths centered around 435 nm, medium wavelength cones (*M-cones*) that react best to wavelengths centered around 530 nm, and long wavelength cones (*L-cones*) that react best to wavelengths centered around 585 nm. Although centered on specific wavelengths, the responsivities of the different cone types are broad and overlapping. Together they span the entire length of the visible spectrum.

The S-, M-, and L-cones are often loosely referred to as "blue," "green," and "red" cones, but it should be kept in mind that the cones encode wavelength data, not color experiences. The two are quite distinct. Color experiences can be had in the absence of wavelength analysis, as in the case of dreams and hallucinations. Conversely, wavelength analysis can occur in the absence of color experience, as in a digital camera attached to a computer. The peak responsivities of the cones do not even align with our color experiences nor do they remain constant over repeated stimulations.

The output of the three cone types accounts for the entirety of the more than two million different colors that we can distinguish. The cone output could, in principle, serve as the axes of a three-dimensional color space spanning the full range of colors we consciously perceive. This is how a computer monitor works, where the full repertoire of perceivable colors is generated as combinations of red, green, and blue. This is not the way the brain works, however. We know this because examination of the psychological nature of our color experiences reveals properties that cannot be accounted for by a color space formed directly from cone outputs. Only after further processing can axes be identified that can form a three-dimensional color space that matches our color experiences.

What Makes Light Visible?

The properties of our cones are not arbitrary. They have been shaped by natural selection. The number of cone types possessed by each species, for example, has resulted from a 540 million-year evolutionary battle between the pressure to maximize wavelength discriminating ability (the more cone types there are, the greater the wavelength discriminating ability) and the pressure to maximize spatial discriminating ability (the fewer cone types there are, the fewer cells need to be jammed into each retinal location). The selection process has produced creatures with as few as one cone type (monochromats) and as many as 10 cone types (mantis shrimp).

The range of wavelengths to which our cones are sensitive has also been shaped by natural selection. What we call "light" is electromagnetic radiation of 400 nm to 700 nm, a range that accounts for only a tiny fraction of the full electromagnetic spectrum. Several factors caused creatures on Earth to become sensitive to this narrow radiation range. First, the light emanating from the sun is centered on the 400 nm to 700 nm range, a range that happens also to include all the wavelengths that can most readily penetrate the Earth's atmosphere. Additionally, sea water, which was the habitat for life when the original photoreceptors evolved, is transparent only to light in this wavelength range. Constrained by these factors, photoreceptors tuned to what we experience as visible are the ones that won out in the battle for survival.

The full range of visible light is somewhat larger than what is visible to humans. Infrared light, which is invisible to humans since its wavelength is just beyond the sensitivity of human L-cones, is in fact visible to certain species of snakes, including rattlesnakes, pythons, and boas, that have photoreceptors sensitive to infrared light located in their jaws. What, we might ask, does infrared light look like to a snake? At present we have no way to know this and must conclude that only a snake knows what a snake sees when it looks at infrared light.

A similar situation is present for ultraviolet light, which has a wavelength that is somewhat shorter than that of violet and is invisible to humans. Again, there are animals that exist that can see ultraviolet light. Such animals are actually widespread in nature, and include many species of fish, amphibians, reptiles, insects, and birds. There is even a recently identified species of bat, residing in Central and South America, that has been found to perceive ultraviolet light. What does this bat experience when looking at ultraviolet light? Again, in keeping with Nagel's classic 1974 paper, only a bat knows what it sees when it looks at ultraviolet light.

There are no organisms yet identified that can detect electromagnetic radiation with wavelengths beyond those of ultraviolet and infrared. Detection of other wavelengths would serve no apparent purpose. On the one hand, radio waves, with their very long wavelengths would provide minimal information regarding objects of the size that animals encounter in their daily life. On the other hand, x-rays, with their very small wavelengths are damaging to biological tissues.

We note that the restricted range of electromagnetic radiation to which our photoreceptors are sensitive is unique to life here on Earth and not a universal constraint. We can imagine encountering life on another planet where the available electromagnetic energy was centered on the terahertz domain, ranging say, from 400 microns to 700 microns rather than the 400 nm to 700 nm range around which it is centered on our planet. If we imagine also that the objects of importance to the alien creatures, as well as the size of the creatures themselves, were a thousand times larger than those on Earth, the creatures' photoreceptors would likely be suitable for measuring the terahertz radiation reflected from the relevant objects in their environment.

Suppose we encountered such an alien species living on a distant planet. What colors would we expect them to see? If their brains had evolved just as ours did, with the only change being that the photoreceptors had adapted to accommodate the longer wavelengths, then we could expect that they experience the very same colors that we do, with the proviso that their experiences would be evoked by micron range electromagnetic waves. Nanometer range electromagnetic waves, which are the ones that are visible to us, would be invisible to them. If, on the other hand, their brains had evolved differently from ours, there would be no way, given the ineffability of conscious experience, of knowing what these creatures experience.

Color Processing by the Ganglion Cells

The output of the cones passes through several intermediate retinal layers and arrives ultimately at the ganglion cell layer. Here, information is encoded by *parasol*, *midget*, and *bistratified* cells that have receptive fields that accord better with our conscious color perceptions than do the receptive fields of the cones. It is here that the division between *chromatic* and *achromatic* colors is made. The chromatic colors, which are encoded by the midget and bistratified cells, are colors like red and blue that are describable in terms of *hue* and *saturation*. The achromatic colors, which are encoded by the parasol cells, are colors like white and black that measure the *luminance* (intensity) of the light and the *brightness* of the perceived colors. The separation of chromatic and achromatic colors continues all along the color processing pathways.

The chromatic colors are computed in terms of *opponent* color pairs. These were first identified in 1872 by the German physiologist Ewald Hering (1834–1918). According to Hering,[27] the two colors of an opponent color pair have the property of being mutually exclusive, with the conscious perception of one color of the pair precluding conscious perception of the other. He postulated that two opponent pairs characterized all of human color vision: a red-green pair and a blue-yellow pair. With

[27] Hering 1872.

the red-green opponent pair, adding little bits of green light to a beam of red light results in the red color becoming progressively washed out, while adding little bits of red light to a beam of green light results in the green color becoming progressively washed out. When red and green light are present in equal strengths, they subtract each other out to yield a yellow percept that contains neither red nor green. Similarly, adding blue and yellow in unequal amounts gives a washed-out shade of one or the other, while adding them in equal amounts gives a white or gray percept that is free of either blue or yellow. Chromatic color combinations other than red-green and blue-yellow do not have this opponent property. Rather than canceling each other out, they combine to yield an intermediate third color that retains elements of the parent colors. Red combined with blue, for example, yields magenta, which retains subjective elements of both red and blue. Similarly, green and blue combine to give cyan, which retains subjective elements of both green and blue.

Hering's theory dealt only with the conscious experience of colors. We know now that a neurobiological correlate for his theory can be found in the functioning of the midget and bistratified cells.[28] Both encode opponent color pairs, the midget cells encoding red-green, the bistratified cells encoding blue-yellow. The opponent character of the midget and bistratified cell responsivities derives from the computations they make on the input from the cones. The responsivity of the midget cells is computed as the difference between the M and L cone outputs (M-L), which yields a red-green opponent sensitivity. The responsivity of the bistratified cells is computed as the difference between the S cone output and the sum of the M and L cone outputs (S-[M+L]), which yields a blue-yellow opponent sensitivity. In both cases, it is the subtractive component in the computation that confers the opponent character upon the cell's responsivity.

The situation with the achromatic colors is different. White and black are not experienced as opponent colors. Rather than being mutually exclusive, white and black combine to form intermediate shades of gray that retain elements of the original white and black. The neurobiological correlate for this behavior is found in the activity of the *parasol* cells. Parasol cell responses to the cone outputs are additive rather than subtractive,

---

[28] Gegenfurtner 2003a.

the cells responding best to the simple sum of the M and L cone outputs (M+L) or its negation-(M+L). Two parasol cell types are used in these computations. One, whose output is computed as (M+L), encodes for white; the other, whose output is computed as-(M+L), encodes for black.[29] The outputs of the two parasol cell types combine to yield all observable shades of gray.

The culmination of all these computations is that the original three cone output variables, S, M, and L, are replaced by three new variables, M+L, M-L, and S-(M+L), these new variables being represented by the activities of the different ganglion cell types. The new variables serve as the "cardinal axes" of a three-dimensional color space that not only spans the full range of colors we consciously experience but also accounts for the opponent aspect of the chromatic colors and for the distinction between chromatic and achromatic colors that characterize our subjective color experiences.[30]

We might at this point ask why the brain goes to the trouble of distinguishing between chromatic and achromatic colors, computing opponent variables, and using cardinal axes to represent color space rather than just relying on the raw cone output data? The answer appears to inhere in the survival advantage that these manipulations confer upon organisms evolving in the natural environments found on Earth. Computational studies show that both the chromatic/achromatic division and the presence of chromatic color opponency provide optimum efficiency of color processing in environments present at the time at which color vision developed.[31] A similar explanation explains the presence of opponent processing in other brain functions, including pain, touch, smell, taste, balance, and emotional expression.

Color Processing in LGN, V1, V2, V4, TEO, and TE

Subsequent to the analysis in the retina, color processing continues in the LGN of the thalamus and then in cortical areas V1, V2, V4, TEO, and TE in succession. In each of these brain regions, neurons tend to be

[29] Gegenfurtner 2003a.

[30] Gegenfurtner 2003b.

[31] Gegenfurtner 2003b

anatomically segregated according to their function. Neurons that assess color tend to aggregate apart from those that assess form and those that assess chromatic colors tend to aggregate apart from those that assess achromatic colors. This is not to say that the segregation is complete. Divergent, convergent, and lateral connections provide for considerable crosstalk between regions. This enriches the processing but a dominant theme of anatomical localization of function still prevails.

The anatomical segregation first appears in the LGN. Here, the midget, bistratified, and parasol ganglion cells of the retina target the *parvocellular*, *koniocellular*, and *magnocellular* cells of the LGN, respectively.[32] The LGN cells are organized in an orderly spatial pattern, the different cell types being segregated into different layers.

In the next processing stage, the LGN neurons send their output to the primary visual cortex, V1, which is partitioned into *blob* and *interblob* regions.[33] The blob regions are clusters of color-sensitive neurons that receive convergent input from the parvocellular and koniocellular LGN cells and exhibit red-green and blue-yellow opponent sensitivity, respectively. The interblob regions consist mostly of achromatic neurons that receive input primarily from the magnocellular LGN cells.

From V1, the outputs of the blob and interblob regions project to *thin*, *thick*, and *pale* stripes in V2, again in a spatially orderly fashion. The thin stripes contain color selective cells that receive convergent input from both the blob and interblob regions of V1 and encode both chromatic and achromatic color information.[34] The pale stripes receive projections from the interblob regions only and encode orientation and form. The thick stripes receive projections from the interblob regions and emit projections to area MT in the dorsal stream where movement is encoded. Since our focus is on the ventral stream, we will not pursue this MT pathway further.

In the next step, the outputs of the thin and pale stripes of V2 project to area V4 where again a specific spatial pattern is evident. In this case, the distinction is between *glob* regions and *interglob* regions.[35]

---

[32] Gegenfurtner 2003b.

[33] Conway 2010.

[34] Gegenfurtner 2003a.

[35] Conway 2007.

The glob regions are several millimeters in diameter and contain neurons that respond more strongly to color than to shape or orientation.[36] The remaining interglob regions respond more strongly to shape and orientation than they do to color.

Color Constancy and the Unique Hues

The neuronal activation in V4 is the final step in a process that fine-tunes our color sensitivities. As we have noted, the ganglion cells employ red, green, blue, and yellow as the primary chromatic colors from which all other chromatic colors are derived. It turns out, however, that these primary colors are not quite in agreement with the primary chromatic colors of our conscious experience. Psychological experiments tell us that slightly different chromatic shades serve as the primary colors of conscious perception. These are referred to as the *unique hues*,[37] which are again arranged as opponent pairs. The unique hues are likely favored by natural selection because they relate to natural light sources in our environment. Notably, sky blue is one of the unique hues. Modifications in the fine-tuning of perceived colors occurs progressively in V1, V2, and V4 so that neurons in V4 and beyond are tuned to the unique hues.[38]

The processing in V4 is also the final step in producing what is called *color constancy*. Color constancy is what makes a red tomato look consistently red, whether illuminated by sunlight, by incandescent light, or by fluorescent light. The wavelength composition of the reflected light is different in each case but the tomato continues to appear red. Color constancy is vital to our categorization ability. Without it, a visual scene would become haphazard and confusing, and vision would lose much of its biological importance.[39]

The brain basis for color constancy begins in V1, continues in V2, and matures in V4. It is attained through a lateral interaction between

[36] Conway 2007.

[37] Conway 2010.

[38] Stoughton 2008.

[39] Zeki 1999.

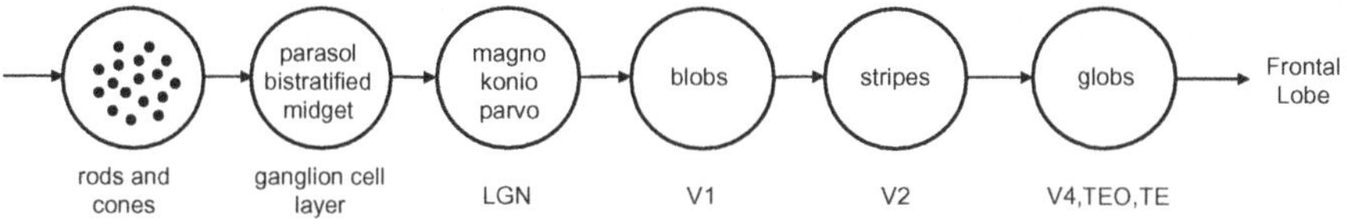

Fig. 3.8 Modular pathway for color perception. Abbreviation: LGN, lateral geniculate nucleus

neurons encoding the color of an object and neurons encoding the luminance of the surrounding background regions.

Subsequent to V4, color processing continues into area TEO, and then to TE, which is the final purely visual stage of the occipitotemporal pathway. Again there is a spatial clustering of color-sensitive neurons.[40] The representations also become more explicit, with neuronal responses signaling colors in the context of whole object perception. From TE, divergent projections target the frontal lobes, the medial temporal lobes, and various subcortical brain structures, where the visual processing joins with processing of other modalities.

Putting it all together we arrive at Fig. 3.8, which summarizes the cortical spatial patterns present in the successive modules of the ventral stream devoted to color processing. A similar case can be made for other types of visual perception as well, including perception of faces, depth, texture, and motion.

The NCC for Conscious Visual Perception

Supposing that visual perception is mediated by processing along hierarchical modular pathways with increasingly explicit representations, what can we say about the NCC for conscious visual perception? Using the directed pathway model, we can frame this question as, "Which module or modules correspond to the NCC for visual perception?" This question was addressed in the 1990s when Nikos Logothetis and colleagues, then at Baylor College of Medicine, employed a *binocular rivalry paradigm* to

[40] Conway 2007.

investigate conscious perception in monkeys.[41] In the binocular rivalry paradigm, subjects are presented with competing visual images to their two eyes. When confronted with such image pairs, subjects will perceive not a fusing of the two images but an oscillation between them: first one image is perceived for several seconds, then the other image is perceived for several seconds, then the first again, and so on. The investigators hoped that by examining the patterns of brain activity present during these image presentations, clues to the nature of the NCC for visual perception might be derived.

In an experiment on monkeys, subjects were presented with images of humans, other animals, and various man-made objects, different ones to each eye. The monkeys were trained to report their perceptions by pulling one of two levers in response to the image presentations. At the same time, single cell activity was recorded for neurons in the various visual areas in the monkey's cortex. The investigators found that in cortical regions V1 through V4, neuronal firing adopted a non-oscillating pattern reflective of retinal processing. In the inferior temporal cortex (areas TEO and TE), on the other hand, neuronal firing adopted patterns that matched the oscillating conscious perceptions.

These findings suggest that visual conscious perception arises only after the processing reaches the modules in the inferior temporal cortex.[42] This does not necessarily mean that the NCC for visual perception is located within the inferior temporal lobes, however. The temporal lobes may be yet another preliminary processor, with the NCC for visual perception located still further along in the perceptual pathway. In fact, neuroimaging studies employing fMRI reveal the presence of oscillating responses to binocular images not only in the inferior temporal cortex but also in the frontal and parietal association cortices.[43] Any subset of these regions is therefore a candidate for the NCC for visual perception.

---

[41] Rees 2002; Leopold 1996.

[42] Logothetis 1998.

[43] Logothetis 1999.

Perception in Other Modalities

What about perception in other modalities? Again we find a ready application of the hierarchical modular pathway model. Each modality is equipped with its own sensory detection organ and in each case the incoming sensory stimuli are converted to electrical signals in the receptors to initiate decoding. The receptor signals are relayed through hierarchical modular pathways in the thalamus and cortex.

With auditory processing the sequence begins in the cochlea in the ear. There, the intensity and wavelength of the sound waves are translated into electrical signals in analogy with the encoding of light waves by the rods and cones in the retina. Unlike the case with the retina, however, thousands of receptor types are used to sample the wavelength composition of the stimulus instead of just the three cone types used in visual processing. Auditory wavelengths can therefore be assessed with high precision but only at the expense of spatial localization, which is encoded only crudely.[44]

From the cochlea, auditory processing passes through several brainstem nuclei, then through the *medial geniculate nucleus* (MGN) of the thalamus, and then on through the auditory areas of the cerebral cortex.[45] More than a dozen auditory processing modules are present in the cortex, arranged in parallel, hierarchical fashion.[46] As with the visual cortex, dual processing streams are present. They are positioned caudally and rostrally, with the caudal stream determining *where* a sound is coming from and the rostral stream determining *what* is being heard.[47]

With somatosensory processing the sequence begins with specialized receptors in the skin, joints, and body organs. There are separate receptor types for touch, temperature, pain, vibration, and joint position. Activation of these receptors generates electrical signals that are processed sequentially by the brainstem, thalamus, and somatosensory cortex. Again, the processing is hierarchical. The thalamus projects in parallel to areas SI, SII,

[44] Hubel 1995.

[45] Koelsch 2005.

[46] Hackett 2011; Smith 2011; Rauschecker 2009; Kaas 2000.

[47] Brancucci 2011; Smith 2010; Rauschecker 2009.

and PV.[48] SI is subdivided into areas 3a, 3b, 1, and 2, with the thalamic inputs projecting to 3a being devoted to position sense and the thalamic inputs projecting to 3b being relayed to area 1 for perception of texture information and to area 2 for assessment of size and shape information. The processing is hierarchical, with 3a and 3b serving as primary somatosensory cortices and 1 and 2 serving as secondary somatosensory cortices.[49]

With olfactory processing the sequence starts with some 10 million olfactory receptors of 1000 different varieties distributed randomly in the nasal lining.[50] Each olfactory receptor connects with its own sensory neuron. Most odorants are composed of mixtures of odorant molecules, with each odorant activating multiple sensory neurons and each sensory neuron being activated by multiple odorants.[51]

Sensory neurons bearing the same receptor converge on a single glomerulus in the olfactory bulb. Populations of activated glomeruli form a spatial array that encodes odor. The olfactory bulb then projects to the anterior pyriform cortex (primary olfactory cortex), which in turn sends cortical output to the frontal and anterior temporal lobes. Olfaction is unique among the senses in that the principal processing pathway does not pass through the thalamus.

With gustatory processing, the sequence starts in the tongue. There are five basic tastes (sweet, sour, salty, bitter, umami), each mediated by its own class of taste receptor cells tuned to a single taste quality.[52] When activated, the taste receptors produce electrical signals that are processed successively by the brainstem nuclei, the thalamus, and the primary gustatory cortex in the insula. In the cortex, the individual tastes are represented in a spatially ordered gustotopic map, with each taste quality assigned its own cortical area.[53] Signals are transmitted from the primary gustatory cortex in the insula to the secondary gustatory cortex in the frontal cortex where the gustatory projections join the olfactory projections to activate neurons that encode flavor.

---

[48] Liang 2011; Eskenasy 2000; Kass 1991.

[49] Eskenasy 2000.

[50] Zhan 2010, p. 16669; Dennis 2004, p. 362

[51] Kay 2011.

[52] Chen 2011b.

[53] Chen 2011b; Miller 2011.

Perception Is Representational

The proposition that perception unfolds over hierarchical modular pathways and that conscious perception involves only a portion of these pathways speaks to a longstanding conceptual issue concerning the relationship between conscious perception and the outside world. Do we experience the outside world directly or do we experience it only through intermediate representations of it in our brain? The contention that we experience the world directly is called *direct realism*, a position that denies the presence of representational intermediaries in the brain. With direct realism, it is the brain as a whole that perceives the outside world and it does so directly.[54] The alternative to direct realism is *indirect realism*, or *representationalism*, where the supposition is that we consciously perceive not the outside world but only a representation of it in our brain.

The directed modular pathway model, as applied to perception, is by its construction manifestly representational in that the various modules each contain their own representation of the outside world based on the information they receive from preceding modules. Conscious perceptions are therefore only indirectly connected to information arriving from the outside world.

While many researchers have readily adopted the representational arrangement in their work, there are some who are disturbed by the division of brain components into those that relay information from the outside world and those that consciously perceive this information. The consciously perceiving components are together referred to as the *homunculus*, or "little man in the brain," whose responsibility it is to observe internal brain states. The introduction of homunculi into brain processing provokes philosophical angst for some in the field. They point out that the demarcation between observer and observed seems arbitrary. On what basis, they ask, can some modules be classified as observing homunculi while others are classified as representations to be observed? What fixes the dividing line between the two types of modules? Additionally, who or what observes the homunculus? Must the homunculus itself be divided into an observing portion and a portion being observed? If so,

[54] Dennett 1991.

then must the observing portion be divided yet again into observing and observed parts, and so on, ad infinitum?

It is because of these objections that eliminative materialists will have nothing to do with representations or homunculi. All there is, they say, is the brain and the environment. The eliminative materialist philosopher Daniel Dennett sums up the direct realism stance:

> The brain is Headquarters, the place where the ultimate observer is, but there is no reason to believe that the brain itself has any deeper headquarters, any inner sanctum, arrival at which is the necessary or sufficient condition for conscious experience. In short, there is no observer inside the brain.[55]

I would suggest that these criticisms lack force since they apply equally well to both direct and indirect realism. With direct realism, it is the sensory receptors that provide the demarcation between observer and observed, a demarcation that is just as arbitrary as that invoked with representationalism. Similarly, the question of "What observes the homunculus?" applies just as well to direct realism as it does to indirect realism, the only difference being that with direct realism the brain as a whole serves as the problematic homunculus.

The stubborn fact, which will become increasingly apparent as we go along, is that empirical evidence strongly favors the presence of homunculi and representations,[56] with modules antecedent to conscious perception encoding increasingly explicit representations of the outside world, and the modules directly mediating conscious perception acting as observing homunculi. I will address this issue further in Chap. 11 when I consider specific physical substrates for conscious experiences.

Representations, we should note, are not as a rule veridical replicas of the outside world. Sounds do not produce noisy nerve cells and odors do not produce smelly brains. The representations are for the most part abstract renderings of the outside world. The situation may be likened to that with a digital camera, where visual patterns recorded on the image sensor are transformed into digital codes that are meaningful to a computer but that have no resemblance to the objects being imaged.

---

[55] Dennett 1991, p. 106.

[56] Kriegeskorte 2013.

Perception Is Active

Proposing that there is a strong hierarchical aspect to perceptual processing does not imply that the process is entirely feedforward and produces only predetermined renderings of external stimuli. Perceptions are, in fact, creative productions, often having as much to do with intrinsic brain activity as with external stimuli.[57] William James emphasized this point: "Whilst part of what we perceive comes through our senses from the object before us, another part (and it may be the larger part) always comes out of our own head.".[58]

To a considerable extent we consciously perceive what we want and expect to perceive. When the stimulus-induced activation patterns fail to match our expectations, our brains typically "*fill-in*" the missing information. Our conscious perceptions are therefore awash with elements of illusion and distortion. The great nineteenth-century Czech anatomist Johannes Purkinje (1787–1869) said as much when he asserted that "illusions of the senses tell us the truth about perception."

The *Kanizsa Triangle* illusion, constructed in 1955 by the Italian Gestalt psychologist Gaetano Kanizsa,[59] provides a compelling example of filling-in (Fig. 3.9). As hard as it may be to believe, there is no upright white triangle at the center of the figure. The upright white triangle you see is in fact a creation of your brain.

Another example of filling-in occurs with the "blind spot," a universal defect in retinal encoding present in each eye. The existence of the blind spot is common knowledge today but, remarkably, it went unnoticed throughout most of recorded history, being discovered in 1682 by the French physicist Edme Mariotte (1620–1684). The blind spot is a disc-shaped visual field defect positioned about 15° lateral from the midline for each eye. The reader can confirm the presence of his or her own blind spot by looking at Fig. 3.10 with the right eye covered. If the page is held at a distance of about 10 inches in front of the left eye and the gaze is directed toward the middle of the row of numbers, the "X" on the left seems to disappear.

---

[57] Treves 2003; Thomas 1999.

[58] James 1890, p. 103.

[59] Kanizsa 1955.

Fig. 3.9 Kanizsa triangle illusion

Fig. 3.10 Demonstration of the blind spot. If you cover your right eye and look at the middle of the row of numbers with your left eye with the page held about 10 inches away, the "X" on the left disappears!

The blind spot is not some sort of trick. It is an actual visual defect resulting from a lack of photoreceptors at the retinal site at which the optic nerve exits the eye. Nature apparently did not see a need to correct for this defect, which is apparently sufficiently small and far enough off to the side to be of no practical significance, especially since in the normal state each eye compensates for the blind spot of the other.

The striking thing about the blind spot is that we are entirely unaware of it, even when we have only one eye open so that the other can't be used to compensate for the defect. Incredibly, the visual field is experienced as continuous, despite the gaping hole actually present. This false perception results from the brain "filling-in" the space with the same color and texture that occupies the surrounding regions.

Single-neuron electrical recordings[60] and fMRI scans[61] show that the filling-in is mediated by actual activation of cortical neurons in the cortical representations of the "blind," unstimulated region. The same mechanisms presumably apply to filling-in occurring with higher order, more abstract mental processing, and may in fact be a guiding principle for cortical processing in general.[62]

In summary, we have learned in this chapter that perception is well modeled as a process that unfolds over parallel, directed, hierarchical modular pathways that ultimately project to the frontal lobes. We turn now to memory, which we will see is another component of conscious processing that can be modeled in terms of directed modular pathways.

[60] Matsumoto 2005; Komatsu 2000; Logothetis 1998.

[61] Meng 2005.

[62] Koch 2004.

4

Memory

The Case of HM

In the previous chapter we focused on the anatomy of conscious experiences evoked by stimuli arriving from the outside world. In this chapter we turn to the anatomy of storage of conscious experiences into memory and their subsequent recall into awareness. We ask again whether these mechanisms can be understood in terms of directed modular pathways.

The key discovery that ignited interest in the anatomy of memory function was made in the mid-twentieth century. The prevailing bias at the time was that all memory operations were spread diffusely throughout the cortex and were therefore not localizable. As late as 1950, Karl Lashley was still asking whether a localized cortical correlate for memory was even possible.[1] In experiments he had conducted spanning 30 years, he was unable to find any cortical area devoted specifically to memory function. The elusive nature of the sought-after engram impelled him to quip that "I sometimes feel in reviewing the evidence on the localization of the memory trace, that the necessary conclusion is that learning is not possible." More seriously, he maintained that the failure to find a

[1] Lashley 1950.

S. Sevush, *The Single-Neuron Theory*,
DOI 10.1007/978-3-319-33708-1_4

localized memory substrate was a consequence of the inherently diffuse nature of the memory trace.

In 1953, Lashley's nonlocalizationist view was shattered. In September of that year, Connecticut neurosurgeon William Scoville (1906–1984) operated on "HM," a 27-year-old man suffering from intractable epilepsy.[2] The surgery targeted the medial temporal lobes, which were removed bilaterally along with the anterior two-thirds of each hippocampus, a pivotal structure residing within the medial temporal lobe (MTL). Scoville's thinking was that, given the known epileptogenic qualities of the MTL, removal of this portion of the brain might lessen the severity of HM's seizure disorder.

After the surgery, HM's seizures were reduced in frequency and severity and he remained in most ways normal. He exhibited no change in personality, no physical deficits, and no loss of intellect (his IQ before the surgery was 104; after the surgery it was 112). There was, however, a striking and unexpected complication from the surgery: HM suffered a profound impairment in memory function. His amnesia included both a *retrograde* component (loss of prior memories) and an *anterograde* component (inability to lay down new memories). The retrograde component was manifest as a complete loss of memory for events immediately preceding his surgery and a partial loss of memory for many events dating back further, such as the fact that his favorite uncle had died three years earlier. The anterograde component rendered him unable to recognize hospital staff members or to learn his way to the bathroom. Later, when his family moved to a new house, he was unable to learn his new address, although he continued to remember his address from before the operation. His mother reported that he would read the same magazines over and over without showing any familiarity with the articles he had just read. And within a half an hour of eating lunch, he was unable to remember anything he had eaten, or even that he had eaten at all. Scoville described HM's memory impairment as "forgetting the incidents of daily life as fast as they occur."

A half century after the operation, HM, then residing at a nursing home in Hartford, Connecticut, continued to exhibit a profound

[2] Scoville 1957.

memory deficit. The world had remained for him fixed at the beginning of the 1950s, with Truman continuing to be the president, World War II continuing to have ended only a few years ago, and television continuing to be a new invention. HM poignantly described his inability to register the flow of events that surrounded him:

> Right now, I'm wondering, have I done or said anything amiss? You see, at this moment everything looks clear to me, but what happened just before? That's what worries me. It's like waking from a dream. I just don't remember.

Over the decades, Scoville and Milner's 1957 paper became one of the most referenced papers in the field. Nearly 100 investigators, first at the Montreal Neurological Institute and after 1966 at the Massachusetts Institute of Technology, participated in studying HM's condition. He died of respiratory failure in 2008, adrift until the end on a "floating island in time." A prominent researcher, reflecting on his contribution to neuroscience, was moved to write:

> We all understand the rare opportunity we have had to work with him, and we are grateful for his dedication to research. He has taught us a great deal about the cognitive and neural organization of memory. We are in his debt.[3]

The immediate significance of HM's case was that it showed that severe memory loss could result from focal cortical damage, decisively refuting Lashley's contention that memory was an entirely diffuse property of the cerebral cortex. His memory loss was not total, however. After the surgery, he could still remember information for short intervals of 20 or 30 seconds and could still recall events from his early childhood. Additionally, he could still perform skills he had learned prior to his surgery and was able to master new ones. Distinguishing between what was impaired and what was spared in HM's case would prove pivotal in the subsequent development of anatomical models of human memory function.

---

[3] Corkin 2002.

Short-Term Memory

HM's case revealed the importance of the time delay between memory acquisition and memory retrieval. In general, memory function over delays of no more than 30 seconds or so is referred to as *short-term memory* (STM), while memory function over longer delays is referred to as *long-term memory* (LTM). Examination of HM's deficit revealed that while his LTM was severely impaired, his STM was entirely intact.

HM was able to use his STM to solve crossword puzzles, engage in intelligent conversation, and watch television with interest. Formal testing corroborated these clinical observations. HM was able, for example, to perform normally on a "digit span" test that required him to listen to a sequence of digits and then immediately repeat them back. When tested, he could repeat six digits reliably, placing him at an average level on this test.[4] He performed similarly on the Seashore Tonal Memory Test. For this test, he first had to listen to a brief series of musical notes played twice in succession, with one of the notes being changed on the second playing. Immediately after the presentation he was asked to identify the nature of the change. On testing with this task, he performed as well as normal control subjects.[5]

Anatomically, the fact that HM's STM function was spared despite the removal of his MTLs showed that the MTLs are not necessary for STM. The question then was which structures are in fact involved? The first clue had come with the classic monkey studies conducted by Carlyle Jacobsen at Yale University in the 1930s.[6] Jacobsen's experimental approach employed a delayed match-to-sample task designed to measure STM function. He began by placing two inverted cups directly in front of an observing monkey. With the monkey watching, he inserted a food reward under one of the cups. He then inserted an opaque partition between the monkey and the cups, temporarily blocking its view of the cups and forcing it to retain the location of the food reward in its mind. After variable delays of 5 to 30 seconds, he removed the opaque partition and permitted the monkey

[4] Keane 1995, p. 1132.

[5] Milner 1966.

[6] Jacobsen 1935.

to choose the cup it thought was hiding the food reward. He found that normal monkeys were able to remember the location of the food reward for up to 20 seconds but made mistakes after longer delays, their performance dropping to chance levels after 30 seconds.

To test the effects of brain damage on this short duration memory ability, Jacobsen employed the same procedure with monkeys who had various parts of their cerebral cortex removed. Most striking were the results observed when the frontal lobes were removed. Monkeys with such removals were unable to select the correct cup after a delay of only a couple of seconds, even if they were allowed to watch the cups continuously throughout the delay period. On the other hand, they performed normally on tasks that did not involve a delay, indicating that their performance difficulty was due specifically to a STM problem rather than to any overall cognitive decline. Similar findings were subsequently observed in brain-damaged humans and the conclusion was consequently drawn that the frontal lobes must be essential for maintaining information in memory for brief intervals.

In the early 1970s, when direct electrical recordings from individual frontal lobe neurons became feasible, the connection between STM and the frontal lobes was strengthened. Investigators identified neurons in the frontal cortex of monkeys that fired at twice their baseline rate throughout the delay period during STM tasks.[7] The finding was initially noted with visual stimuli but was later observed with auditory and tactile stimuli as well. The frontal connection was further supported when functional neuroimaging became available in the 1990s. Increased frontal cortical activity on fMRI and PET scans was observed during STM processing for each of the visual, auditory, and tactile sensory modalities.[8] Electrical recording and functional neuroimaging studies revealed an expanded anatomical correlate, with not only the frontal but also the parietal and temporal association cortices being activated during STM tasks. By the end of the twentieth century, all three major association cortices, frontal, parietal, and temporal, had been implicated in STM function. The MTLs were, notably, not included on this list.

[7] Fuster 1971.

[8] Fletcher 2001.

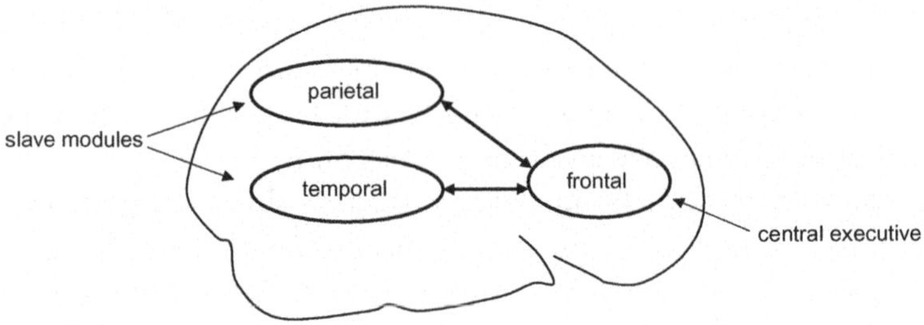

Fig. 4.1 Anatomy of working memory

Working Memory

Knowing the anatomical structures involved in STM was well and good but what was still needed was the mechanism by which they interacted. In 1974, the British psychologists Alan Baddeley and Graham Hitch satisfied this need with their highly influential *working memory model* of STM.[9] The working memory model supposes that STM is mediated by the actions of three modular constituents: a *central executive module* and two *slave modules*. The slave modules are deemed passive memory storage areas, one for storing acoustic memories, the other for storing visual memories. The *central executive* is cast as the overseer of the slave modules, charged with the responsibility of maintaining the memories stored within them and recalling the memories to conscious experience at a later time. The working memory model is particularly useful in that its individual components have plausible anatomical correlates (Fig. 4.1).[10] Substantial experimental work has implicated the frontal lobes in central executive function,[11] and has identified the temporal[12] and parietal[13] association cortices as the anatomical correlates for the slave modules.

[9] Baddeley 1974.
[10] Baddeley 2003.
[11] Jonides 2008, p. 204.
[12] Pasternak 2005, p. 97.
[13] Hoffman 2002.

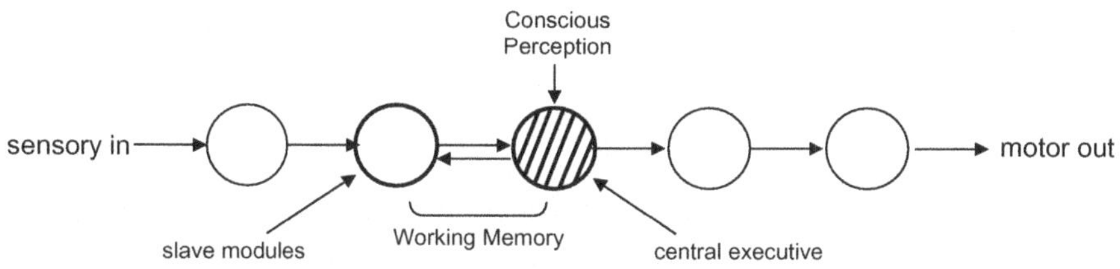

Fig. 4.2 Working memory, which is composed of posterior slave modules interacting with a frontal central executive, is incorporated within the perceptual pathway

Given these anatomical associations, the working memory model can be grafted smoothly onto the hierarchical perception model we developed in the last chapter. Specifically, the slave modules can be equated with the portion of the perceptual pathways preceding the conscious perception module, while the central executive (frontal lobes) can be equated with the conscious perception module itself (Fig. 4.2).

Unique to humans, working memory provides for mental rehearsal, a manipulation that keeps a memory alive for longer than the usual 20- or 30-second span of short-term memories. This appears to involve a frontal-posterior-frontal loop, present only in the language hemisphere of humans, that refreshes the short-term memories stored in the posterior cortices. Evidence for such a loop is most persuasive for auditory/verbal rehearsal,[14] where Wernicke's area and the frontal cortex provide the two poles of the loop. The subjective experience accompanying the operation of this loop is that of "talking to one's self in one's head." A rehearsal loop is also hypothesized for visual material but the anatomical details are yet to be worked out.

LTM and the MTL

With the working memory model and the connection between STM and conscious experience in hand we can now turn to the anatomy of LTM, which to a large extent is the same as that for STM, with the difference being that with LTM the memory traces are permanent rather than fleeting.

[14] Baddeley 2003.

Microscopically, this entails changes in the connections between neurons that develop through repeated exposure by a process called Hebbian learning (which we will examine in Chap. 8). If learning is gradual, new memories can be "interleaved" with old ones in a manner that causes little interference within the network. If, however, rapid learning is required, new memories will be laid down too quickly for interleaving to be possible. Theoretical arguments and computer simulations show that in such cases *catastrophic interference* ensues, with new memories obliterating old ones.[15] Since humans and many other animals clearly possess the capability of laying down long-term memories rapidly without incurring catastrophic interference, some modification of the memory mechanism must be in play. This is where the MTL comes in. It offers an auxiliary set of structures that obviate the problem of catastrophic interference.

Our understanding of MTL function has been gained through assessment of patients who, like HM, have suffered MTL damage, and through lesion experiments on monkeys and from neuroimaging and single-cell recording data obtained on humans and laboratory animals. Anatomically, the MTL is attached to the working memory slave modules (the parietal and temporal association cortices) as a directed modular loop (Fig. 4.3). It functions by siphoning off information about the ongoing activity in the slave modules and using this information to lay down memory traces and then to transmit return signals back to the slave modules.

The flow of information through the MTL loop is strongly feedforward and hierarchical.[16] Information is processed first by the parahippocampal and perirhinal cortices, then by the entorhinal cortex, and then by the hippocampus, which itself comprises a succession of modules: dentate gyrus, areas CA3 and CA1, and subiculum. Information is then passed back from the hippocampus to the entorhinal cortex, then to the parahippocampal and perirhinal cortices, and ultimately back to the slave modules from which the loop originated.[17]

Information processing within the MTL loop is rapid and flexible, allowing for single-trial learning and an ability to individually retrieve

[15] McClelland 1995, p. 433.

[16] Rolls 2010; Rolls 2000a.

[17] Eichenbaum 2012.

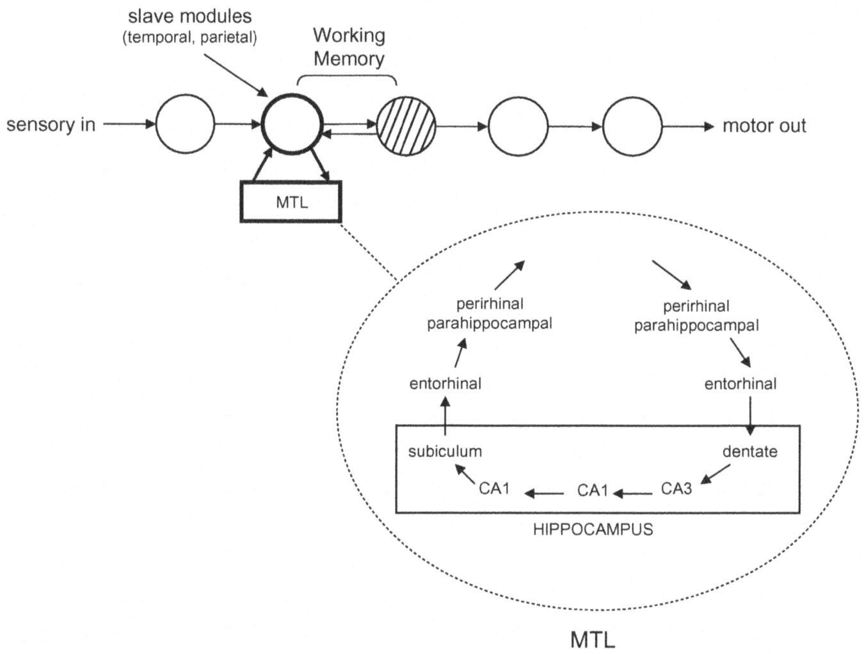

Fig. 4.3 The MTL loop is grafted onto the perception pathway as a directed modular loop that receives information from the working memory slave modules, processes the information in feedforward modular fashion, and returns the processed signals back to the working memory slave modules. Abbreviation: MTL, medial temporal lobe

and manipulate separate memory components. The modules within the loop each have their own role. Information first passes through the dentate gyrus, which serves as a "pattern separator" that recodes the incoming information so as to minimize any overlap between different memories. From the dentate gyrus, information passes to area CA3, where memory fragments form associations with whole memories in a process described as "pattern completion." From CA3, information passes to CA1, where memories are recoded in preparation for return transmission back to the slave modules. The return transmission is mediated by back projections from the subiculum to the entorhinal cortex, then to the perirhinal and parahippocampal cortices, and then back to the slave modules in the temporal and parietal cortices.[18] In all, the pathway comprises a succession of modules containing increasingly abstract and compressed representations.

The memory traces encoded in the MTL are not, it should be noted, simply duplicates of the LTM traces present in the slave modules. What is stored, rather, is the associations between LTMs, which provides the organism with the ability to retrieve whole memories from partial fragments. By storing only the linkages between memories and not the memories themselves, the MTL apparatus can store a huge number of memories with only a small allocation of resources.

As was the case with perception, the information flow through the MTL is segregated into dorsal and ventral streams. These are a continuation of the dorsal and ventral streams present in the parietal and temporal cortices that we encountered in Chap. 3. In the case of the MTL, the "what" pathway processes information about objects and events and runs from the inferior temporal cortex into the perirhinal cortex, then through the lateral portion of the entorhinal cortex, and finally into the hippocampus. The "where" pathway, which processes information pertaining to spatial and other contextual material, runs from the parietal cortex into the parahippocampal cortex, then through the medial portion of the entorhinal cortex, and finally into the hippocampus. The hippocampus then merges the "what" and "where" streams into composite memories that consist of events within their surrounding contexts.

The overall arrangement is one in which STM and LTM both utilize the working memory apparatus. For both, information in the slave modules in the posterior association cortices is harnessed by the executive module in the frontal lobes to produce conscious retrieval. The distinction is that with STM the content of the slave modules is dictated primarily by ongoing sensory perception, while with LTM the content in the slave modules is determined in part by MTL memory traces. We note, additionally, that MTL activation is involved not only in LTM retrieval but in perception as well, where it provides a continuous return flow of information to the slave modules that has the effect of "flavoring" ongoing perception with memories derived from past perceptions.[19]

[18] Rolls 2000a.

[19] Fuster 1999.

Recognition Memory

The type of memory we have so far been considering, called *recall memory*, consists of recall of previous conscious experience. There is, as well, another memory function, called *recognition memory*, that is used to determine merely whether a given stimulus has been encountered before. Recognition memory comes in two forms. The first, called *recollection memory*, is just another form of recall memory, with the recall of a previously experienced event allowing one to recognize that that the episode has previously occurred. The second, called *familiarity memory*, works differently. Here, recognition is signaled by a *feeling of familiarity* rather than by a recollection of a previous event. With familiarity memory one may, for example, recognize a face as familiar without being able to recall the time, place, or context of the original encounter.

Both types of recognition memory have conscious experience as their endpoint and both are experienced routinely in everyday life. The two interact productively. For example, a feeling of familiarity provoked by a stimulus might ignite a search for corresponding recollection memories. William James described his own experience of a familiarity memory leading to a recollection memory search:

> I enter a friend's room and see on the wall a painting. At first I have the strange, wondering consciousness, "surely I have seen that before," but when or how does not become clear. There only clings to the picture a sort of penumbra of familiarity,—when suddenly I exclaim: "I have it, it is a copy of part of one of the Fra Angelicos in the Florentine Academy—I recollect it there!"[20]

The anatomy of familiarity memory differs from that of recollection memory. Whereas recollection memory involves the entire LTM loop from the slave modules through the MTLs and back again, familiarity memory involves only the initial portion of the memory pathway leading up to and including the perirhinal cortex. Memory traces stored in the perirhinal cortex lead to a sense of familiarity without any involvement

---

[20] James 1890, p. 658.

of the rest of the MTL loop. The other anatomical structures involved in familiarity memory are not yet known for certain but are likely to include the amygdala, the thalamus, and the frontal cortex.[21]

The role of the perirhinal cortex in familiarity memory is in keeping with its ability to recognize stimuli rapidly albeit imprecisely, thereby providing a selective advantage in situations where quick stimulus assessment is needed. Computational studies suggest that by disregarding context, the perirhinal cortex allows for a rapid rate of stimulus assessment and an ability to store large numbers of memories in a relatively small region of cortex. From an evolutionary standpoint, familiarity memory likely evolved as a means of quickly identifying known objects and situations and distinguishing them from novel ones.

Déjà Vu

The distinction between recollection and familiarity memory sheds light on the intriguing phenomenon of *déjà vu*. Déjà vu is the feeling one experiences when an object or situation feels familiar but there is no memory of where or when the previous encounter occurred. Charles Dickens' description of the phenomenon in David Copperfield is a classic:

> We have all some experience of a feeling, that comes over us occasionally, of what we are saying and doing having been said and done before, in a remote time—of our having been surrounded, dim ages ago, by the same faces, objects, and circumstances—of our knowing perfectly what will be said next, as if we suddenly remembered it![22]

The experience does not have to be visual. The unexplainable familiarity feeling can, for example, be provoked by an odor. A person who grows up near the ocean and years later visits a town by the ocean may experience a feeling of déjà vu evoked by the subliminal smell of the ocean air. Similar experiences can be provoked by auditory stimuli, yielding "déjà

[21] Eichenbaum 2012.

[22] Dickens 1850, Chapter 39.

entendu" ("already heard"), and gustatory stimuli, yielding "déjà goute" ("already tasted"). There is also "déjà pense" ("already thought"), which is the feeling that one has thought this thought before, and "déjà fait" ("already done"), which is the sense of having performed the same actions before. The common feature is a context-free feeling of familiarity inducing an unexplainable feeling of having experienced the situation before.

Déjà vu is attributable, at least in part, to the activation of perirhinal cortex without further processing by the hippocampus. Evidence for this was provided by cortical stimulation studies performed in the 1950s by Wilder Penfield on awake patients undergoing brain surgery. Penfield's work, combined with electrical stimulation studies done more recently,[23] indicate that stimulation of the regions in and around the perirhinal cortex is most likely to evoke feelings of déjà vu in humans.

A phenomenon that is the opposite of déjà vu, called "jamais vu" ("never seen"), is explainable as a recollection memory of a past event unaccompanied by a feeling of familiarity in response to a stimulus that should be recognized as familiar. A clinically distressing form of jamais vu is Capgras syndrome,[24] in which the affected individual believes that a family member has been replaced by a look-alike imposter. Here, the subject acknowledges the complete resemblance of the person with the family member but the absence of a feeling of familiarity produces an incongruity that provokes distress. This condition occurs in schizophrenia, Alzheimer's disease, and in patients suffering from damage to the right side of their brain.

Feeling of Knowing and the Tip-of-the-Tongue Phenomenon

Another type of memory that involves consciously experienced feelings is the *feeling of knowing* that signals that an item is stored in our memory despite our inability to explicitly retrieve it. A feeling of knowing may, in turn, trigger a "tip-of-the-tongue" phenomenon in which a subject is unable to retrieve a target word but is certain that the word is present in

[23] Bartolomei 2004.

[24] Capgras 1923.

memory, just out of reach. We call again on William James for an eloquent description of the phenomenon:

> Suppose we try to recall a forgotten name. The state of our consciousness is peculiar. There is a gap therein; but no mere gap. It is a gap that is intensely active. A sort of wraith of the name is in it, beckoning us in a given direction, making us at moments tingle with the sense of our closeness, and then letting us sink back without the longed-for term. … It is an intense feeling. The rhythm of a lost word may be there without a sound to clothe it; or the evanescent sense of something which is the initial vowel or consonant may mock us fitfully, without growing more distinct. Every one must know the tantalizing effect of the blank rhythm of some forgotten verse, restlessly dancing in one's mind, striving to be filled out with words.[25]

Feelings of familiarity and feelings of knowing can be referred to as *cognitive feelings*. They both involve conscious experience and they both involve directed pathways that ultimately target the frontal lobes. In the next chapter we will examine other types of feelings and will find that they have a comparable anatomy.

Memories Are Reconstructive

Synaptic Consolidation

MTL memory traces are unstable when first laid down, being subject to spontaneous degradation and to interference from subsequently acquired memories. The brain corrects for this deficiency by stabilizing the traces through a process called *consolidation*. Consolidation comes in two forms: *synaptic consolidation*, which occurs in the MTL loop, and *systems consolidation*,[26] which occurs in the temporal and parietal cortices. The first of these, synaptic consolidation, involves the rapid conversion, over seconds, of MTL electrical activity into semi-stable chemical traces and then, over minutes to hours, conversion of the chemical traces

[25] James 1890, p. 251.

[26] Dudai 2004.

into permanent structural traces. Disruption of MTL activity while these changes are taking place causes memory loss in both anterograde and retrograde directions. The anterograde loss, which continues as long as the MTL is nonfunctional, occurs because no new memories can be laid down during the period of disruption. The retrograde loss, which extends minutes to hours backward from the time of injury, results from the fact that memories that were in the process of being consolidated do not get the chance to complete the process and so are lost.

A common example of disrupted synaptic consolidation is the clinical syndrome of *concussion*, which is defined as a temporary alteration in consciousness following a blow to the head. If severe enough, a concussion can impair LTM function and cause both an anterograde and retrograde memory loss. An amusing case of such memory loss occurred in 1992 in a football game between the Miami Dolphins and the Seattle Seahawks. With the Dolphins trailing 17–12 late in the fourth quarter, Hall of Fame quarterback Dan Marino was orchestrating one of his legendary late-game comebacks when he was struck in the jaw by an oncoming linebacker. Stunned by the blow, Marino had to come out of the game temporarily but returned one play later and proceeded to hit wide receiver Freddy Banks with a pass in the end zone, scoring the winning touchdown. When questioned after the game, Marino did not remember the touchdown pass and showed little recollection of the rest of the game. "Who won?" he asked. "I did what? You mean we scored? Yes!"

This anecdote typifies the concussion syndrome, with Marino exhibiting both an anterograde and a retrograde amnesia following a blow to his head. The anterograde amnesia developed because of his inability to lay down new memories following the impact, resulting in a loss of memory for the final touchdown pass. The retrograde amnesia developed because his memories from earlier in the game were not consolidated and were therefore lost.

Note that Marino's conscious perception and STM memory remained intact throughout the period of anterograde amnesia. He was able to call the winning play in the huddle, to keep it in mind for a few seconds, and then to execute the complex visual and motor programs necessary to read the defense and connect for the touchdown pass. This emphasizes the point that STM and LTM are dissociable processes, with the MTLs being required only for LTM function.

Systems Consolidation

The second form of consolidation, systems consolidation, occurs over a longer time span. With systems consolidation, LTM traces that initially include the MTL are gradually transformed into memory traces entirely confined to the posterior association cortices. The MTL in effect "teaches" the memories to the posterior association cortices.[27] The teaching sessions take place each time an LTM is retrieved and then returned to storage. With each retrieval and return to storage, traces within the posterior association cortices are strengthened. Eventually, the memory traces in the posterior association cortices become strong enough to recreate the original memories on their own, without the help of the MTL.

Systems consolidation disruption, like synaptic consolidation disruption, results in both anterograde and retrograde memory deficits but the specifics of the mechanism and of the nature of the memories that are lost are different. The pattern of the deficit with systems consolidation disruption depends on which of two subtypes of LTM is being considered. The first of these, *episodic memory*, is memory for personal events that occur at a particular time and place and that are accompanied by surrounding contextual associations.[28] An example would be an encounter you had with a friend earlier in the day. In this case, the episodic memory would include not only the fact of the encounter but also the time and place of its occurrence, what the friend was wearing, what was said, and so on. The second subtype, called *semantic memory*, is memory for facts, such as who was the president of the United States at the end of World War II. Such memories are devoid of contextual components.

MTL damage affects both episodic and semantic LTMs but does so differently for the two LTM subtypes. With episodic memory, the deficit is both anterograde and retrograde. The anterograde component accounts for the inability to lay down new LTMs; the retrograde component accounts for the inability to recall past events. The retrograde

---

[27] McClelland 1995.

[28] Tulving 1972.

impairment follows what is known as *Ribot's Law*,[29] with recent memories being lost and remote ones being retained. This pattern was seen in HM's case and is seen as well in Alzheimer's disease (which in the early stages selectively damages the MTL), with episodic memories of events in the recent past being lost but with episodic memories from childhood being unaffected.

For semantic memory, MTL damage causes only an anterograde memory deficiency. Thus, HM remained able to recall facts he had learned prior to his surgery but could not recall facts he was taught subsequently. For example, he could do crossword puzzles that involved pre-1953 knowledge but could not do ones involving later knowledge. Similarly, he retained knowledge of the meaning of words in common use prior to 1953 but could not assimilate new words as they entered the language subsequently. When presented with such new words, he could only guess their meaning. He interpreted "acid rain" as "heavy rain," a "closet queen" as a "moth," and a "flower child" as a "young person who grows flowers." In all, HM's semantic memory impairment left him unable to update his knowledge of the world around him, rendering him, as one researcher described it, "an alien in his own land and time."[30]

The difference in patterns of retrograde memory loss for episodic and semantic LTM can be explained on the basis of a difference in systems consolidation rate for the two LTM subtypes. In the case of episodic memories, systems consolidation proceeds slowly, with the result that recent episodic memories do not have time to consolidate and are therefore lost with LTM damage, while remote episodic memories, which have time to consolidate and become free of MTL dependency, remain intact. In the case of semantic memories, the systems consolidation rate is rapid, such that both recent and remote semantic memories are free of MTL dependency and are therefore spared. The physiological mechanisms by which semantic memories consolidate more quickly than episodic ones is presently under debate, with a variety of proposed explanations on offer.[31]

---

[29] Ribot 1881.

[30] Gabrieli 1988.

[31] Winocur 2011.

Memory Traces Evolve Over Time

A common misconception is that episodic memories are retrieved in the form of a simple reactivation of stored traces. Episodic memories are in fact reconstructive events. Each time a memory is retrieved and then returned to storage, the memory trace is freshly reconsolidated, with new connections created between the MTL and posterior association cortices. Memory traces, and the conscious experiences evoked by them, therefore change over time.

That episodic memory retrieval is a reconstructive event was suggested by Sigmund Freud with respect to childhood memories. Freud noted that we sometimes remember childhood events not from a first-person perspective, which is how they were originally experienced, but from a third-person perspective in which we observe ourselves as actors in a scene as viewed by an outside observer. Childhood memories, Freud noted, must have been "worked over" and are then recalled in altered form. The potential unreliability of stored memories led Freud to wonder whether we can trust them at all:

> It may indeed be questioned whether we have any memories at all from our childhood: memories *relating* to our childhood may be all that we possess. Our childhood memories show us our earliest years not as they were but as they appeared at the later periods when the memories were revived. In these periods of revival, the childhood memories did not, as people are accustomed to say, emerge; they were formed at that time. And a number of motives, which had no concern with historical accuracy, had their part in thus forming them as well as in the selection of the memories themselves.[32]

Several decades later, the British psychologist Sir Frederick Charles Bartlett (1886–1969) found further evidence of the reconstructive nature of memory recall. In a famous experiment, Bartlett had subjects read a Native American story entitled, "The War of the Ghosts," and then retell the story repeatedly after various delays. He found that subjects who were unfamiliar with the nuances of Native American culture altered or

[32] Freud 1999.

omitted some events and falsely inserted others to make the stories fit their own experience and culturally induced expectations. In his classic 1932 monograph he wrote:

> Remembering is not the re-excitation of innumerable fixed, lifeless and fragmentary traces. It is an imaginative reconstruction or construction, built out of the relation of our attitude towards a whole active mass of organised past reactions or experience, and to a little outstanding detail which commonly appears in image or in language form. It is thus hardly ever really exact, even in the most rudimentary cases of rote recapitulation, and it is not at all important that it should be so.[33]

False memories can be created by imagining events that never actually happened. Similarly, imagining a conversation with someone may lead to a false memory that the conversation actually took place. False memories can also be produced by "social contagion," where one's own memories are infected by those of others. If an individual participates in a group recollection effort, he or she may later report personal memories for events that never happened but were implanted during the group effort.

The inaccuracy of normal memory function applies even to major events. Consider, for example, the following two descriptions that were written in response to the question, "How did you first hear of the news of the Challenger disaster?" referring to the ill-fated space shuttle mission in 1986[34]:

> DESCRIPTION 1: I was in my religion class and some people walked in and started talking about it. I didn't know any details except that it had exploded and the schoolteacher's students had all been watching, which I thought was so sad. Then after class I went to my room and watched the TV program talking about it and I got all the details from that.
> DESCRIPTION 2: When I first heard about the explosion I was sitting in my freshman dorm room with my roommate and we were watching TV. It came on a news flash and we were both totally shocked. I was really upset and I went upstairs to talk to a friend of mine and then I called my parents.

[33] Bartlett 1932.

[34] Zola 1997.

These responses were among those given by 44 students at Emory University in Atlanta during a study in which each student was asked the question twice, first on the morning after the event and again two and a half years later. Remarkably, the two descriptions given were the responses of a single student at the two different times. It is striking how different the two versions are, especially considering that the student expressed great confidence in the recollections. In fact, about one-third of the students in the study exhibited a substantial change in their recollection of the event over the two-and-a-half-year-delay, yet with many students expressing great confidence in the accuracy of their accounts.

Once a false memory is inserted into storage, repeated retrieval of the specious memory will serve to strengthen the trace and increase the confidence with which the memory is subsequently recalled. The end product may be vivid and filled with detail and be difficult to distinguish from veridical memories. The malleability of memory is staggering when compared with our intuitive notions. As one researcher put it, "Memory, like silly putty, can be molded to support entirely false beliefs."[35] With all the distortion incurred during retrieval, it is a wonder that there are any reliable memories at all. Cognitive psychologist Elizabeth Loftus summarized the situation this way:

> People's memories are not only the sum of all that they have done but … are also the sum of what they have thought, what they have been told, what they believe. … Who we are may be shaped by our memories but our memories are shaped by who we are and what we have been led to believe.[36]

Modern memory researchers have embraced Bartlett and Freud's contention, deeming retrieved memories to more closely resemble an artist's painting than a camera-like reproduction. If a film credit were being given for the process, it would read, "Memory based on or inspired by real events." Conscious memory retrieval, like conscious perception, is a pattern completion process in which missing elements are "filled in" according to expectations based on past experience. Cognitive psychologist

---

[35] Rosen 2004.

[36] Loftus 1997.

Ulric Neisser has likened this reconstructive process to that employed by a paleontologist who recreates a dinosaur from fragments: "Out of a few stored bone chips we remember a dinosaur."[37]

Frontal Lobes and Memory

Confabulation Due to Frontal Lobe Damage

As unreliable as consciously recalled memories are in normal individuals, they are even more unreliable following frontal lobe brain damage. The greatest deficiencies result from damage to the orbital and ventromedial frontal lobes caused by cerebral hemorrhages, head trauma, or severe alcoholism. Patients with such damage exhibit a bizarre form of conscious memory distortion referred to as *confabulation*. The clinical reports are compelling. For example, in a case reported by Armin Schnider, a neurologist at the University Hospital in Geneva,[38] a 58-year-old woman who had suffered a cerebral hemorrhage from an anterior communicating artery aneurysm rupture became convinced that she was at home and had to feed her baby, even though she was in the hospital and her "baby" was over 30 years old at the time. In a second case, a tax accountant suffering from extensive traumatic destruction of his frontal cortex absconded from the hospital under the false belief that a taxi was waiting downstairs to take him to a meeting with the county's financial director. In yet another case, a dentist who had suffered an aneurysm rupture repeatedly left the hospital, convinced that patients were waiting for him at his clinic.

One of my own patients, who I examined following an episode of Wernicke's encephalopathy associated with alcoholism, believed that he was living at home with his wife when in fact she had divorced him two years earlier and he was actually residing in a nursing home. He described matter-of-factly how he had spent the previous night at home watching television with his wife and how he had had a "few beers" over the course

[37] Neisser 1967.

[38] Schnider 2003, p. 663.

of the evening. In fact, these were memories constructed from events that had occurred years earlier.

In cases like these, the principal defect resides in the temporal organization of the retrieved memories, such that events from a remote time period are displaced to the more recent past. Not all confabulations have this basis, however. Confabulators can also include details of events that never happened, such as in a case of alcohol-induced amnesia reported by the Boston behavioral neurologist D. Frank Benson (1928–1996):

> She described, in detail, previous conversations with physicians she had never met, gave or accepted incorrect names for her own children, described recent visitors who had not been there, and gave details of trips she had made out of the hospital that had not occurred.[39]

Confabulations resulting from frontal lobe lesions can be quite bizarre, as in several cases seen at the Boston Veterans Administration Hospital.[40] One patient approached another patient and told him that "he had seen on television the previous night footage of the other patient's home being ripped out of the ground by a giant crane and of the patient himself running from the house." Another patient falsely recalled a drowning accident involving one of his children and yet another described variously how his family had died in his arms or had been killed before his eyes and would relate in lurid detail his sexual experiences with his daughters. In each of these cases, the bizarre recollections were entirely fictitious.

Behavioral neurologist Antonio Damasio described cases in which frontal damage produced "wild fabrications."[41] One patient believed he was a spaceship commander at the time of the Columbia space shuttle mission and that he occasionally became a space pirate. The same patient also described a personal meeting he supposedly had with Egyptian President Sadat. "He believed Sadat had visited him recently in the hospital and described a visual memory of Sadat sitting in the corner of the room by the foot of his bed. Only occasionally did the patient seem to

---

[39] Benson 1996.

[40] Stuss 1978.

[41] Damasio 1985.

realize that his recalled experiences were not real." Another patient, when asked about the then current Falkland Islands crisis, "described a trip she thought she had made to the Islands. She pictured herself strolling with her husband down the main street of the Falklands' capital and recalled buying 'local trinkets' in a general store." Of course, she had never set foot on the Falkland Islands.

Particularly bizarre were the confabulations produced by a patient with frontal and parietal lesions reported by Frank Benson. The patient's conceptions featured fantastic displays of spatial illogicality:

> He exhibited, however, a distinct abnormality of orientation for place. While he quickly learned and remembered that he was at the Jamaica Plain Veterans Hospital (also known as the Boston Veterans Administration Hospital), he insisted that the hospital was located in Taunton, Massachusetts, his home town. Under close questioning, he acknowledged that Jamaica Plain was a part of Boston and admitted it would be strange for there to be two Jamaica Plain Veterans Hospitals. Nonetheless, he insisted that he was presently hospitalized in a branch of the Jamaica Plain Veteran Hospital located in Taunton. At one time he stated that this branch hospital was located across the street from his own home. Once he even stated that the hospital was located in a spare bedroom of this own home. When asked the size of the branch hospital, he said that it was fourteen stories (the correct size of the Jamaica Plain hospital). Questioned whether he had actually seen the hospital in his own home he became vague but on several occasions stated that he had talked to workmen in a hallway of his own home. These workers, who had been building the hospital, had mentioned the size and location the building.[42]

Despite the bizarre and illogical nature of their productions, confabulators have an absolute conviction of the veracity of their erroneous consciously experienced memories, reflecting defective monitoring of their retrieved memories. This contrasts with normal individuals who, when faced with such contradictions, show insight into the conflict between their reason and their feelings.

---

[42] Benson 1976.

The exact mechanism by which confabulations are produced is as yet uncertain. The clearly erroneous displacements in time and space without the slightest concern for consistency or plausibility implicates frontal lobe dysfunction since the frontal lobes are vital to encoding the temporal order of events.

Frontal Lobes and Memory

When considering the anatomy of conscious LTM, the focus is usually on the MTLs, no doubt because damage to the MTLs causes a severity of LTM impairment unmatched by damage anywhere else. The frontal lobes receive less emphasis since frontal lesions do not cause the profound amnesic syndromes that MTL lesions do. The frontal lobes are nevertheless essential for conscious memory function. There is abundant evidence supporting a prominent role for the frontal lobes in all forms of conscious STM and LTM.

An underappreciation of the role of the frontal lobes in conscious memory processing may be attributable to the fact that frontal function is less crisply modular than is posterior cortical function. Because of the vague modularity, frontal lesions must be large if they are to produce significant memory impairments. Large lesions, in turn, cause extensive cognitive impairment that may overshadow specific memory deficits and make them difficult to detect.

A critical role for the frontal lobes in conscious memory has nevertheless been established. The principal contribution of the frontal lobes to conscious memory processing is its executive action on the posterior cortices. Additionally, the frontal lobes provide top-down guidance to MTL processing. Anatomically, the frontal lobes are heavily connected with the posterior cortices, the connections being for the most part bidirectional. It is generally assumed that the connection that runs from the frontal lobes back to the posterior cortices mediates the top-down influence that the frontal lobes exert on posterior processing. On the other hand, it seems reasonable to hypothesize that the connection that runs from the posterior cortices to the frontal lobes mediates conscious memory recall.

Imagery, Procedural Memory, and Conscious Experience

An important form of conscious experience associated with memory is *imagery*, which is conscious experience that occurs in the absence of external stimuli. Included is both volitional imagery, as in daytime musings, and non-volitional imagery, as in hallucinations and dreams. Hallucinations are forms of imagery for which the conscious experiences are vivid and seem real. Dreams are hallucinations that occur in association with sleep.

Imagery resembles perception to a great extent. This was noted by the eighteenth-century philosopher David Hume who wrote of the "great resemblance" between the two, "except [for] their degree of force and vivacity."[43] Anatomically, imagery and conscious perception utilize overlapping modular pathways.[44] The difference is that whereas conscious perception is driven by both the incoming stimulus and LTM fragments, imagery is driven by LTM fragments alone.

In contrast with imagery are components of memory that are clearly separate from conscious experience. An example of such unconscious memory function was evident in HM's case by his retained ability to learn to trace figures under mirror guidance and to read words reflected in a mirror at rates comparable to that for normal controls. The latter task is not easy, as the reader can verify with the mirror-reflected words in Fig. 4.4, although performance does improve with practice. The learning process is for the most part unconscious. Thus, while HM showed steady improvement over successive training sessions, he would deny at the start of each session that he had ever attempted the task before and would be surprised by his excellent performance. This type of memory, called *procedural memory*, is encoded in the basal ganglia and other subcortical structures. It is a form of implicit memory, a category that includes skills, habits, and conditioned responses. In each of these operations, conscious perception is brought to bear on the task at hand to improve performance and facilitate learning but the memory retrieval products are not themselves conscious experiences.

---

[43] Hume 1739, p. 2.

[44] Naseralis 2015.

Fig. 4.4 Mirror-reflected words

In summary, we have seen that, after working through all the complexities of memory function, two memory categories stand out with respect to conscious experience. First, there is the act of recall, which brings memories of past events into conscious experience. Second, there are feelings of familiarity and knowing, in which the feelings are themselves conscious experiences. For both categories, the underlying anatomy consists, as it does for conscious perception, of directed pathways that project ultimately to the frontal lobes. We now turn to feelings other than the cognitive ones addressed here and ask whether the underlying anatomy for these can be modeled similarly.

5

Feelings

Introduction

Over the course of the last two chapters we saw how perception, memory, and imagery could be cast as directed modular processes. In this chapter we turn to *feelings*, by which I mean the subjective experiences associated with emotions and related phenomena. It would seem that feelings, unlike perceptions, are too amorphous to be effectively modeled in terms of directed pathways. The purpose of this chapter is to show that they can.

Emotional Feelings

Foremost among our feelings are those associated with emotion, which can be defined as a mental and physical *valenced* state induced by an environmental stimulus, where a valenced state is one that can be rated as pleasant or unpleasant. Emotion thus differs from perception, which is neutral with regard to valence. In behaviorist terms, *an emotion is a state evoked by a rewarding or punishing environmental stimulus*, where a

S. Sevush, *The Single-Neuron Theory*,
DOI 10.1007/978-3-319-33708-1_5

rewarding stimulus is anything that the organism will work to obtain and a punishing stimulus is anything that the organism will work to avoid.[1]

We note that emotions are both mental and physical. The mental component is the subjective feeling. The physical component is the accompanying physiological state of the body. The emotion provoked by an encounter with a bear, for example, consists both of a subjective feeling of terror and a corresponding physiological reaction (dilating pupils, increasing heart rate, turning to flee).

Besides feelings associated with emotion, there are also feelings of pleasure and pain, as well as feelings that are experienced in relation to drives, such as hunger or thirst. Feelings associated with the drives are distinguished from feelings associated with emotions by the fact that the former are elicited by external stimuli while the latter are evoked by conditions of the body.[2] The anatomy of the two is highly overlapping, however, and will be considered together.

There are also *cognitive feelings*, which are *valenced conscious experiences that accompany cognitive operations.* We saw examples of cognitive feelings in the last chapter in the form of feelings of familiarity associated with recognition memory and feelings of knowing associated with the "tip-of-the-tongue" phenomenon.

Interoception and the Insular Cortex

Portraying emotional feelings and feelings associated with the drives in terms of directed modular pathways has recently become possible. The original insight came with the writings of William James and the Danish physician Carl Lange in the 1880s. They offered a theory of emotion that contradicted the then prevailing intuitions regarding cause and effect in emotional reactions.[3] The generally accepted sequence of events was that when a person encounters an emotion-inducing stimulus, he or she first experiences an emotional feeling and then reacts with behavioral and

---

[1] Rolls 2000.

[2] Rolls 2005.

[3] James 1884; Lange 1885.

physiological responses. If you encounter a snarling bear, you experience terror and then your pupils dilate, your heart rate increases, and you turn to flee.

The James–Lange theory inverts the sequence. It supposes that the physiological and behavioral responses come first and the emotional feelings come after. On an encounter with a snarling bear, your pupils dilate, your heart rate increases, you turn to flee, and only then do you experience terror. The idea is that the subjective experience of terror can be seen as *the perception of the physical reaction of the body*.

As William James put it[4]:

> Our natural way of thinking about these standard emotions is that the mental perception of some fact excites the mental affection called the emotion, and that this latter state of mind gives rise to the bodily expression. My thesis on the contrary is that *the bodily changes follow directly the perception of the exciting fact, and that our feeling of the same changes as they occur* IS *the emotion.* Common sense says, we lose our fortune, are sorry and weep; we meet a bear, are frightened and run; we are insulted by a rival, are angry and strike. The hypothesis here to be defended says that this order of sequence is incorrect, that the one mental state is not immediately induced by the other, that the bodily manifestations must first be interposed between, and that the more rational statement is that we feel sorry because we cry, angry because we strike, afraid because we tremble, and not that we cry, strike, or tremble, because we are sorry, angry, or fearful, as the case may be. Without the bodily states following on the perception, the latter would be purely cognitive in form, pale, colourless, destitute of emotional warmth. We might then see the bear, and judge it best to run, receive the insult and deem it right to strike, but we could not actually *feel* afraid or angry.

The validity of the James–Lange theory has been disputed ever since its publication. In the 1920s, Walter Cannon challenged the theory on the grounds that afferent signals coming from the bodily organs are insufficiently differentiated to account for the full variety of emotional feelings that we experience. In the 1960s, coincident with the emerging cognitive

[4] James 1884, p. 189.

revolution in psychology, the theory was again challenged, this time on the grounds that cognitive interpretations of external stimuli were responsible for the specific emotional feelings that the stimuli evoke. In the past two decades the theory has undergone a resurgence, with plausible anatomical correlates having been discovered.

The pivotal revelation was the discovery of the role of the insular cortex in emotional processing. The insula is the "hidden" lobe of the cerebral cortex, snuggled beneath overlying flaps of the frontal, parietal, and temporal cortices. Its functions have only recently been delineated. Central is the notion of *interoception*, a term introduced by Bud Craig, a neuroscientist at Barrow Neurological Institute in Phoenix. Interoception refers to the perception of the physiological condition of the body.[5] Among the interoceptive feelings are sensations of pain, itch, tickle, touch, temperature, hunger, thirst, flushing of the skin, shortness of breath, nausea, and muscular and internal organ sensations.[6] Interoceptive feelings also include sensations evoked by circulating levels of oxygen, carbon dioxide, glucose, insulin, and those evoked by core temperature assessed by direct sampling of the blood in the hypothalamus and brainstem.[7]

The anatomy of interoception centers on the insular cortex, where it proceeds along a hierarchical modular pathway comparable to those that mediate ordinary perception.[8] The first step in the pathway is the activation of peripheral sensory nerve fibers that innervate almost all living tissue in the body and whose activation pattern represents the body's overall physiological status. Signals from the sensory nerves are relayed via brainstem nuclei to the thalamus and insula cortex, and then on to the frontal lobes.[9]

Within the insula there is a posterior-to-anterior (caudal-to-rostral) hierarchical gradient in the complexity of the interoceptive representations (Fig. 5.1).[10] Information enters the insula in its posterior portion,

[5] Craig 2009.
[6] Craig 2002.
[7] Critchley 2013.
[8] Craig 2011.
[9] Critchley 2013.
[10] Craig 2011.

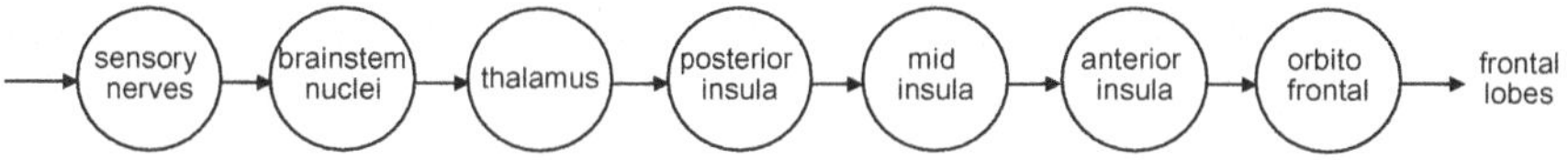

Fig. 5.1 The modular pathway for interoception runs from sensory input through the brainstem and thalamus, then through three hierarchical stages within the insula, and then on to the orbitofrontal cortex and other portions of the frontal lobes

which serves as the primary interoceptive cortex. Information is then rerepresented in the mid-insula, and yet again in the anterior insula. Activation in the anterior insula correlates most closely with subjective feelings of the body state.

Emotion and the Orbitofrontal Cortex

The principal projection target for the insula is the *orbitofrontal cortex* (OFC), which is on the undersurface of the frontal lobes. Information arriving at the OFC joins information arriving from the ventral stream and from the amygdala. In the anterior OFC, reward value, both positive and negative,[11] is assigned to the environmental and interoceptive stimuli. Reward value provides incentive for making decisions.[12]

Incentive values can be adjusted both in the short term and over evolutionary time intervals. For example, there is a greater short-term experience of pleasure following ingestion of food when one is hungry than when one is satiated. On the other hand, genetically preprogrammed incentive weighting allows natural selection to influence an animal's behavioral repertoire over geological time intervals.

The OFC directs behavior toward what is socially acceptable.[13] OFC damage results in socially inappropriate actions, with decreased impulse control and regressed, childlike behavior. The OFC also is involved in instincts. Damage to the caudal OFC in monkeys produces a decreased

[11] Rolls 2003.

[12] Damasio 1994.

[13] Damasio 1994.

aggressive response to snakes and a reduced tendency to reject foods, such as meat, that are normally rejected.

Projections of the OFC target, among other destinations, other parts of the frontal lobes, thus completing a directed pathway for emotional feelings and feelings associated with the drives that leads from the brainstem to the thalamus to the insula to the OFC and on to other regions in the frontal lobes.

The Ventral Striatum and the Neurobiology of Pleasure

At the core of all our feelings are pleasure and pain. Identifying brain correlates for pleasure has long been problematic. An important step forward was the heralded experiments performed in the mid-twentieth century by James Olds (1922–1976), then a post-doctorate psychology fellow at McGill University in Montreal. In conjunction with his undergraduate student, Ralph Morrison, he identified a set of brain regions where electrical stimulation was strongly reinforcing, such that, once stimulated, an animal would go to great lengths to make the stimulation recur. The finding caught public attention, with the region being heralded as the "pleasure center" in the brain.

The crucial discovery occurred during preparation for an experimental setup designed to study the effects of electrical brain stimulation on the motivation of rats. One Sunday morning prior to the start of a formal testing session, Olds went into the laboratory for a last-minute check on the makeshift electrode he had implanted in the brain of a rat that was to be tested the next morning. During his preparations, he observed a behavior he had not previously noticed: following a brain shock the animal returned repeatedly to the location where the shock had occurred. Alert to the significance of the observation, Olds returned home to announce that "he had made a discovery, a real one, one that would not evaporate the next day."[14]

[14] Thompson 1999.

Years later, one of Olds' post-doctoral fellows, Paul Shinkman, reminisced about his mentor's discovery:

One day in the lab he [Olds] was telling a few of us about the way he had discovered rewarding brain stimulation 12 years earlier. He delivered the brain stimulus with a hand-held button. On one particular occasion the (newly implanted) rat crept cautiously across the floor of the testing chamber. At this point in telling this story, Jim assumed the role of the rat, moving furtively across the room while continuing the narrative. When the first brief stimulation was delivered, the rat stopped abruptly, took two careful steps backwards, and peered up directly at Jim. (Here Jim looked up over his shoulder in a bemused position). "The rat," said Jim, "seemed to say, 'I don't know what I just did, but whatever it was, I want to do it again.'" Jim immediately stopped thinking about elicited behaviors and began on the spot to attempt informal shaping of emitted behaviors.[15]

In the next step, Olds developed a setup that allowed the rat to self-activate the electrode by pressing on a pedal. By varying the location in the brain at which the electrode was inserted, he was able to identify the brain areas that were most rewarding. If the electrode was positioned in one of these brain areas the rat would, following an initial chance pressing of the pedal, eagerly sniff in all corners of the box and hastily manipulate any objects in its path until it stepped on the pedal a second time. It would then cease wandering and remain at the site of the pedal, actively pressing it at a rate of one or two presses per second and thousands of presses per hour.[16]

By selectively manipulating the timing of the electrical jolts, Olds found that he was able to rapidly shape the animal's behavior. Rats could be induced to learn to run mazes or to endure painful foot shocks in order to get to the self-stimulating treadle. Like a crack addict on a weekend binge, the animals would persist in lever pressing, foregoing eating, drinking, or sex for as long as 48 straight hours or until physical exhaustion set in. Nor did the response ever habituate: the rats "usually maintained the same rate of self-stimulation throughout the hour and for as many days or months as they were tested." Later on, Olds repeated the experiments

[15] Thompson 1999.

[16] Olds 1958.

with monkeys and obtained similar results. Other investigators replicated the findings with goldfish, guinea pigs, dogs, cats, goats, and dolphins.

Through systematic evaluation of the effects of brain location on the rate of intracranial self-stimulation, Olds and his colleagues determined that about 60 percent of the rat brain is motivationally neutral, 5 percent produces avoidance reactions, and 35 percent provokes repeated bar pressing. Electrodes implanted in the posterior hypothalamus yielded 5000 bar presses per hour, while those in the interpeduncular nucleus of the tegmentum yielded 7000 bar presses per hour.

The results of his investigations led Olds to fancifully describe the area of stimulation sensitivity as the "pleasure center" in the brain. In the 1960s, the electrical self-stimulation paradigm was extended to humans, with the reported findings comparable to those in laboratory animals. Anatomical regions that have since been found to respond to self-stimulation include the ventral striatum, the ventral pallidum, the ventral tegmentum, and the ventral thalamus.[17]

Wanting Versus Liking

But was the region discovered by Olds really a "pleasure center?" University of Michigan researcher Kent Berridge has reported that careful scrutiny of the descriptions offered by subjects of their experiences during brain stimulation bring into question whether the subjects actually experienced pleasure. Take this account, for example:

> The patient, in explaining why he pressed the septal button with such frequency, stated that the feeling was "good"; it was as if he were building up to a sexual orgasm. He reported that he was unable to achieve the orgastic end point, however, explaining that his frequent, sometimes frantic, pushing of the button was an attempt to reach the end point. This futile effort was frustrating at times and described by him on these occasions as a "nervous feeling."[18]

---

[17] Berridge 2003.

[18] Heath 1963.

And in the case of another subject:

> The button most frequently pushed provided a stimulus to the centromedian thalamus. This stimulus did not, however, induce the most pleasurable response; in fact, it induced irritability. The subject reported that he was almost able to recall a memory during this stimulation, but he could not quite grasp it. The frequent self-stimulations were an endeavor to bring this elusive memory into clear focus.[19]

Berridge has suggested that individuals such as these experience only an intense desire to obtain pleasure,[20] not a feeling of pleasure per se. He points out that the subjects' descriptions in Olds' experiments were vague and devoid of clear declarations of subjective pleasure. When pressed to give details of how they felt, the subjects simply repeated, "I just feel good." There were no exclamations of delight or reports of intense pleasure thrills.

Berridge has introduced the terms "liking" and "wanting" to capture the distinction between these states.[21] Whereas "liking" indicates a pleasurable experience, "wanting" indicates only the presence of a motivational state directed toward obtaining a pleasurable experience. He suggests that these can be distinguished in animals and in human infants by certain behaviors that routinely accompany pleasurable experiential states. He notes that human infants respond to the sweet taste of sugar with lip smacking and rhythmic tongue protrusions but respond to the bitter taste of quinine with grimaces involving retraction of the lips, flailing of the hands, and shaking of the head. Analogous responses are observed also in rodents and nonhuman primates. It is the "liking" responses that Berridge takes as indicating a pleasurable experience.

"Liking" and "wanting" have different chemical correlates. It appears that the neurotransmitter, *dopamine*, which has been hailed as "the pleasure molecule," does not actually cause a feeling of pleasure or "liking" at all. Rather, it generates a "wanting" reaction that leads to the compulsive

---

[19] Heath 1963.

[20] Berridge 2003.

[21] Berridge 2003.

behaviors of drug addiction, eating disorders, and related pursuits.[22] On the other hand, opiates, such as opium, heroin, and morphine, do produce "liking" reactions. In the 1970s it was discovered that the brain produces its own opiates.

The ventral striatum and ventral pallidum are the sites where the principal actions of the opioids and other pleasure-inducing drugs are effected. A portion of the ventral striatum called the shell region is particularly responsive to opioid. Activation of the opioid receptors in this region will by itself produce a "liking" response.

The ventral striatum is part of a cortico-striato-thalamo-cortical loop that has been postulated to be involved in the generation of pleasurable feelings. The loop begins with information encoded in the OFC being passed to the ventral striatum. The information flow then proceeds via the ventral pallidum to the mediodorsal nucleus of the thalamus, a region that has been implicated in emotional processing and that is the target of the "feeling of familiarity" pathway originating in the perirhinal cortex of the temporal lobe. The loop is then completed by the well-known pathway from the mediodorsal nucleus of the thalamus back to the OFC. The information flow through this loop is strongly feedforward, with modulatory feedback flow present for some of the steps. The loop has been hypothesized to act by selectively inhibiting responses to unrewarded, and therefore inappropriate, stimuli.[23]

Feelings and the Anterior Cingulate Cortex

A distinction between sensory experiences and feelings is brought out by a consideration of the experience of pain. The subjective experience following a pinprick or a slap would seem to be both a sensation (indicating the location, intensity, and duration of the stimulus) and a feeling (engendering a valence and a motivational state). The anatomy is consistent with this duality. On entering the central nervous system, the pain signals arriving from the periphery diverge into two distinguishable

---

[22] Berridge 2013.

[23] Price 1999, p. 391.

pathways, one for pain as a sensation, the other for pain as a feeling. The pathway for pain as a sensation runs from the thalamus to the primary somatosensory area in the parietal lobe. The pathway for the experience of pain as a feeling passes through the *anterior cingulate cortex* (ACC).

The dissociation of the two pathways was dramatically revealed by a surgical procedure developed in 1962 by Eldon Foltz in an attempt to relieve intractable pain. The procedure, called a "cingulotomy," involved the intentional destruction of a small portion of the rostral ACC on both sides of the brain. Incredibly, patients who underwent this procedure would report that they still could feel the pain but that it didn't bother them! A dramatic example of this procedure was described by Damasio.[24] The patient suffered from tic douloureux, a condition in which spasms of excruciating pain affect one side of the face, with even trivial stimuli, such as a puff of wind, setting off spasms of pain. All attempts to treat the symptoms with medication proved ineffective and so the cingulotomy procedure was performed on the patient by the neurosurgeon Almeida Lima. Damasio writes:

> I will not forget seeing the patient on the day before the operation, afraid to make any movement that might trigger a new round of pain and then seeing him two days after the operation, when we visited him on rounds; he had become an entirely different person, relaxed, happily absorbed in a game of cards with a companion in his hospital room. When Lima asked him about the pain, he looked up and said quite cheerfully that "the pains were the same," but that he felt fine now. I remember my surprise as Lima probed the man's state of mind a bit further. The operation had done little or nothing to the sensory patterns corresponding to local tissue dysfunction that were being supplied by the trigeminal system. The mental images of that tissue dysfunction were not altered and that is why the patient could report that the pains were the same. And yet the operation had been a success. It had certainly abolished the emotional reaction that the sensory patterns of tissue dysfunction had been engendering. Suffering was gone. The facial expression, the voice, and the general deportment of this man were not those one associates with pain.[25]

---

[24] Damasio 1999.

[25] Damasio 1999, p. 74.

Interaction of Emotion and Cognition

Although we often tend to emphasize the role of cognition in behavior, emotion is at least as critical. Psychologist James Russell quips that "psychology and humanity can progress without considering emotion—about as fast as someone running on one leg."[26] Emotions constitute an ancient brain system devoted to a fast and automatic evaluation of stimuli and a rapid behavioral response.

There is a rich intrinsic frontal connectivity that provides the basis for a linkage between cognition and emotion. The linkage has behavioral correlates. On the one hand, emotions act on cognition to filter our thoughts: when we are sad, we tend to think of sad things and when we are happy, we tend to think of happy things. On the other hand, cognition can act on emotions by suppressing or otherwise modifying them, thus forming the basis for cognitive therapy.

Emotions are critical for decision making. OFC lesions block the interaction between emotions and decision making, with the result that patients are unable to choose from available alternatives. Damasio, in describing a case in which this was the problem, relates that the patient, when asked when he would like to come for his next appointment, proceeded to analyze the different possibilities for a full 20 minutes without coming to a decision. His indecisiveness was crippling. Yet, when asked by the examiner, "How about Tuesday at 1 PM?" the patient instantaneously responded, "Fine."

Amygdala and Fear

The complete pathways underlying emotional feelings are only partly understood. Among the better studied of these are the pathways involved in emotional feelings of fear. There are three fear pathways that converge on the OFC. First, there is the feedforward pathway through the insula to the OFC. Second, there is the feedforward pathway of the ventral stream and its projection to the OFC. Third, there is a pathway involving

[26] Russell 2003.

the amygdala, which is an almond-shaped subcortical nucleus that lies within the anterior temporal lobe, deep to the cortex. The pathway runs from the ventral stream to the anterior temporal cortex and from there to the basolateral and central nuclei of the amygdala, and then on to the OFC. This third pathway mediates Pavlovian classical conditioning, with incentive values generated by the amygdala being rigid and learning taking many trials to be achieved.

The connection between the amygdala and conscious feelings was first noted by Heinrich Kluver (1897–1979) and his neurosurgeon colleague Paul Bucy (1904–1992) in the 1930s.[27] They described what is now known as the Kluver–Bucy syndrome, which results from bilateral destruction of the anterior temporal lobes, including the underlying amygdala. Animals with the Kluver–Bucy syndrome exhibit dietary changes (eating inappropriate items, including feces), hyperorality (a compulsive tendency to examine objects by mouth), hypersexuality (increased sexual drive, tendency to engage in sexual acts with anything in reach, both living and nonliving), and visual agnosia ("psychic blindness," an inability to recognize the emotional significance of familiar objects).

Many of the behavioral symptoms observed in the Kluver–Bucy syndrome are attributable to damage to the anterior temporal cortex, which is part of the ventral stream. This damage results in "psychic blindness," which can account for the animal's tendency to approach objects such as food or sexual partners indiscriminately. The most prominent behavioral symptom in the Kluver–Bucy syndrome, however, is the dramatic loss of aggression and fear that results from the damage to the amygdala. The striking change in emotional behavior of the "wild and aggressive" macaque monkeys that were operated on by Kluver and Bucy illustrate this point. Prior to the removal of their anterior temporal lobes, the monkeys displayed great emotional excitement, in keeping with their nature. On approach, they would scamper away and quickly find a place to hide. If their hiding place was uncovered, they would cower for a moment and then dash to another, hopefully safer spot. After the surgery, the monkeys' behavior was entirely different. Instead of trying to escape, they would readily approach the investigator as well as other animals. They allowed

[27] Kluver 1939.

themselves to be picked up and stroked. And if they were attacked and even bitten by another animal, they would continue to approach the attacker again and again to their own misfortune. In general, the previously aggressive monkeys became tame and docile.

Once it was recognized in animals, the Kluver–Bucy syndrome began to be detected in humans as well. The first reported instance of the condition in a human was that described by Terzian and Ore in 1955[28] in a 19-year-old man who underwent neurosurgical removal of both his temporal lobes to treat uncontrolled epileptic attacks. Over subsequent decades, the syndrome came to be viewed as a regularly occurring condition in humans, resulting from bilateral destruction of the temporal lobes caused by head trauma or by naturally occurring conditions such as Pick's disease, which is a progressive non-Alzheimer's dementia that damages the frontal and anterior temporal lobes.

The observations originally reported by Kluver and Bucy have been amply confirmed and the connection between the amygdala and both fear and aggression is now well established. Recordings of electrical field potentials in humans with implanted amygdala electrodes reveal increased activity during viewing of unpleasant scenes but not of pleasant or neutral scenes.[29] Additionally, functional neuroimaging has shown that the amygdala is activated during fear.[30] Direct electrical stimulation of the amygdala in humans induces intense fear reactions.[31] It is likely, however, that the amygdala is not only specialized for fear but is important for other emotions as well, a contention that is a current target of scientific investigation.

In summary, then, feelings, including those of pleasure and pain, those associated with emotions and drives, and those associated with cognition, are all plausibly modeled by directed modular pathways that ultimately target the frontal lobes. This completes our survey of perception, memory, and feelings and our assessment of their compatibility with the directed modular pathway thesis. In the next chapter we ask whether there might be more than one set of these directed modular pathways per brain.

---

[28] Terzian 1955.

[29] Oya 2002.

[30] Phillips 2003.

[31] Lanteaume 2007.

6

The Split-Brain Paradigm

History of the Split-Brain Procedure

Introduction

Until now we have focused our attention on the assertion that the brain is an information processer that does its work over directed modular pathways, and that the processing over these pathways leads eventually to the neural substrate for conscious experience. This assertion, while still open to debate, remains within the bounds of mainstream conjecture. In this chapter we venture into less charted territory by taking on the question of whether there might be more than one neural substrate for conscious experience present in a given brain at any given moment. Specifically, we ask whether separate brain substrates for conscious experience are present in the left and right cerebral hemispheres.

As a matter of terminology, I will throughout the book follow the common convention of using the designation "left hemisphere" to indicate the hemisphere that is "dominant" for grammatical language function, which is on the left side of the brain in most people. I will address the less common cases of reversed dominance and mixed dominance later in this chapter.

S. Sevush, *The Single-Neuron Theory*,
DOI 10.1007/978-3-319-33708-1_6

The possibility of separate conscious experiences in the two hemispheres arose on February 6, 1962 at White Memorial Hospital in Los Angeles, when a surgical procedure that had been tried and abandoned some 20 years earlier was revived. The surgery involved cutting the white matter tract connecting the two cerebral hemispheres of the brain of a patient with uncontrollable seizures. The surgery suppressed the seizures but caused profound alterations in behavior and mental function that carried powerful implications regarding the nature of the NCC. The history leading up to the surgical event is of interest.

The Early History of the Split-Brain Procedure

The structure of concern is the *corpus callosum*, a dense white matter tract that serves as the principal anatomical connection between the two cerebral hemispheres. About two hundred million axons pass through the corpus callosum, making it by far the largest fiber tract in the human brain. Despite its girth, the function of the corpus callosum remained a mystery until well into the twentieth century.

Back in the seventeenth century, the corpus callosum had been deemed a candidate for "seat of the soul."[1] In the nineteenth century a more modest role was suggested, that the corpus callosum might serve to unite the activities of the left and right halves of the brain. By the early twentieth century, however, an absence of clinical defects in patients suffering damage to portions of their corpus callosum led to the opinion that the structure served no purpose at all, at least not in the adult. British psychologist William McDougall (1871–1938) was so sure that this was the case that he openly volunteered to have Sir Charles Sherrington, the great neurophysiologist, sever his corpus callosum if he ever contracted an incurable disease. He predicted that despite such a procedure, his consciousness would remain whole.[2]

McDougall's opinion gained empirical support when in the 1930s the renowned Johns Hopkins University neurosurgeon, Walter Dandy, severed almost the entirety of the corpus callosum in several patients

[1] Bogen 1997.

[2] Bradshaw 1999.

to get to deep lying brain tumors. Following the surgeries the patients appeared entirely normal, prompting Dandy to declare: "This simple experiment at once disposes of the extravagant claims to function of the corpus callosum."[3]

In 1939, University of Rochester neurosurgeons William Van Wagenen and R. Yorke Herren cut the corpus callosum in a series of 10 patients suffering from severe epilepsy.[4] They performed the procedure with the intention of preventing localized seizure activity from growing into brain-wide electrical paroxysms. On the basis of their routine post-operative observations they concluded that "section of the commissural pathways contained in the corpus callosum may be carried out without any untoward effect on the patient."

Following the surgeries, neurologist Andrew Akelaitis (1904–1955), also at the University of Rochester, tested the patients formally and extensively for possible impairments in mental functioning. In keeping with Van Wagenen and Herren's clinical observations, he found no consistent adverse effects on the patients' cognition or behavior and published his findings in a series of articles in the 1940s.

The negative results reported by Akelaitis were widely quoted. They appeared to establish unequivocally that the corpus callosum played no observable role in the functioning of the mature brain. In 1949, the American neurophysiologist and cyberneticist Warren McCulloch (1899–1969) quipped that the only demonstrated function for the structure seemed to be that of transmitting seizure activity from one side of the brain to the other. A little later Lashley chimed in, declaring facetiously that the principal function of the corpus callosum must be merely "to keep the two hemispheres from sagging."[5] Indeed, by mid-century the structure had acquired the reputation for "being, among all brainy structures, the largest, most useless."[6] Moreover, the surgical procedure was found to be ineffective in controlling the patients' seizures and was therefore abandoned.

---

[3] Dandy 1936, p. 40.

[4] Van Wagenen 1940.

[5] Wickens 2005.

[6] Sperry 1961a, p. 43.

That might well have been the end of it but for the audacity of neurobiologist Roger Sperry (1913–1994) and his doctoral student Ron Myers who, undaunted by the pervasive skepticism, decided to revisit the split-brain issue, this time in animals. In work that started at the University of Chicago in 1953 and continued from 1954 onward at Caltech in Los Angeles, Sperry and Myers demonstrated that cutting the corpus callosum in rats, cats, and monkeys did in fact have observable effects. They were able to show that after the division of the corpus callosum, memories stored in one half of the brain could not be transferred to the other half.[7]

In 1962, Boston neurologist Norman Geschwind, aware of Sperry and Myers' new animal work, set out to find a case in which a split-brain effect could be identified in a human. His search was successful. In collaboration with neuropsychologist Edith Kaplan he examined patient "PJK," a 41-year-old police officer who had undergone surgery to remove a brain tumor that had engulfed his anterior corpus callosum. Geschwind and Kaplan's report of the emergent autonomous behavior exhibited by the patient's disconnected left hand has become a classic:

> It was striking to observe that when handling objects [with his left hand and with his eyes closed] he would move them actively about with his fingers and would focus on their salient features. For example, he inserted his finger into a thimble, ran his thumb over the teeth of a comb, rubbed the bristles of a tooth brush, and retracted the point of a ballpoint pen. Despite his appropriate handling of the dominant features of these objects, he misnamed them all. … It appears to us that the simplest description of this patient's most striking disturbances is that he behaved as if his two cerebral hemispheres were functioning nearly autonomously.[8]

That same year, in White Memorial Hospital in Los Angeles, neurosurgeon Philip Vogel, together with his neurosurgery resident Joseph Bogen (1926–2005), resurrected the split-brain surgical procedure that had been introduced and then discontinued in Rochester. The patient was WJ, a World War II veteran paratrooper who suffered from uncontrollable seizures. Vogel and Bogen noted that in the Rochester series the

[7] Sperry 1961a.

[8] Geschwind 1962, p. 678.

sectioning of the corpus callosum had been incomplete and had been performed in stages. This, they suggested, might have limited its effectiveness in treating the seizure disorders. Accordingly, they opted to sever WJ's entire corpus callosum and anterior commissure (an additional tract connecting the left and right anterior temporal lobes), and to do so in just a single sitting. The surgery was a clinical success, with complete eradication of the patient's seizures.

Vogel and Bogen's decision to resurrect the split-brain procedure was a bold one. Bogen later told of how he had written to the chief of neurosurgery at the University of Rochester asking for information about the patients that had been operated there in the 1940s. He received the terse reply that the operating surgeon Dr. Van Wagenen was forever sorry about what he had done to those patients. Bogen noted that when he and Vogel went ahead and performed the split-brain procedure in Los Angeles, there were those in the field who referred to them as "the West Coast butchers."[9]

The final link in the chain of events came when Bogen, who had spent time at Caltech earlier in his training and had met Sperry and learned of his split-brain animal work, asked Sperry to assess patient WJ for possible split-brain effects. Sperry agreed, and, in conjunction with his new first year psychobiology graduate student Michael Gazzaniga, performed the landmark investigations that revealed for the first time the full split-brain phenomenon in a human. Gazzaniga, whose ingenious experimental strategy made the work possible, expressed the flavor of the moment:

> Nothing can possibly replace a singular memory of mine: that of the moment when I discovered that case WJ could no longer verbally describe (from his left hemisphere) stimuli presented to his freshly disconnected right hemisphere. An experiment I had designed, executed and carried out alone as a mere graduate student at Caltech had worked. With it, the modern split-brain story was born, and I was to spend the next five years in a sort of sublime state, working every day at the finest scientific institution in the world with one the greatest biologists of all time, Roger Sperry.[10]

---

[9] Bogen 1997.

[10] Gazzaniga 2005.

Over the subsequent decades, further research on the patients operated on by Bogen and Vogel, as well as on other patients operated on at Dartmouth Medical School, laid out the details of the split-brain syndrome. The right brain/left brain distinction highlighted by the split-brain research took on a popular appeal that reached a frenzied peak by 1980. The importance of the work to modern neuroscience was underscored when Sperry was awarded the Nobel Prize in Physiology or Medicine in 1981.

Unfortunately, the clinical effectiveness of the split-brain procedure as a surgical treatment for epilepsy has turned out to be only marginal. Although seizure severity and frequency are reduced, only a minority of the patients show an overall improvement in the quality of their lives. The surgery is nevertheless still performed occasionally, with hundreds of cases having accrued.

Gazzaniga and Sperry's Ingenious Experiment

Why did Gazzaniga and Sperry succeed in revealing the split-brain effect where Akelaitis failed? Part of the explanation resides in Bogen and Vogel's decision to cut the corpus callosum in its entirety in a single surgical session. This enhanced the clinical effectiveness of the procedure and probably exaggerated the split-brain effects as well.

Equally important, however, was the clever method used by Gazzaniga and Sperry in testing patients. In their setup, the patient sits before a display apparatus that flashes images of objects to the right or left visual fields, or sometimes to both half-fields simultaneously, while the patient's gaze remains fixated on a central point. Importantly, the images are displayed only briefly so as to preclude the patient from shifting gaze to compensate for any defects. In the early days of split-brain research the brief presentations were effected by a mechanical device called a tachistoscope. In modern studies, tachistoscopes have been replaced by computer display screens.

In a typical session, an image is flashed on the screen and the patient is required to immediately report on what he has just seen, either by saying the name of the object out loud or by using one or the other hand to

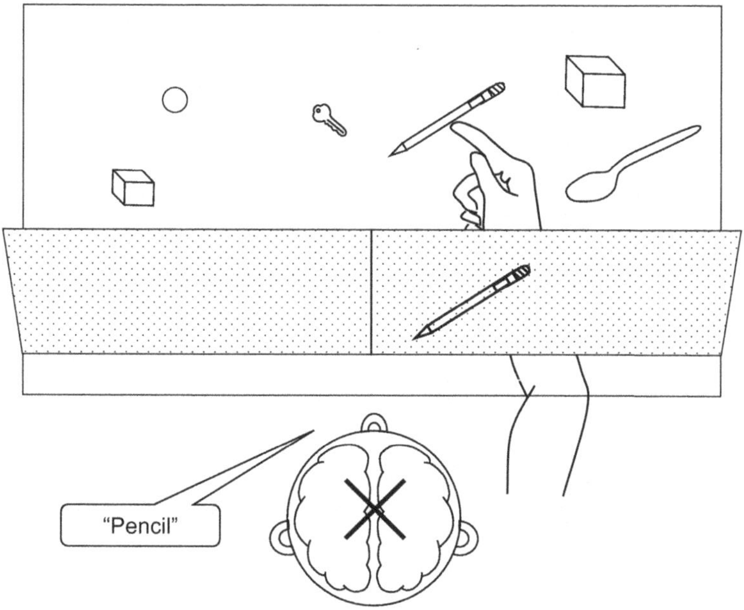

Fig. 6.1a Response of a split-brain patient to a pencil seen in the right visual field: says "pencil" while pointing to the pencil with the right hand

select the object from a set of choices lying on a table, the patient's view being blocked by the screen. The remaining hand is in the meantime kept under the table to prevent it from participating.

Figures 6.1 (a–c) depict the typical split-brain phenomenon. In Fig. 6.1a, a picture of a pencil is flashed to the patient's right visual field and he responds manually by accurately directing his right hand to select, by feel, the pencil sitting on the table out of view. At the same time, when asked to say out loud what it was that he saw on the screen, he appropriately responds that he saw a pencil.

In Fig. 6.1b, a picture of a key is now flashed to the patient's left visual field. He again responds manually, this time by accurately directing his left hand to select, by feel, the key sitting on the table out of view. But when asked to say out loud what it was that he saw on the screen, he reports that he saw "nothing," despite the ongoing accurate performance of his left hand.

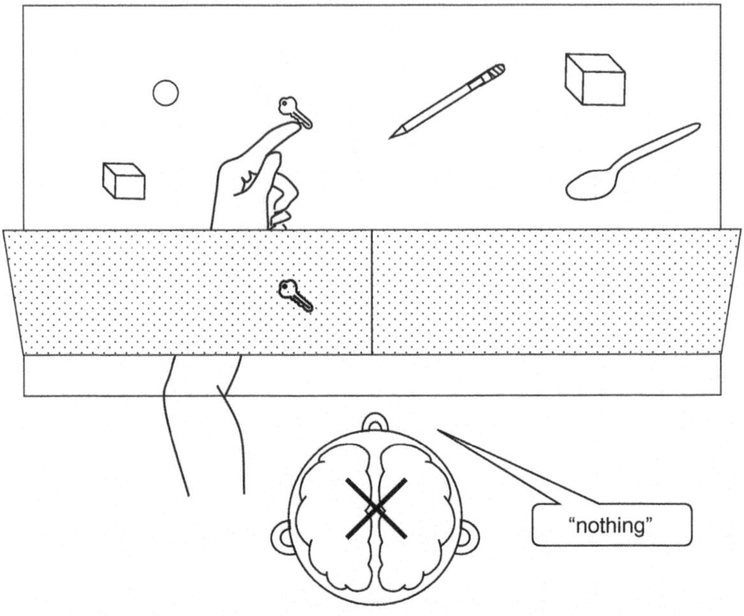

Fig. 6.1b Response of a split-brain patient to a key seen in the left visual field: says "nothing" while pointing to the key with the left hand

In Fig. 6.1c, which combines the procedures of 6.1a and 6.1b, we see the split-brain phenomenon in its most compelling form. Here, the pictures of the key and pencil are simultaneously flashed on the screen in the left and right visual fields, respectively, to which the patient responds by simultaneously selecting the key, by feel, with his left hand while saying out loud that he sees a pencil, oblivious to the selection action of his left hand.

The Brain Mechanism Responsible for the Split-Brain Effect

A ready explanation for these observations follows from the concept of information flow developed over the previous chapters. To see how this works, we consider first a normal individual's reaction to the experimental setup. Initially (Fig. 6.2a), each hemisphere receives input corresponding

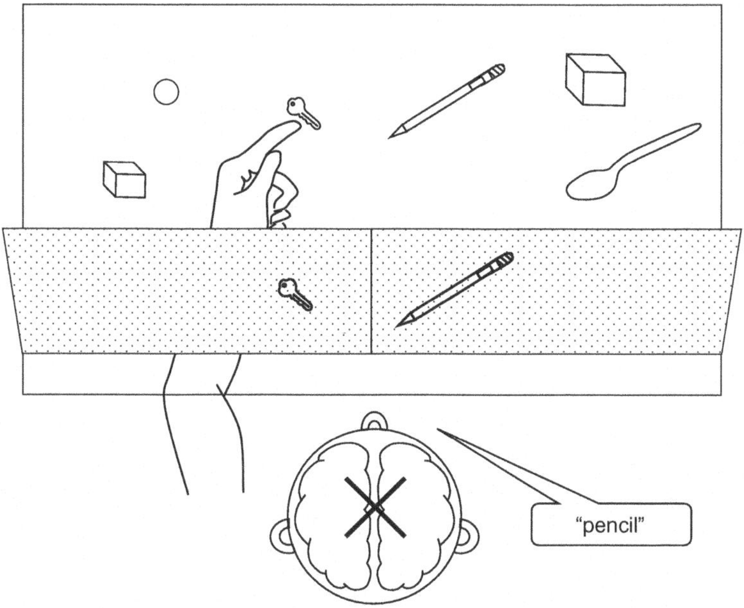

Fig. 6.1c Response of a split-brain patient to the simultaneous presentation of a key in the left visual field and a pencil in the right visual field: says "pencil" but points to the key with the left hand

to what it sees in the contralateral (opposite side) visual field: the right hemisphere initially receives visual input about the key, while the left hemisphere initially receives visual input about the pencil. Over the next few milliseconds, signals are transferred across the intact corpus callosum, providing each hemisphere with information about the ipsilateral (same side) visual field. As a result, each hemisphere is able to see both the key and the pencil. The intact corpus callosum also enables each hemisphere to control movements made by either hand. The net outcome is that the normal individual is able to respond correctly to either the key or the pencil, and can do so both verbally and manually with either hand.

We now consider what happens when the individual's corpus callosum is severed (Fig. 6.2b). The callosal damage results in a loss of transfer of visual information between the hemispheres such that each hemisphere receives input only from the contralateral stimulus. Unlike the case with an intact callosum, there is no transfer of information between

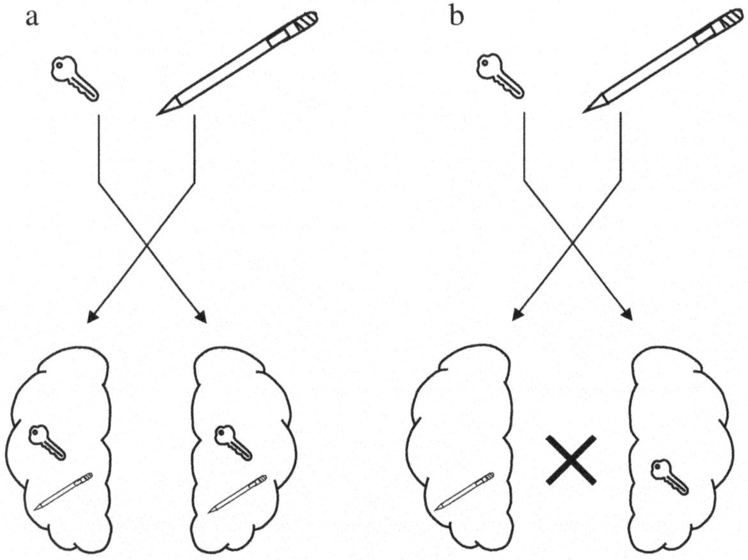

Fig. 6.2 Brain mechanisms underlying the split-brain effect

the hemispheres. Therefore, each hemisphere sees only what is presented in the contralateral visual field. And since only the left hemisphere can verbally describe what it experiences, it reports seeing the pencil in the right visual field but says nothing about the key in the left visual field. Additionally, since the pathways for cortical control over fine motor movements of the hands and fingers are crossed, the callosal damage renders each hemisphere capable of controlling only the opposite hand.

Other Examples of the Split-Brain Effect

Sensory modalities other than vision also show the split-brain effect. For example, split-brain patients cannot verbally report on figures or letters traced on the skin of their left hand or left foot. Similarly, they show a split-brain effect with respect to their sense of smell, although the situation with odors is atypical because the olfactory pathways do not cross. Consequently, only odors sniffed through the left nostril can be accurately named since only these odors gain access to the left hemisphere speech mechanisms. On the other hand, odors sniffed through the right nostril can only be identified via a right-hemisphere-mediated left hand pointing response.[11]

Another split-brain effect is the inability of operated patients to recognize or retrieve with one hand objects identified with the other hand. Nor can split-brain patients use their right hand to imitate postures imposed on the left hand. Also, if the patient's hands are kept out of view and the examiner stimulates a spot on the palm or fingers of one hand, the patient cannot point with his thumb to the corresponding site on the opposite hand.[12]

Interhemispheric comparisons are defective in the visual sphere as well. If, for example, colors are simultaneously flashed in the right and left visual hemifields, the patient cannot say whether they are the same or different.

The split-brain effects are most dramatic when stimuli are presented to both hemispheres simultaneously. A patient who is presented with the compound word "hatband" and is asked to select the corresponding object from a set of choices will select a hat with the left hand while verbally reporting that he sees the word "band." When asked what kind of band he has in mind, the patient offers guesses such as "rubber" or "rock and roll" but not "hat."

In some situations, the corpus callosum division actually works to the patient's advantage. For example, if the two hands are required to simultaneously copy different figures shown on the two sides of the screen, the presence of the damaged callosum improves the performance.

In summary, cutting the corpus callosum has the effect of splitting the cortex into two independently functioning domains: a linguistically competent left hemisphere that can perceive targets located on the right side of space and can express itself either verbally or by movements of the right hand; and a mute right hemisphere that can only perceive targets located on the left side of space and can only express itself by left hand movements.

[11] Gordon 1969.

[12] Sperry 1966–1967.

Separate Willfulness

One of the more intriguing features of the split-brain syndrome is the separate willfulness of the two hemispheres that is observed in the post-operative period. The phenomenon was first noted at the beginning of the twentieth century by Kurt Goldstein in 1908 in a neurologically impaired woman who exhibited an unruly left hand:

> On one occasion the hand grabbed her own neck and tried to throttle her, and could only be pulled off by force. Similarly, it tore off the bed-covers against the patient's will...She soon is complaining about her hand, that it is a law unto itself. ... when once it has got hold of something, it refuses to let go. "I myself can do nothing with it: if I'm having a drink and it gets hold of the glass, it won't let go and spills the drink out. Then I hit it and say: 'Behave yourself, hand'...I suppose there must be an evil spirit in it."[13]

In 1962, Geschwind and Kaplan were the first to attribute the syndrome to a corpus callosum interruption and in 1972, the French neurologists, Brion and Jedynak stated that this type of left hand behavior was common in callosal patients and they gave it the name "la main estrangiere" or "the alien hand."

A number of illustrative cases have been described, such as this one by Geschwind:

> A surgical callosal patient whom I had the opportunity to examine extensively over a month pointed out that since his operation he would sometimes suddenly strike his wife, but only with his left hand, which caused him extreme chagrin, since he was normally a mild-mannered man with no tendencies for such activity.[14]

In the 1960s, Gazzaniga noted this example of post-operative left hand willfulness:

---

[13] Goldstein 1908.

[14] Geschwind 1981.

> The patient would pick up the evening paper with the right hand, but put it down abruptly with the left and then have to pick it up again with the right. ... it was as if the control of the left hand were strongly centered in the minor hemisphere at such times and hence isolated from the main intent and prevailing directorship of the dominant hemisphere.[15]

He later added an additional case:

> One patient, for example, described the time he found his left hand struggling against his right when he tried to put his pants on in the morning. One hand was pulling them up while the other hand was pulling them down. In another incident the same patient was angry and forcibly reached for his wife with his left hand while his right hand grabbed the left in attempt to stop it.[16]

Another illustrative example of the opposition behavior of the two hemispheres involved a 17-year-old split-brain patient studied by psychologist Jerre Levy in Sperry's laboratory. In one of the experimental sessions, a pipe was placed out of sight in the patient's left hand and he was then asked to write with his left hand the name of the object he had been holding. He began by laboriously writing the letters P and I. The hand then suddenly became relaxed and the writing sped up. The I was quickly converted to an E, and the letters N, C, I, and L were then added with ease. The interpretation of this behavior was that initially the right hemisphere, which knew what was being held in the left hand, assumed dominance but struggled mightily to produce the letter P and I, its writing ability being primitive. But then the dominance switched, with the left hemisphere assuming dominant ipsilateral control of the left hand but, having no knowledge of what the left hand was holding, making an educated but erroneous guess that it was a pencil.[17]

In the early 1980s I had the opportunity to view a film in which one of Sperry and Gazzaniga's split-brain patients exhibited the characteristic interhemispheric conflict. The patient was being tested with the block design subtest of the Wechsler Adult Intelligence Scale, which requires that the

[15] Gazzaniga 1962.
[16] Gazzaniga 1970.
[17] Levy 1971.

subject assemble 16 half-colored cubes so as to match a sample figure. This is a task the right hemisphere performs better than the left. On one of the trials, while the patient was attempting in vain to clumsily and laboriously arrange the blocks with his right hand (left hemisphere), his left hand (right hemisphere) suddenly entered from off screen, pushed his right hand away, and proceeded to quickly arrange the blocks into their correct position.

The examiner then intervened, pushing the left hand off screen and asking the patient to try once more to arrange the blocks with his right hand. But within a few seconds, the impatient left hand again entered from off screen and again pushed the right hand away and attempted to take over the task. This time the patient's right hand grasped his left hand firmly by the wrist and forcibly pushed it away. A moment later, however, the petulant left hand emerged once more and again the right hand had to forcefully push it away. Eventually, the patient had to sit on his left hand to keep it from intruding and allowing the right hand to finish the task in peace.

In another film, a woman who had suffered a corpus callosum disconnection secondary to a cerebral hemorrhage repeatedly put a cigarette in her mouth with her right hand and then took it out with her left hand. In both these examples, which are typical for split-brain patients in the months after surgery,[18] a degree of right hemisphere willfulness is evident matching that present in the left hemisphere. Which hemisphere exerts dominance is to some degree determined by the nature of the task involved. If visuospatial skills are required by a task, then the right hemisphere dominates; if a verbal response is called for, the dominance shifts abruptly to the left hemisphere.

Dual Conscious Experience in the Commissurotomized Brain

The Split-Brain Patient Has Two Foci of Conscious Experience

Having outlined the highlights of the split-brain syndrome, we now consider its relevance for conscious experience and the mind/brain problem. The central issue here is whether there might be more than one conscious

[18] Sperry 1966.

experience present per brain. The possibility that split-brain patients might have two separate spheres of conscious experience has been entertained ever since the early work of Sperry and Gazzaniga in the 1960s. The argument is straightforward. Since only the left hemisphere of the split-brain patient is able to speak, whenever a split-brain patient makes a verbal response, it must be his or her left hemisphere that is doing the talking. If we make the assumption that verbal reports are reflective of conscious experience, then we can conclude that the left hemisphere mediates at least one unitary conscious experience.

The question then is whether the split-brain patient's right hemisphere provides a second, separate substrate for conscious experience. Some have denied this possibility. The argument is generally that the disconnected right hemisphere is nothing more than an "automaton," a mindless apparatus that is incapable of conscious experience.[19] This distinction between a smart, conscious left hemisphere and a subservient, robotic right hemisphere grew out of the common observation that patients who suffer extensive left hemisphere damage show little residual cognitive ability, suggesting that the cognitive level of the remaining right hemisphere is primitive at best. Overlooked, however, was the possibility that left hemisphere damage might itself interfere with right hemispheric function, the result being an underestimation of the right hemisphere's true cognitive capacity.

Decades of split-brain research has amended this oversight. Indeed, the unfettered right hemispheres of split-brain subjects manifest far better cognitive ability than had previously been thought possible. Sperry, in his 1981 Nobel Prize acceptance speech, summarized the transition in thinking about the right hemisphere that resulted from split-brain research:

> With few exceptions, the bulk of the collected lesion evidence up through the 1950's into the early 1960's converged to support the picture of a leading, more highly evolved and intellectual left hemisphere and a relatively retarded right hemisphere that, by contrast, in the typical right-hander brain, is not only mute and agraphic but also dyslexic, word-deaf, and apraxic, and lacking generally in higher cognitive function. It thus came as a considerable surprise in the early 1960's when tests on commissurotomy or "split-brain" patients seemed to indicate the presence in the right,

[19] Morin 2002; Eccles 1965.

> so-called "minor" hemisphere of a considerable capacity for cognitive understanding and the comprehension of language, both written and spoken.[20]

We know now that the right hemisphere perceives, learns, and remembers at an unequivocal human level. Estimates are that the right hemisphere has the comprehension capability of a young child,[21] sufficient, for example, for comprehending simple verbal instructions during testing. The right hemisphere of the commissurotomy patient can, via the left hand, identify objects named aloud by the examiner, such as a square, a rectangle, a cone, a cylinder, a pyramid, a fork, a coin, a tack, a clown, an Indian, a screwdriver, a pair of pliers, a pair of scissors, a safety pin, a flashlight bulb, and a door latch. It can indicate an understanding of such concepts as "rough," "smooth," and "round." It can also identify objects described by the examiner with descriptions such as "used to light fires with" for a match, "used to tell time" for a clock, "a measuring instrument" for a ruler, and "a liquid container" for a glass.[22]

Although the right hemisphere cannot speak or write,[23] it does have a rudimentary reading ability. It can, for example, match objects such as a cup, fork, and apple with corresponding written words. The right hemisphere also has the ability to think associatively. For example, when a picture of a cigarette is flashed in the left visual field, the left hand will correctly choose an ashtray or a box of matches from among a group of unrelated items. Similarly, if a picture of a dollar sign is flashed, the left hand will select a metal coin while rejecting other items without monetary associations. The right hemisphere has memory abilities as well. If, after a time delay, the right hemisphere is required to select an item from memory, it is able, by using the left hand, to retrieve from a large array of objects an object previously palpated by blind touch.

The right hemisphere is actually superior to the left hemisphere for some activities. For example, the right hemisphere performs better than

---

[20] Sperry 1982, p. 1223.

[21] Zaidel 1977.

[22] Sperry 1961; Gazzaniga 1967.

[23] Sperry 1969; Gazzaniga 1967; Trevarthan 1987.

the left on visuospatial tasks, such as those requiring recognition of shapes and configurations of objects[24] or judgment of a whole circle's size from a small arc.[25] Additionally, the right hemisphere is superior to the left in recognizing familiar faces and in discriminating musical chords.[26] The right hemisphere also excels in scanning bilateral stimulus arrays. For example, split-brain patients exhibit identical reaction times whether responding to a unitary visual discrimination task or to two such tasks presented simultaneously in the left and right fields, whereas normal controls show large decrements in reaction time to the dual stimuli.[27]

The right hemisphere also manifests distinctively human emotional sensitivity and expression[28] and generates typical human emotional responses when confronted with affect-laden stimuli or emotionally charged situations.[29] This is evident in its signaling of displeasure by frowning, wincing, and head shaking when it hears the left hemisphere making stupid verbal mistakes.[30] More generally, the right hemisphere of the split-brain patients can, with appropriate emotional reactions and social evaluations, readily recognize and identify pictures of themselves, of family members, of acquaintances, of pets, of familiar scenes, of political, historical and religious figures, and of television and screen personalities.[31]

In summary, the right hemisphere exhibits a remarkable range of cognitive abilities, such that regarding the right hemisphere as devoid of conscious experience would be tantamount to denying conscious experience to a young child or to an intelligent non-human primate, both of which most researchers associate conscious experience. This certainly reflected Sperry's opinion:

> We have not been able to see any real justification in our test findings for denying consciousness to the disconnected mute hemisphere. Everything we have observed in many kinds of task performances over many years of

[24] Trevarthan 1987.

[25] Sperry 1982.

[26] Sperry 1982.

[27] Ellenberg 1980.

[28] Sperry 1969.

[29] Sperry 1984.

[30] Sperry 1984; 1966–1967.

[31] Sperry 1984.

> testing reinforces the conclusion that the mute hemisphere has an inner experience of much the same order as that of the speaking hemisphere though differing in quality and cognitive faculties…After watching repeatedly the superior performance of the right hemisphere in tests like the above, one finds it most difficult to think of this half of the brain as being only an automaton lacking in conscious awareness.[32]

Given these considerations, it is hard to avoid the conclusion that, at least in the split-brain case, there are two independent anatomical spheres of conscious experience, one situated in the left hemisphere, the other situated in the right. This contention has in fact been favored by most writers on the subject and almost all those who have worked directly with split-brain patients.[33]

A Matter of Terminology

Before proceeding, there is a matter of terminology that needs attention. In view of there potentially being more than one sphere of conscious experience present in a given brain, a potential ambiguity may arise with respect to which conscious experience is being referred to at any given time. To circumvent this difficulty, I will make a temporary distinction between what I will call "*verbally reportable conscious experience*" (vr-conscious experience) and "*non-verbally reportable conscious experience*" (nvr-conscious experience). By vr-conscious experience I mean the uniquely human form of conscious experience whose content is available for verbal report and whose production is mediated by the split-brain patient's left hemisphere. Conscious experiences of this kind are associated with logical thinking, grammatical competence, a sense of future and past, and a well-developed sense of self. An example would be the type of conscious experience that you, the reader, are having right now as you read this paragraph and reflect upon what I am saying.

In contrast, by nvr-conscious experience I will mean the kind of conscious experience assumed to be present in nonhuman animals and very

[32] Sperry 1984, p. 665.

[33] Koch 2009; Tononi 2008.

young children, and in the right hemisphere of the split-brain patient. Conscious experiences of this sort lack logic, grammar, sophisticated self-awareness, or sense of future and past.

Note that I am making this distinction solely for the purpose of facilitating the discussion that will take place in the next few chapters. I do not intend it as supportive of any specific philosophical position, such as, for example, Ned Block's distinction between *access* and *phenomenal* consciousness.[34] Later, in Chap. 11, when a workable mind/brain theory is in hand, I will in fact argue that all conscious experiences share the same basic mechanism.

Potential Obstacles to the Thesis of Dual Conscious Experience

Ostensible Normality of Split-Brain Patient Behavior

If the thesis that split-brain patients have dual conscious experiences is to be deemed scientifically feasible it must be reconciled with several peculiar characteristics of the split-brain syndrome. One is the nearly normal behavior split-brain patients exhibit in their everyday activities. In most circumstances, split-brain patients speak and behave as normal individuals do. Recall that when Akelaitis examined the split-brain patients in Rochester, he was unable to identify any cognitive or behavioral deficits, even with extensive neuropsychological testing. Roger Sperry regarded the unexpected normality of split-brain patients as extraordinary:

> The most remarkable effect of sectioning the cerebral commissures continues to be the apparent lack of change with respect to ordinary behavior. The least affected…patients…exhibit no gross alterations of personality, intellect or overt behavior two years after operation. Individual mannerisms, conversation and bearing, temperament, strength, vigor, and coordination are all largely intact and seem much as before surgery.[35]

[34] Block 2007.

[35] Sperry 1969, p. 275.

Split-brain patients remain able to perform activities requiring bilateral coordination, such as swimming, buttoning a shirt, or playing the piano.[36] They can continue to run a household, do the family cooking, go to the market, and watch movies with no difficulty.[37] Sperry observed that, "in casual conversation over a cup of coffee and a cigarette one would hardly suspect that there was anything at all unusual."[38] Or as Gazzaniga has put it: "One would miss the departure of a good friend more, apparently, than the left hemisphere misses the right."[39]

How can such ostensibly normal behavior be produced by a pair of disconnected and independently experiencing hemispheres? Some have argued that such normal behavior cannot in fact be achieved and have accordingly rejected the notion that split-brain patients have two independent loci of conscious experience. Yet, as Geschwind pointed out, unified performance by independently behaving individuals is actually not that hard to attain:

> The one feature of the case that may at first appear to be somewhat perplexing is the retained ability of the patient to perform certain learned activities that require the cooperation of the two hands, such as threading a needle. It can readily be demonstrated, however, that two normals, one using the right hand and the other using the left, can combine to perform successfully such activities.[40]

The development of bilaterally cooperative behavior is facilitated by the fact that the two hemispheres reside in the same body, eat the same food, meet the same people, wake up and go to sleep at the same time, and, in general, proceed through life with the synchronicity of a wizened old couple. Additionally, bilaterally coordinated behavior is facilitated by *cross-cueing*, a maneuver in which one hemisphere produces a behavior that informs the other hemisphere of what is going on. For example, the left hemisphere might mumble the name of an object it is palpating with

---

[36] Nagel 1979.

[37] Sperry 1966, p. 301.

[38] Sperry 1964, p. 46.

[39] Gazzaniga 1970, pp. 71–72.

[40] Geschwind 1962.

the right hand (controlled by the left hemisphere), thereby cueing the right hemisphere, which can hear and understand the mumbled name. Or one hemisphere may inform the other hemisphere about an object it is examining by having the fingers manipulate it so that it makes a recognizable sound, such as in the case of jingling keys. The pervasive tendency to cross cue, and to do so cleverly, is characteristic of all split-brain patients.[41]

Finally, some activities are mediated by brain regions that are anatomically connected via subcortical pathways that are spared in the surgery. This is the case for stimuli presented in the midline, for auditory and gustatory processing, and for emotional responses where lateralized input spreads rapidly across subcortical stations to involve both hemispheres.[42]

Unawareness of Perceptual Loss

A second peculiar characteristic of the split-brain syndrome is the unawareness that split-brain patients have of their demonstrable perceptual deficits. Take the visual field cut suffered by the split-brain patient's left hemisphere, for example. Since the left hemisphere of a split-brain patient receives visual input only from the right visual field and is therefore blind to the happenings in the left visual field, one might expect to hear verbal complaints of a loss of vision on the left side of space. But such is not the case. The split-brain patient denies left-sided perceptual deficiency,[43] contending that his or her perception is integrated and whole.[44]

How can we explain such unawareness of a glaring visual deficiency? An answer derives from an extension of the phenomenon of filling-in that we ran across in Chap. 3. The reader will recall that unawareness of the blind spot and misperceptions that occur with certain visual illusions are attributable to the brain creatively filling in the absent data with an extension of the stimulus pattern present in the surrounding regions. With the split-brain patient, the filling-in consists of a completion of a half object to a whole object by extrapolation of the seen to the unseen half.

---

[41] Gazzaniga 2013.

[42] Sperry 1982, p. 1225.

[43] Sperry 1966, p. 301.

[44] Sperry 1969.

The operation of a filling-in mechanism is made evident by the reactions of split-brain patients to chimeric figures. These are compound figures created by joining the left side of one object with the right side of another object. If a chimeric figure composed of a left-half-rose with a right-half-eye is presented to a normal individual with an intact corpus callosum, both hemispheres separately encode the entire chimeric object and the individual can describe the figure verbally or report awareness of its presence by a manual pointing response. If a chimeric rose/eye is presented to a split-brain patient, however, the left hemisphere, which actually sees only the right-half-eye, uses a filling-in mechanism to consciously perceive a whole eye and reports this verbally. In the meantime, the right hemisphere, which actually sees only the left-half-rose, uses a filling-in mechanism to consciously perceive a whole rose and reports this manually with a pointing response.

The Illusion of Sentient Control Over Unconscious Acts

A third peculiar characteristic of split-brain patients is the insistence by the verbal left hemisphere that it is in control of behaviors that are actually produced by the right hemisphere. When asked why they engaged in the behavior they offer confabulatory responses. As an example, when the word "laugh" was flashed in the left visual field of one split-brain patient he began laughing, even as his verbal left hemisphere reported seeing nothing. When asked why he was laughing the patient replied, "Oh, you guys are too much." Then, when the command "rub" was flashed in his left visual field, he rubbed the back of his head with his left hand. When asked what he thought the command was, he said, "itch." And when the word "kiss" was presented to his left visual field, he blurted out, "Hey, no way, you've got to be kidding." But when asked what word was flashed, a look of puzzlement came over his face as he offered, "Oh, 'nurse' I guess." In each case the patient's left hemisphere produced a confabulatory reason for the behavior instead of admitting that it saw nothing.[45]

---

[45] Gazzaniga 1977, pp. 1146, 1147.

With another patient, a picture of a snow scene was flashed in the left visual field and a picture of a chicken claw was simultaneously flashed in the right visual field. When asked to choose objects from an array laid in full view before him on a table, the patient's left hand appropriately chose a shovel (to go with the snow scene) and his right hand appropriately chose a chicken (to go with the chicken claw). But when asked why he made those choices, the patient's verbal left hemisphere, unaware of what the right hemisphere had seen, replied, "Oh, that's simple. The chicken claw goes with the chicken, and you need a shovel to clean out the chicken shed."[46] The patient's left hemisphere thus confabulated a reason for the left hand's pointing to the shovel. In fact, the left hemisphere, which could not see the snow scene, should have admitted that it had no idea why the shovel was chosen by the left hand. Instead it confabulated a concocted explanation based on the information available to it.

A particularly compelling confabulation was one filmed by Sperry and colleagues and described by David Galin:

> One film segment shows a female patient being tested with a tachistoscope. In the series of neutral geometric figures being presented at random to the right and left fields, a nude pinup is included and flashed to the right (nonverbal) hemisphere. The girl blushes and giggles. Sperry asks, "What did you see?" She answers, "Nothing, just a flash of light," and giggles again, covering her mouth with her hand. "Why are you laughing then?" asks Sperry. She laughs again and says, "Oh, Dr. Sperry, you have some machine!" The episode is very suggestive; if one did not know her neurologic history, one might see this as a clear example of perceptual defense and think that she was "repressing" the perception of the conflictual sexual material—even her final response (a socially acceptable nonsequitur) was convincing.[47]

The confabulatory responses of split-brain patients are emitted spontaneously and frequently. They have been taken as evidence of a drive, present in normal individuals as well as in split-brain patients, to seek explanations for why events occur.[48] Gazzaniga calls the left hemisphere

---

[46] Gazzaniga 1995, p. 225.

[47] Galin 1977, p. 398.

[48] Gazzaniga 1978.

module that generates these confabulations the *interpreter*.[49] He suggests that it is operative not only in split-brain patients but in the normal population as well. According to Gazzaniga, the interpreter "generates the storyline as to why we do the things we do, feel the things we feel, and see the patterns in our behavior that contribute to our theory about ourselves. Once you see it at work in this simple experiment, you see it everywhere." He goes on to say:

> So, we humans are built in certain ways and indeed have certain moral rules that are there in newborn babies and aging adults. What is different about us is that we all cook up different beliefs about why we respond the way we do. Our variation comes from that interpreter giving each person his own spin and story—because each of us draws on different experiences. Many times the stories of others seem preposterous. It can be their religious story, their political story, or their philosophy of life. They can annoy and irritate and leave one trembling with the sense of superiority, the sense that the other person is uninformed while one alone has it right. Yet, as the great physicist Max Born said, "The belief that there is only one truth, and that oneself is in possession of it, is the root of all evil in the world." Take a step back when you feel this way. Think about it a minute and appreciate that after all everything is a story—yours as well as the other guy's.

In summary, the split-brain patients' confabulatory illusions of sentient control over their left hand actions, together with their unawareness of left-sided perceptual deficits and ostensibly normal general behavior, can be plausibly incorporated into a dual-consciousness model of split-brain function. We now move on to consider whether a dual-consciousness model applies to normal brains as well.

Dual Conscious Experience in the Normal Brain

If the split-brain patient has two centers of conscious experience, what can we say about a normal individual with an intact corpus callosum? The common opinion is that the state of dual conscious experience argued to

[49] Gazzaniga 1989, 1995.

be present in the split-brain patient does not carry over to normal individuals. Implied is that an intact corpus callosum somehow congeals the activity in the two hemispheres into a single center of conscious experience. This was Sperry's opinion:

> I myself have favored the view that the conscious mind is normally single and unified, mediated by brain activity that spans and involves both hemispheres.[50]

According to this perspective, however, there is the awkward implication that the abrupt splitting of the corpus callosum instantaneously divides a single center of conscious experience neatly in two. It is difficult to contemplate a mechanism by which such a perfect schism might be so easily achieved. A simpler explanation is that the dual experiences are already present in the normal state and that the split-brain surgery merely acts to disrupt communication and coordination between them. The left hemisphere would then mediate the same verbal, self-reflective consciousness and the right hemisphere the same nonverbal, non-self-reflective consciousness both before and after the surgery. The role of the corpus callosum would be no more than a conduit for information transfer between hemispheres and not as a mechanism for fusing left and right hemisphere subjective experiences.

The possibility that normal individuals might have two separate spheres of conscious experience was first suggested in the nineteenth century by the London physician Arthur Ladbroke Wigan (1785–1847) in 1844.[51] Wigan contended that each cerebral hemisphere supported a fully developed mind and that a normal individual has two of them, each maintaining its own stream of thought. He regarded each hemisphere as capable of engaging in all the thoughts and emotions usually ascribed to the brain as a whole. He noted that he had come up with the idea 25 years before the writing of his book and that in the intervening time he had not found a single valid or even plausible objection.

---

[50] Sperry 1984.

[51] Wigan 1844.

Wigan's conjecture was cited by others throughout the 1800s but faded into obscurity toward the end of that century, likely because of the discovery of language lateralization and the rise of the doctrine of left hemisphere dominance during that era. The view that held sway in the twentieth century prior to the split-brain research was that there was only one conscious experience in the normal brain and it was lateralized to the left hemisphere.

With the advent of the split-brain research, however, Wigan's conjecture was revitalized by the observation that split-brain patients exhibited the same perceptions, memories, and feelings after the surgery that they had exhibited before the surgery. Absent were any reports of mental splitting or duplication, as might be expected if only one center of conscious experience were present before the surgery. In 1981, Rolando Puccetti offered a logical basis for positing dual conscious experiences in normal brains, suggesting that the function of the corpus callosum was duplicative rather than integrative. His arguments were published in the journal, *Behavioral and Brain Sciences*, along with an extensive discussion by 17 commentators.[52] Opinions varied, with some objecting to Puccetti's arguments and some supporting them but with no resolution achieved.

If two streams of conscious experiences are in fact present in the normal individual then why do not we sense the duality? An answer derives from the same arguments as those offered in the split-brain case. We saw in our discussion of split-brain patients that the mechanisms of filling-in, cross-cueing, and other compensatory processes rendered the patients unaware of their dual experience state. These same processes may serve the same end in the normal individual with an intact callosum.

Puccetti raises the interesting question: "If we cerebrally intact twin-brained human beings are really compounds of two persons, which is me? Am I the person whose conscious unity is rooted in left brain information-processing and right hand motor control; or am I the person whose consciousness is based in right brain activity and subordinate left hand control?" The answer is that the entity that is asking the question is the left hemisphere, because only the left hemisphere is capable

[52] Puccetti 1981.

of self-reflection. A similar question will arise in later chapters when we consider the presence of not just two but many consciousnesses in the brain at any given time.

What about people who have reversed lateralization or mixed hemisphere dominance? In the rarely encountered reversed lateralization case, everything we have noted would apply unaltered, except with right and left reversed. In the mixed dominance case, on the other hand, the situation is more complex and relatively unexplored. To discuss it further at this time would take us too far afield. Suffice to say that the existence of such anomalous conditions remains entirely consistent with the assertion that there are two separate streams of conscious experience in both the split-brain and normal states. In what follows we will adopt this position and see where it leads us in our search for the vr-NCC.

7

Frontal Convergence

Is a Focal VR-NCC Possible?

In Chap. 6, we reviewed the arguments in favor of there being separate NCCs in the two hemispheres, the verbally reportable one being lateralized to the left hemisphere. We now ask whether the vr-NCC might be localized still further. The received view is that it cannot. The consensus is that the vr-NCC must be widely distributed, extending across many cortical and subcortical brain regions.[1] The possibility of a spatially compact vr-NCC has been roundly rejected by most in the field, the rallying cry being that "there are no convergence zones in the brain, no locations where it all comes together."[2] Damasio sums up this contention:

> The unavoidable conclusion is that, while it is possible to conceive of the integration of sensory processes within a few neuronal regions necessary to define a single entity, it is apparent that no single area in the human brain receives projections from all the regions involved in the processing of an

[1] Baars 2005; Seth 2005; Libet 2004; John 2001; Llinas 1998; Dehaene 1998; Damasio 1989.
[2] Crick 2003; 1990; Dehaene 1998; Dennett 1991; Damasio 1989; Goldman-Rakic 1988.

S. Sevush, *The Single-Neuron Theory*,
DOI 10.1007/978-3-319-33708-1_7

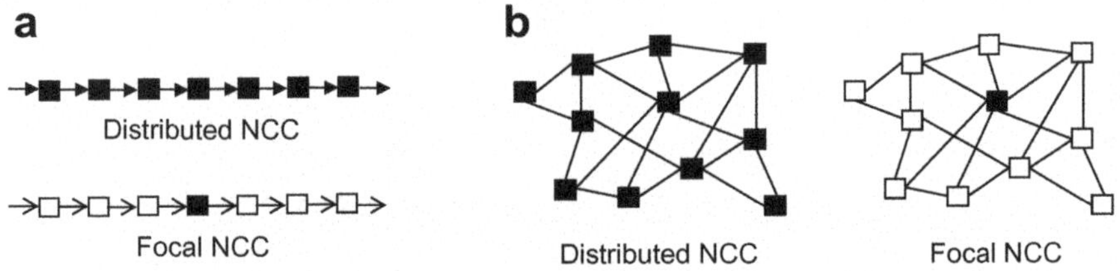

Fig. 7.1 For any continuously distributed NCC, a corresponding focal NCC is also possible, whether the information flow is unidirectional, as in (**a**), or omnidirectional, as in (**b**)

> event. More importantly, it is inconceivable that any single region of the brain might integrate spatially all the fragments of sensory and motor activity to define a set of unique events.[3]

The appeal of this view is understandable. It is difficult to imagine how a single brain region could be sufficiently rich in connections and processing capacity that it could by itself account for the intricate and varied nature of vr-conscious experience. Studies using neuroimaging and electrical recording techniques seem to support this contention, with multiple brain regions lighting up in even the simplest instances of vr-conscious experience.

Yet, a focal vr-NCC is not as far-fetched as it may seem. The possibility of a focal vr-NCC is in fact logically implicit in any distributed model. This is so because, for any set of sufficiently interconnected cortical regions that might serve collectively as the substrate for a distributed vr-NCC, the alternative is always possible that just one region is the true vr-NCC and that all the other regions function merely to send signals to or receive signals from this one region.[4] The argument is generally applicable, regardless of whether one accepts the presence of directed modular pathways (Fig. 7.1a) or favors instead a system with omnidirectional connectivity (Fig. 7.1b).

During a conscious visual task, for example, functional neuroimaging, single-cell recordings, and clinical observations consistently reveal

[3] Damasio 1989, p. 38.

[4] De Graff 2012.

widespread activation of occipital, temporal, parietal, and frontal cortices, and of multiple diencephalic and brainstem structures as well. Since, however, these disparate regions are highly interconnected, the possibility that only a subset or even just one of the identified regions actually subserves conscious experience, and that the other regions function only to provide input into or output from this single region, cannot be dismissed without further consideration.

The Left Lateral Prefrontal Cortex as VR-NCC

A strong case can be made that the vr-NCC is at least confined to within the territory of the frontal lobes. The frontal lobes are the recipients of information pertaining to every component of vr-conscious experience. This was recognized in the nineteenth century by John Hughlings Jackson who hypothesized even then that the frontal lobes might serve as the "the seat of consciousness."[5] Jackson's conception was reiterated and explored in more detail by the renowned neuroanatomist Walle Nauta (1916–1994) in a paper published in 1971 entitled, "The Problem of the Frontal Lobe: A Reinterpretation." Nauta contended that the frontal lobes are unique in being the recipients of information derived from both the outside world and from the world within the body.[6] His "frontocentric theory" placed the frontal lobes as the common end point for all information coming into the brain. I read Nauta's paper in the late 1970s and was strongly influenced by it. I have regarded the frontal lobes as the likely locus of the vr-NCC ever since.

In the time since Nauta's publication, a frontal lobe localization for the vr-NCC has garnered further support.[7] Even Damasio in his 1989 paper acknowledged that a frontal lobe vr-NCC was possible, his contention being only that no smaller region within the frontal lobe is capable of serving as a suitable convergence zone.[8] In 1995, Francis Crick and

[5] Penfield 1947; 1938.

[6] Goldman-Rakic 1988; Nauta 1971.

[7] Elston 2003; Miller 2001; Barbas 2000; Crick 1995.

[8] Damasio 1989.

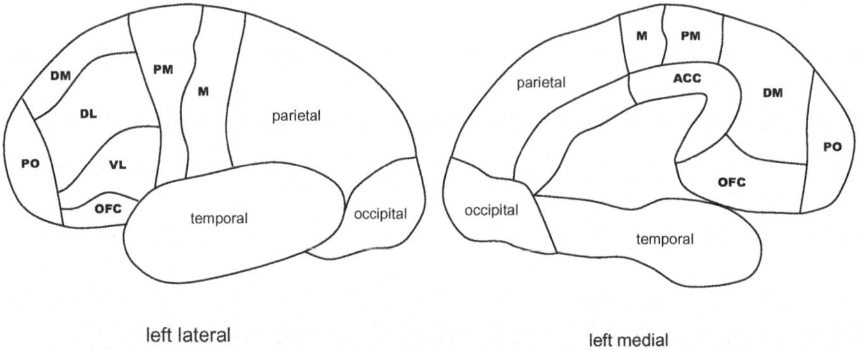

Fig. 7.2 Frontal lobe subdivisions. Abbreviations: ACC, anterior cingulate cortex; DL, dorsolateral; DM, dorsomedial; M, motor; OFC, orbitofrontal cortex; PM, premotor; PO, polar; VL, ventrolateral

Christof Koch weighed in with their dictum that for a neuron to be aware of an object, it must project directly to some part of the frontal cortex in front of the primary motor area.[9]

If the vr-NCC can be localized to the frontal lobes, the question arises as to whether it can be localized still further. Not that any further localization would be necessary for the arguments I will be presenting in the coming chapters to be valid. A single-neuron model of vr-conscious experience would work just as well with a vr-NCC that was spread over the whole frontal lobe as it would with one that was localized to just one subregion of the frontal lobe. The question we need to answer is not whether a focal or a distributed frontal lobe vr-NCC is possible but what is the arrangement actually adopted by the brain? With this in mind, we now assess the plausibility of a focal vr-NCC being situated within a subregion of the frontal lobes. First, we undertake a brief review of frontal lobe anatomy.

The frontal lobe can be subdivided into eight regions (Fig. 7.2). Posteriorly, there are the *premotor* (PM) and *motor* (M) *cortices*, which serve primarily as output modules, sending signals downward to the brainstem and spinal cord to exert control over bodily movements. Medially, there is

[9] Crick 1995.

the ACC, and on the undersurface there is the OFC. Recall that we have already encountered the ACC and OFC in Chap. 5 in connection with the perception of feelings. The broad upper surface of the frontal lobe can be divided into the *dorsomedial* (DM), *dorsolateral* (DL), *ventrolateral* (VL), and *polar* (PO) *cortices*. These four regions together with the OFC comprise the *prefrontal cortex* (PFC).

Which of these regions might by itself serve as the vr-NCC? For a focal region of the frontal lobes to be regarded as the vr-NCC, it would need to satisfy at least the following criteria: (1) the region should be the recipient of afferent connections pertaining to all of the perceptions, memories, and feelings that make up vr-conscious experience; (2) the region should have the appropriate efferent connectivity to account for the production of vr-conscious speech and behavior; (3) complete destruction of the region should result in a loss of vr-conscious experience; and (4) activation of the region should be demonstrable on neuroimaging scans and with single-cell recording techniques during engagement by a subject in a vr-conscious task.

I believe there is a region, namely the left VL-PFC, that satisfies all these criteria. Let's look at the specifics.

Afferent Connectivity

In Chaps. 2–5, we saw how a directed modular pathway model could be applied to the processing of perceptions, memories, and feelings. For the case of perception, we saw in Chap. 3 that the ventral stream, which processes visual, auditory, and tactile stimuli and which is the stream associated with vr-conscious experience, projects ultimately to the PFC. Although not mentioned specifically in the chapter, a substantial portion of the projection targets the VL-PFC subregion in particular.[10]

With regard to memory, we saw in Chap. 4 that a link between the PFC and both STM and LTM is well established. For STM, we saw that the PFC was the location of the central executive, the specific module in

[10] Romanski 2007.

the working memory model that is associated with vr-conscious experience. For LTM, we saw that vr-conscious recall of visual, auditory, and tactile memories could be modeled by a pathway that traverses the MTL loop and then joins the ventral stream in projecting ultimately to the PFC. The VL-PFC subregion is a particularly prominent target of these projections.[11]

On the other hand, for olfactory and gustatory stimuli, the perceptual pathways target the OFC, not the VL-PFC.[12] Moreover, the pathways for vr-conscious feelings, whether they be those associated with emotion, drives, familiarity, pain, or pleasure, target both the OFC and the ACC, and not the VL-PFC.[13] Sense can be made of these projections if we take into account that there are strong projections from the OFC and ACC to the VL-PFC.[14] A plausible model could be envisioned in which direct OFC projections to the VL-PFC complete a pathway for the vr-conscious experiences of smell, tastes, and feelings. The ACC projection to the VL-PFC, on the other hand, would complete a pathway for VL-PFC activation when mental effort is required to make decisions during cognitive tasks (Fig. 7.3).[15]

Efferent Connectivity

On the efferent side, the left VL-PFC sends outputs to the frontal eye fields, PM cortex, basal ganglia, cerebellum, and superior colliculus. Most importantly, the left VL-PFC itself contains Broca's area (Brodmann's areas 44 and 45),[16] the brain region known for a century and a half to be critical for grammatical language output.[17] The left VL-PFC is therefore well positioned to access the motor programs that mediate vr-conscious output.

---

[11] Blumenfeld 2006.
[12] Johnson 2000.
[13] Damasio 1999.
[14] Rushworth 2007.
[15] Gasquoine 2013; Rushworth 2008.
[16] Frey 2014.
[17] Broca 1861.

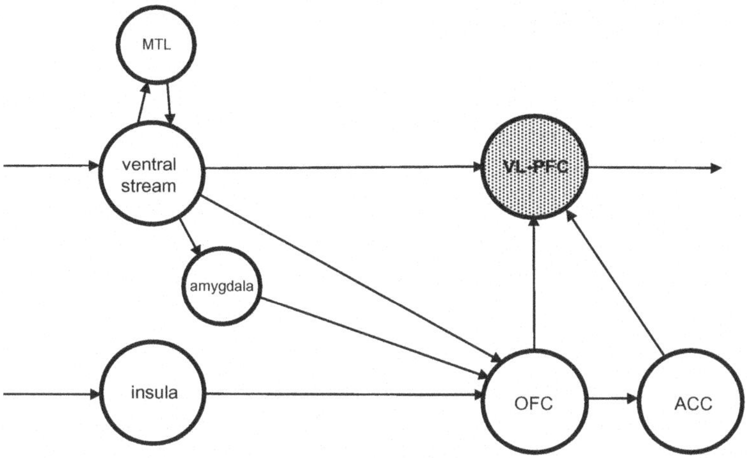

Fig. 7.3 A directed modular pathway model of perception, memory, and feelings is shown. The NCC is assumed to be localized within the VL-PFC (shaded region), which receives perceptual input from the ventral stream (both directly and via the amygdala, OFC and ACC), and input leading to feelings from the insula (via the OFC and ACC). Short-term memory is mediated by the same pathways as those that mediate perception, while long-term memory is mediated by an auxiliary loop passing through the MTL. Abbreviations: ACC, anterior cingulate cortex; MTL, medial temporal lobe; OFC, orbitofrontal cortex; VL-PFC, ventrolateral prefrontal cortex

On the basis of afferent and efferent connectivity, then, the VL-PFC is a reasonable candidate for the vr-NCC. Other regions within the frontal lobe lack the appropriate connectivity. In the case of the OFC, direct output projections to PM cortex or any of the other motor output pathways are lacking[18] and the region is not as intimately associated with Broca's area as is the VL-PFC. In the case of the ACC, on the other hand, afferent connections are inadequate, with no direct input coming to the ACC from the posterior cortical regions mediating vr-conscious perception, memory, and feelings. Likewise, neither the PO-PFC, the DM-PFC, nor the DL-PFC have the input connectivity to allow them to encode the contents of vr-conscious experience.

---

[18] Rushworth 2007.

The Ablation Paradigm

If the left VL-PFC is posited to be, by itself, the mediator of vr-conscious experience, then its complete destruction should result in a total loss of such experience. This would constitute an application of the *ablation paradigm*,[19] which specifies that *if a given brain region directly mediates a given cognitive function, then complete destruction of that brain region should result in the loss of that cognitive function*. Logically, the contrapositive of this statement is true as well: *if destruction of a brain region does not result in the loss of a given cognitive function, then the given brain region cannot be the direct mediator of that cognitive function.*

The ablation paradigm has been applied to the mind/brain problem for centuries. Patients with well-defined anatomical damage from disease, trauma, or surgery are assessed cognitively and conclusions are drawn regarding the importance of the damaged tissue for a specified cognitive function. Care must be taken when drawing inferences using this approach, however. To begin with, there is the danger of falling prey to the *ablation paradigm fallacy*. This is the illegitimate belief that if damage to a region impairs a certain cognitive function then that region must be the mediator of that function. This in fact is usually a faulty inference. For example, destruction of the retina results in loss of vr-conscious perception, yet no one thinks that the retina directly mediates vr-conscious perception. Nor can one conclude that the nose and mouth are the respiratory centers because their occlusion results in catastrophic respiratory failure. In general, when damage to a region causes loss of a function, all that can be concluded is that the region is a candidate for the mediator of that function. Other data would be needed to determine whether the region is actually the vr-NCC or is merely a region bringing information to or emitting information from the vr-NCCC, or is a modulatory region that is required for the proper functioning of the vr-NCC.

As applied to mind/brain studies, it is the contrapositive form of the ablation paradigm that is most useful in the search for the vr-NCC. Applied correctly, it removes from consideration brain regions whose destruction does not eliminate vr-consciousness, thereby narrowing the field of

---

[19] I learned this term from Ken Heilman during my fellowship at University of Florida at Gainesville.

vr-NCC aspirants. For example, we can say with confidence that the cerebellum is not part of the vr-NCC since its complete removal does not abolish vr-conscious experience.

The contrapositive form of the ablation paradigm has been invoked in six published cases in which supposed extensive damage to the frontal lobes produced little change in vr-conscious experience. The conclusion drawn in these cases has been that the frontal lobe could not by itself be the vr-NCC. This conclusion must be questioned, however. For example, there is the widely quoted case of Phineas Gage, a New England railway worker who in 1858 suffered frontal lobe trauma secondary to an iron tamping rod piercing his skull. It was reported that after the incident, Gage began using profanity and acting impulsively, and had become unable to adapt to social settings. Friends and acquaintances noted that "Gage was no longer Gage."[20] On the other hand, Gage's vr-conscious experience was entirely unaffected. The conclusion repeatedly drawn from this case has been that, since Gage retained normal vr-conscious experience subsequent to supposedly complete frontal lobe damage, his vr-conscious experience could not have been mediated by his frontal lobes.

In fact, the case is of little value in our search for the vr-NCC. The problem is that the frontal lobe damage in Gage's case was far from complete. The damage was severe enough to alter Gage's personality, constrict his emotional responsiveness, and diminish his goal-oriented behavior, but these deficits could be attributable to a lesion limited to the OFC. A reconstruction of Gage's brain based on the position of the fractures in his skull has in fact demonstrated that the damage in his case was likely confined to the medial OFC.[21] The left VL-PFC was completely spared.

The Gage case illustrates that a correct application of the ablation paradigm requires *complete* destruction of the candidate brain region. Partial destruction will not do, since the remaining tissue may be able to manage the function even when the damage is fairly extensive.[22] Additionally, if

[20] Stuss 1992.

[21] Damasio 1994.

[22] Buxhoeveden 2002.

sufficient time is allotted, the function in question may be transferred to neighboring brain regions, as happens, for example, in childhood developmental disorders.

The method used to determine the extent of brain damage comes into question as well. Neuroimaging and autopsy data, if they are to be trusted in assessing the effective extent of damage, must be supplemented by clinical observation. Thus, if neuroimaging and autopsy results indicate that damage to a cortical region is complete but clinical assessment reveals retained cognitive abilities known to be dependent on that region, the conclusion must be that the damage was in fact incomplete, irrespective of the neuroimaging and autopsy findings.

Other Published Cases

Unfortunately, these caveats have frequently been neglected.[23] The neuroscience literature is replete with assertions that vr-conscious experience is not localizable based on clinical cases in which PFC lesions were incomplete. The five other published cases further illustrate this. First, there is Brickner's "Patient A," a 39-year-old stockbroker who had a considerable portion of his frontal lobes surgically eliminated in the course of removing a large brain tumor that was compressing his frontal lobes.[24] As reported by Damasio,[25] the neurosurgeon, Walter Dandy, "had to perform an extensive bilateral resection of frontal tissue in two stages. On the left side all the frontal tissue rostral to Broca's area was removed. On the right, the excision was even larger and included all the brain anterior to the motor area." Like Gage, Patient A showed post-surgical alterations in personality and emotional reactivity and manifested diminished goal-oriented behavior, yet retained vr-conscious experience.[26]

This case has repeatedly been offered as support for the contention that the frontal lobes cannot be the direct mediators of vr-conscious experience.

[23] Crick 1998.
[24] Brickner 1939.
[25] Damasio 1998.
[26] Damasio 1993.

Yet, the boundaries of the surgical excision were described only loosely. Furthermore, the tumor was a slow growing meningioma, a type of growth that takes decades to reach a size that causes symptoms. There was therefore ample time for compensatory re-wiring of the cortex to occur and with it a restructuring of anatomical/functional relationships. And critically, the lack of language impairment indicates that the left VL-PFC was at least partially spared.

Then there is the case reported by Ackerly and Benton in 1948,[27] which involved a 37-year-old man who suffered frontal lobe damage around the time of his birth. At age 19 he was found to have impairments in personality, emotional reactivity, and goal-oriented behavior, but had normal language function and retained vr-conscious experience. He ultimately underwent exploratory neurosurgery, when a cystic degeneration of his left frontal lobe and an absence of a right frontal lobe were discovered. Again, the conclusion was drawn that the extensive damage to his frontal lobe structures implied that vr-consciousness could not have been mediated by his frontal lobes. This conclusion is faulty, however, in view of the enormously long time allowed for re-wiring of his cortex and because his unaffected language function indicated that damage must have spared Broca's area and the adjacent VL-PFC.

The next case was that reported by Hebb and Penfield in 1950,[28] in which a normal 16-year-old boy suffered traumatic damage to both his frontal lobes, after which he suffered from a severe seizure disorder and exhibited personality changes and mild impairments in initiative and long term planning. At age 28, he underwent neurosurgery to treat his seizures and in the course of the surgery, "at least a third of the frontal lobes was removed." Following the surgery the seizures were gone and there were no changes in cognitive or emotional status. At no time did the patient manifest any abnormality in vr-conscious experience.

That this case is included in the literature as evidence that the frontal lobes do not mediate vr-conscious experience is hard to understand. If a third of the patient's frontal lobes were removed, then two-thirds of the

[27] Ackerly 1948.

[28] Hebb 1950.

frontal lobes, including the left VL-PFC, remained intact, more than enough tissue to continue mediating vr-conscious experience.

Next is the case reported by Markowitsch.[29] This involved a 27-year-old woman with extensive degeneration of her frontal lobes of unknown cause and duration. On neuropsychological testing she showed impairments in a variety of cognitive functions and exhibited a lack of concern for her illness. On MRI scan, there was extensive atrophy of the frontal lobes, more on the right than on the left.

This case was taken by Tononi and Koch[30] to provide evidence that PFC ablation does not impair vr-conscious experience. Their conclusion is dubious, however, given the unknown pathology, the gradual progression of the condition over years, and the absence of any autopsy findings. Moreover, the lack of any language impairment indicates that the left VL-PFC was spared.

Finally, there is the case reported by Mataro.[31] The patient was a 20-year-old university student whose head was impaled by an iron spike. The spike had "penetrated the left frontal region, passed through both frontal lobes injuring the left eyeball, and emerged from the right side." Incredibly, the patient remained conscious following the impalement and even helped with his own rescue. Following the trauma, he went on to live a near normal life. He married, fathered two children, and worked in the family business. At age 54 he suffered a right parietal contusion from a fall and was noted subsequently to have worsened memory and attention. Neuropsychological testing when he was 81 years old indicated deficits in memory, attention, and goal-oriented behavior. An MRI scan revealed extensive frontal lobe damage.

This is an additional case that was quoted by Tononi and Koch in support of their contention that vr-conscious experience does not require the PFC. Again, however, the patient suffered only partial frontal damage with only modest impairments in frontal lobe function and unaffected language function. Its relevance to the question of localization of the vr-NCC to the left VL-PFC is tenuous at best.

---

[29] Markowitsch 2000.

[30] Tononi 2008.

[31] Mataro 2001.

Cases with Massive Frontal Lobe Damage

In summary, we have six sketchily described cases in which frontal lobe damage was present yet vr-conscious experience remained intact. In none of the cases, however, did the damage involve the entirety of the left VL-PFC, nor did any of the patients exhibit language impairment, as would be expected with extensive damage to the left VL-PFC. In most of the cases, there was, additionally, a long clinical course that could have allowed for compensatory re-wiring, undermining the ability to accurately localize the damage. Consequently, these cases are in fact entirely consistent with a localization of the vr-NCC to the VL-PFC.

On the other hand, cases in which brain damage is abrupt and more extensive than in these reported cases are not hard to find. These include individuals who have suffered large strokes or extensive anoxic damage, or who have undergone massive surgical ablations similar to those reported by Dandy.[32] Such patients exhibit a total loss of vr-conscious experience, quite in keeping with the thesis that vr-conscious experience is mediated by the left VL-PFC.

One must take care in these cases not to misinterpret residual conscious behavior as evidence of spared vr-conscious experience. In the case of massive left hemisphere damage, residual non-vr-conscious experience would be expected and attributable to the undamaged right hemisphere. Similarly, in the case of damage extending to the entirety of both hemispheres, the clinical picture would be that of a persistent vegetative state accompanied by a primitive kind of non-vr-conscious experience. In both these situations, residual conscious experience of a nonverbal variety would be present but vr-conscious experience would be absent, a pattern completely consistent with a VL-PFC basis for vr-conscious experience.

In all, the ablation paradigm, when properly applied, has produced results that are entirely consistent with a vr-NCC that is localized to the left VL-PFC. The same could, for that matter, be said for certain other frontal lobe regions, including the DL-PFC, DM-PFC, ACC. Additional arguments are therefore needed to eliminate these other frontal regions from vr-NCC contention. On the other hand, the ablation paradigm

---

[32] Dandy 1946.

does exclude the OFC, or at least any but its most lateral portion, from vr-NCC status, since OFC lesions extensive enough to produce profound changes in social and emotional behavior do not eliminate vr-conscious experience.[33]

The Activation Paradigm, REM Sleep, and the Goblot Conjecture

A complement to the ablation paradigm is the *activation paradigm*: *if a given brain region directly mediates a given cognitive function, then that region should exhibit activation, as evident with neuroimaging scans or single-cell recordings, during engagement in that cognitive function.* The activation paradigm, like the ablation paradigm, suffers from non-specificity. Thus, many brain regions will typically "light up" on fMRI scans or with single-cell recordings during episodes of vr-conscious experience.[34] Only a subgroup of these regions would actually be a part of the vr-NCC, the other regions serving to bring information into, carry information out of, or permit the proper functioning of the vr-NCC, or even being completely unrelated to the vr-NCC altogether.

In general, when a given brain region shows activation during a given task, the only conclusion that can be drawn is that the given region is a *candidate* for vr-NCC status. It would be incorrect to conclude that the brain region is a part of the vr-NCC. To do so would be to fall prey to *the activation paradigm fallacy*. As with the ablation paradigm fallacy, mistaken inclusion of brain regions under the auspices of the activation paradigm fallacy fosters an overestimation of the spatial extent of the vr-NCC.

As with the ablation paradigm, the principal application of the activation paradigm is in its contrapositive form: *if a structure does not show activation during a task, then that structure is ruled out as a candidate for the neural correlate of that task.* The role of the activation paradigm in this contrapositive form is principally exclusionary.

---

[33] Damasio 1999.

[34] Dehaene 1998; Llinas 1998; Crick 1990.

In keeping with the activation paradigm, there have been, to my knowledge, no credible studies in which subjects that were engaged in tasks involving vr-conscious experience failed to exhibit activation of their left VL-PFC. There have been, however, several reports of absence of left VL-PFC activation on functional neuroimaging scans during rapid-eye-movement (REM) sleep.[35] Since REM sleep is known to be associated with dreaming, and since dreams are presumably a form of vr-conscious experience, the implication of these studies is that the quiescence of the VL-PFC during REM sleep indicates that the VL-PFC cannot be the locus of the vr-NCC.

The reasoning here is again dubious, however. It is based on the widely held assumption that dreams occur throughout REM sleep. Do we actually know this to be true? In fact, all we have on awakening are memories that tell us that we have been dreaming. But how can we tell if these memories are veridical or if they are artifactual constructions generated during the waking process? This question is difficult to answer since we have no direct knowledge of what transpires during most of the REM sleep periods. All we know is that on awakening we recall that we were just in the middle of a dream. The possibility that the memory is itself a product of the waking process cannot be ruled out. This possibility was put forth as a hypothesis by the nineteenth-century French philosopher and logician, Edmond Goblot (1858–1935). Goblot's conjecture stemmed from the famous "guillotine dream" reported by the French physician Louis Ferdinand Maury:

> I was rather unwell and lying down in my room with my mother at my bedside. I dreamed of the Reign of Terror. I witnessed massacres. I appeared before the Revolutionary Tribunal. I saw Robespierre, Marat, Fouquier-Tinville, and all the most wicked figures of that terrible era. I talked to them. Finally, after many events that I only partly remember, I was judged, condemned to death, taken out in a tumbril through a huge throng to the Place de la Revolution. I mounted the scaffold. The executioner tied me to that fatal plank and tipped it up. The blade fell. I felt my head separating from my body. I woke up, racked by the deepest anguish, and felt the bedpost on my neck. It had suddenly come off and had fallen on my cervical vertebrae just like the guillotine blade.[36]

---

[35] Maquet 2005.

[36] Maury 1865.

In this dream, time was compressed. Numerous events unfolded over what seemed to be a long interval but, since the falling bedpost apparently initiated the dream, the interval was actually quite short. Dreams such as Maury's are commonplace. They indicate that, at least in some cases, the memory of a dream is a reconstruction, just as memories in general are reconstructions.[37]

The compelling intuition that dreams stretch far back into the period of REM sleep cannot be relied upon. In a recent article, Nir and Tononi[38] acknowledge that the possibility that subjects are actually unconscious throughout sleep and merely confabulate the dream content during the transition into wakefulness is hard to refute. The situation evokes a refrigerator light analogy: the light is on whenever the door is open but that does not prove that the light is on when the door is closed.[39]

Are Other VR-NCCs Possible?

I have in this chapter presented a line of reasoning in support of the left VL-PFC being a locus for the vr-NCC. It is not clear, however, that that the left VL-PFC is the only structure involved. It may be possible that portions of neighboring left frontal regions participate as well. It is possible, for example, that the PO-PFC (which you will recall is the most anterior frontal cortex) and even a portion of the OFC might contain neurons that participate in the vr-NCC. Especially attractive is the possibility that the PO-PFC mediates vr-conscious experiences consisting of "higher-order thoughts." The French neuroscientist Etienne Koechlin at the Université Pierre et Marie Curie in Paris has proposed a "cascade model" of PO-PFC function according to which the region exerts flexible cognitive control over decision making that is implemented by the more caudal PFC structures.[40] The PO-PFC does not receive direct input from the perceptual pathways, however, nor does it have direct access to output

[37] Ardito 2000.

[38] Nir 2010.

[39] Dehaene 2001.

[40] Koechlin 2007; Fletcher 2001.

pathways, but it could conceivably receive input from and send output to the more caudal VL-PFC region and in this manner contribute vr-conscious experience of an abstract nature. Discovering the exact boundaries of the vr-NCC on the macroscopic level is ultimately an empirical matter, requiring studies dedicated to identifying those frontal neuronal populations whose activities directly correspond to vr-conscious experience. With this caution in mind, we now shift our search for the vr-NCC from the macroscopic to the microscopic level of cortical function.

8

Neuronal Networks

Neuronal Networks

Neuron Doctrine

In our search for the vr-NCC we have so far focused on the macroscopic level of brain functioning. We have seen that cortical information processing at that level can be modeled in terms of directed modular pathways, and that the left VL-PFC is a plausible location for the vr-NCC. We now shift our attention to the microscopic level and ask what is going on within the VL-PFC that might illuminate the nature of the vr-NCC. Our focus in this chapter will be on *neuronal networks*, which are webs of interconnecting neurons that carry out the information processing that takes place in the cortex.

The elemental unit of the neuronal network is the individual neuron, which was originally discovered in the late 1830s following the invention of the achromatic microscope. Aided by advances in tissue fixing and staining, the new microscope was used to visualize not only the neuronal cell bodies but also filamentous strands (which we now know as

S. Sevush, *The Single-Neuron Theory*,
DOI 10.1007/978-3-319-33708-1_8

axons and dendrites) attached to the neuronal cell bodies.[1] The discovery of these strands inspired the German anatomist Joseph von Gerlach (1820–1896) to put forth his *reticular theory* of cortical functioning in 1872. Gerlach's theory, which represented the first attempt to model cortical function in terms of neuronal networks, envisioned a continuous syncytium of interconnected neuronal filaments that permitted electrical currents to flow freely across the cortex, unperturbed by membranes or other barriers. His contention was that these filaments did the work of the mind and that the neuronal cell bodies served only a nutritive role.

Gerlach's theory, propelled by its satisfying assumption of a continuous and amorphous physical correlate for what was presumed to be a holistic and pliable mind, quickly became the dominant view. It received the support of the great Italian physician and histologist Camillo Golgi (1843–1926) who was enticed by the idea of a unitary action of the nervous system. Its domination continued until the late 1880s, when contrary evidence began to surface. The decisive blow came from the work and writings of the Spanish anatomist Santiago Ramon y Cajal (1852–1934) who, using a modification of Golgi's own silver staining technique, demonstrated that the neuronal filaments reached out to their neighbors but did not physically fuse with them. Cajal rejected the idea that neuronal filaments were joined into a continuous syncytium, suggesting instead that the cortex consisted of an assembly of separated units joined only by the coordination of their activity, not by anatomical continuity. Cajal's new theory became known as the *neuron doctrine*. In short order the neuronal elements received their modern names: the term *neuron* was used to refer to the nerve cell together with its attached processes[2]; the processes themselves were called *dendrites*[3] and *axons*[4]; and the junctions between the axons and the dendrites were called *synapses*.[5]

The neuron doctrine rapidly eclipsed the reticular theory. As intuitive as was the conception that a single mind must be mediated by a

---

[1] Deiters 1865.

[2] Named by Wilhelm Waldeyer 1891.

[3] Named by William His 1889.

[4] Named by Rudolph Albert von Koellicker 1896.

[5] Named by Sherrington 1897.

single interconnected syncytium, this was apparently not how the cortex functioned. The refutation of the reticular theory was an exemplary case of Thomas Huxley's "great tragedy of science: the slaying of a beautiful hypothesis by an ugly fact."[6] As Cajal reminisced:

> We who were active in histology then saw networks everywhere…True, it would be very convenient and very economical from the point of view of analytical effort if all the nerve centers were made up of a continuous intermediary network between the motor nerves and the sensitive and sensory nerves. Unfortunately, nature seems unaware of our intellectual need for convenience and unity, and very often takes delight in complication and diversity.[7]

Ironically, Cajal and Golgi shared the Nobel Prize in Physiology or Medicine in 1906, the first such prize given for work in neuroscience. At the awards ceremony, the debate between the reticular theory and the neuron doctrine was showcased one last time, with Golgi's address devoted to a stubborn attempt to resurrect the past, and Cajal's address serving as a springboard for the future.

The neuron doctrine has withstood the passage of time. It is now generally accepted that the neuron is the basic computational unit in the brain. The number of neurons in each brain is vast, equaling the number of stars in the Milky Way, about 100 billion. Each neuron has three anatomical components: a highly branched *dendritic tree* (present in all species with a nervous system)[8]; a cell body or *soma*, about 20 microns in diameter[9]; and a single *axon* (Fig. 8.1). This basic structure has been preserved ever since it first appeared at the jellyfish stage of evolution. Changes have come primarily in the size and complexity of neuronal networks, not in the alteration of individual neurons.[10]

---

[6] Huxley 1870.
[7] Cajal 1937.
[8] Hausser 2000.
[9] Crick 1994.
[10] Swanson 2003.

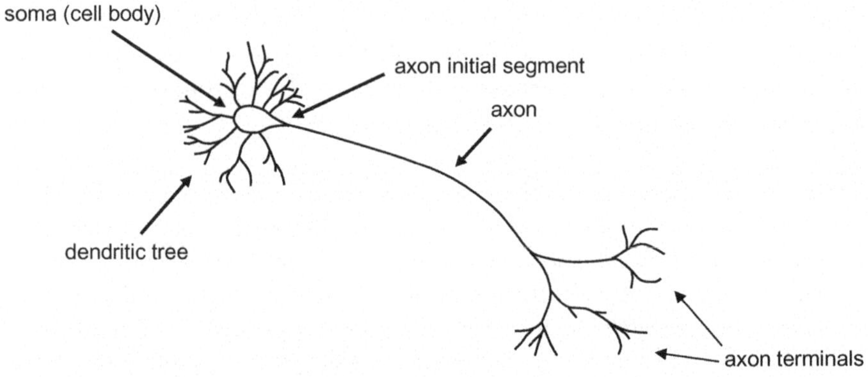

Fig. 8.1 The neuron

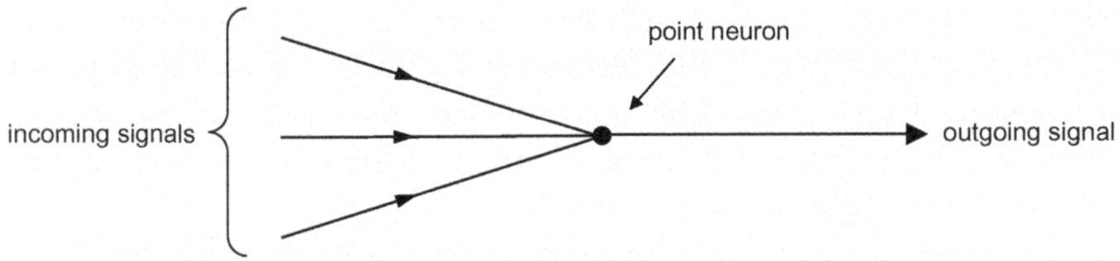

Fig. 8.2 Point neuron model

Point Neuron Model

The intricate branching of neuronal dendrites provide neurons with the potential for complex information processing. For our first pass through the subject of neuronal networks, however, we will ignore this complexity and adopt what is called the *point neuron model* in our discussions.[11] With this model, the entire neuron, including its complex dendritic tree, is approximated by a single point toward which all inputs converge and from which a single outgoing signal is emitted (Fig. 8.2). The point neuron model, despite its simplicity, has been remarkably effective in accounting for a good deal of cortical function.

[11] McCulloch 1943.

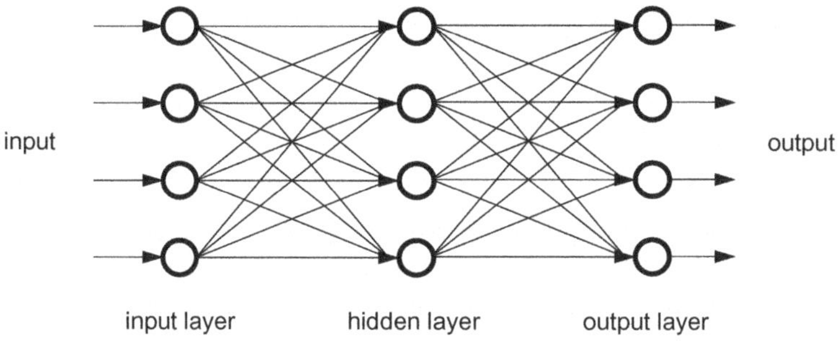

Fig. 8.3 A simple feedforward PDP neuronal network. Abbreviation: PDP, parallel distributed processing

Neurons in the network transmit signals to one another in terms of trains of electrochemical signals called *action potentials* or "*spikes*," which we will examine in detail in the next chapter. Most of the information carried by a spike train is encoded as the time-varying rate at which the spikes are produced.

Neurons typically receive thousands of incoming signals each second. To handle this enormous information input, the point neuron model is equipped with an *integrate-and-fire* mechanism.[12] According to this mechanism, inputs to a neuron are merged as a weighted sum that is compared to the cell's threshold for firing. If the weighted sum is less than threshold, the target neuron remains quiescent and merely continues to gather more spikes. When the weighted sum reaches the firing threshold, the target neuron emits a spike.

Neuronal Networks

The point neurons join together to form neuronal networks.[13] The most well-developed neuronal network model, and the one we will adopt, is the *parallel distributed processing* (PDP) model of neuronal network operation.[14] Figure 8.3 depicts a portion of a simple feedforward PDP

[12] Brunel 2007; Lapicque 1907.

[13] Yuste 2015.

[14] Rumelhart 1986.

neuronal network. The network consists of cortical neurons (circles) arranged as three successive layers (vertical columns) leading from input to output. Signals entering the network via the input layer are transmitted along feedforward, convergent and divergent connections to a hidden layer, and are then transmitted along feedforward convergent and divergent connections to the output layer, from which signals are sent out from the network. In the figure, each layer is portrayed as containing only four neurons. In real cortical networks, layers typically contain thousands to millions of neurons each.

A flexible feature of neuronal networks is that the strength of the connections between the neurons in successive layers can vary. This is incorporated into the model by assigning weights to the various connections, with some connections being so strong that they can activate a target neuron all by themselves, others being of intermediate strength and able to activate a target neuron only with the help of other simultaneous inputs, and still others with zero weighting and no connections with the target neuron at all.[15]

Neuronal networks provide the microscopic makeup of macroscopic cortical modules. The directed cortical modular pathways that we have been examining can be effectively modeled as arrays of simple neuronal networks arranged in sequence. Network models of this sort exhibit impressive computational capabilities and are able to approximate cortical function surprisingly well.

Memory in Neuronal Networks

Alexander Bain

A fundamental feature of cortical neuronal networks is their ability to learn from experience. The memory mechanisms underlying this learning ability have been slow to reveal themselves, the first theorizing on the subject coming in the form of the insightful writings of the nineteenth

[15] Maia 2005.

century British utilitarian philosopher Alexander Bain (1818–1903).[16] Bain's prescient formulation followed on the heels of the discovery of nerve cells and their interconnecting filaments in the middle of the century. Central to his thinking was the supposition that memories are stored in the same nerve cell populations that are activated during perception. He envisioned two types of memory. The first was a fleeting continuation of a conscious perception mediated by persisting electrical currents. He characterized this type of memory as a "continuing impression of a feebler kind" and gave as examples the brief auditory impression that remains after the peal of a thunderclap or the momentary mental echo of a clanging bell after it has stopped sounding. The second type of memory was an enduring structural change in the connections between nerve cells that allowed for the reactivation of the original perceptual experience at a later time. He hypothesized that the two types of memory occurred in sequence. First, an external stimulus produces a conscious perception mediated by electrical activation of a group of neurons in the population. Subsequently, a weakened form of the electrical activation (the "continuing impression of a feebler kind") persists for a brief period. Repeated activation of the neuronal group then leads to a structural change in the connections between group members that renders the memory trace permanent. Later, the original current pattern can be reactivated in an act of memory retrieval in which the original perceptual experience is recalled after a delay.

Bain proposed that the structural change required for enduring memories consisted of "specific growths in cell junctions" that enabled electrical currents to flow more easily throughout the neuronal group, thereby facilitating the group's later reactivation. He suggested that the growths between cells were formed whenever cells in the group were activated simultaneously or in rapid succession. To add complexity to his model, he proposed that multiple cell groups could themselves be joined together by additional growths, providing for associations between different memories. He postulated that the strength of the connections between cells was dependent on repeated activation, and that a lack of repeated activation would result in their decay. Connections could thereby be both

[16] Bain 1868, 1873.

created and destroyed, giving the model the flexibility it needed to meet changing environmental circumstances.

In all, Bain's suggestion of how the brain stored and retrieved memories was extraordinarily insightful, anticipating by more than a century the basic tenets that guide contemporary neurobiological theories of memory. His emphasis on the connections between cells as the site where enduring memories were encoded and stored was particularly prophetic. He could not, however, improve upon his vague notion of "growths in cell junctions" given the primitive state of neurobiological knowledge at the time. An attempt to take the idea further was made in 1893 by the Italian neurologist Eugenio Tanzi (1856–1934), who incorporated the new discovery of synapses into his own memory model. Tanzi proposed that growths in cell junctions might consist of amoeba-like protrusions of incoming axons into the synaptic spaces, and that these would be produced whenever a synapse became active. The protrusions, Tanzi reasoned, would have the effect of reducing the size of the synaptic gap, thereby increasing the efficiency of interneuronal communication. Variants of Tanzi's neuronal amoeboidism were soon adopted by other investigators, including the great Ramon y Cajal. With the coming of the twentieth century, however, the idea of neuronal amoeboidism began to languish, leading ultimately to the assertion by Lashley in 1950 that there was no evidence to support any of the growth theories, and that they were not plausible anyway since the proposed cell growth would be too slow to account for the rapidity with which learning takes place.[17] Another two decades would transpire before an alternative, chemical mechanism of synaptic memory would be identified.

Synaptic Memory, Hebb's Postulate

In 1949, Lashley's student, the Canadian psychologist Donald Hebb (1904–1985), added an important detail to Bain's model by offering his renowned *neurophysiological postulate*[18]:

---

[17] Lashley 1950.

[18] Hebb 1949.

> When an axon of cell A is near enough to excite a cell B and repeatedly or persistently takes part in firing it, some growth process or metabolic change takes place in one or both cells such that A's efficiency, as one of the cells firing B, is increased.

Hebb's postulate, which constituted a precise statement of Bain's conjecture, provided a specific mechanism that could explain how neuronal groups might be constructed. The way Hebb's postulate works is shown in Fig. 8.4. In the initial condition, indicated to the left in the figure, neurons A and A' are already strongly connected to neuron B and together can cause B to fire. Neuron C, in contrast, is only weakly connected to B and is unable by itself to make B fire. Random firing of C, no matter how often, doesn't change the situation. If, however, C happens to fire just before or simultaneously with A and A', then C "takes part in firing" B and, according to Hebb's postulate, the synapse between C and B is strengthened (as indicated to the right in the figure). Neuron C can thereafter participate more strongly in the firing of B, and by so doing join the neuronal group previously formed by A and A'. An associative memory trace is thereby established between C and B, in line with the dictum, "*cells that fire together wire together*." I will refer to this memory trace as a *Hebbian engram*, and to the memory process as *Hebbian learning*.

By a reiterative application of Hebb's simple procedure, whole networks of overlapping neuronal groups can form, just as envisioned by Bain. Hebb referred to these hypothetical neuronal groups as "cell

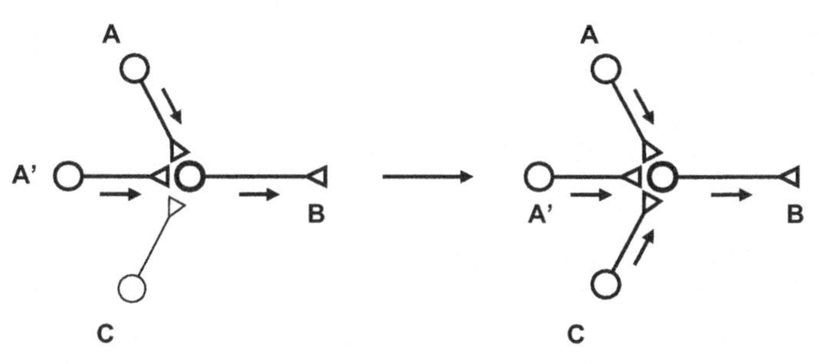

Fig. 8.4 Hebb's postulate

assemblies," which he conceived of as sets of thousands of neurons organized into reverberating loops. For Hebb, each reverberating loop formed a thought, and sequences of reverberating loops were the basis for thinking. He proposed that the persistence of a reverberating loop accounted for a transient form of immediate memory (similar to Bain's "continuing impression of a feebler kind"), and that the reactivation of a reverberating loop after a delay represented retrieval of a previously stored memory. Like Bain, Hebb added flexibility to his model by assuming that synaptic connections could be both created and destroyed: created by the repeated activation of a reverberating loop, destroyed by prolonged inactivity of the loop.

Memory Molecules and the Memory Transfer Experiments of the 1960s

Although Hebb's formulation was appealing and would in the long run be adopted, it could not be tested with the then available technology. This opened the way for alternative theories to be considered. One such alternative theory briefly grabbed the spotlight. This was the infamous theory that memories might be stored in intracellular molecules.

The search for memory molecules had begun in 1953 when James McConnell (1925–1990), then a psychology graduate student at the University of Texas, became interested in the memory function of a species of primitive freshwater flatworm called planaria. Planaria are one-inch worms that are among the simplest creatures to possess what we might call a brain. Over a ten-year period, McConnell conducted a series of studies involving these worms, first at the University of Texas and then at the University of Michigan, providing evidence that memory transfer across animals was a possibility. The initial step in his project was to establish memories in the form of conditioned reflexes. He used as an unconditioned reflex the innate tendency for planaria to contract their bodies when electrically shocked. By pairing electrical shocks with exposure to light, Pavlovian conditioning was induced, such that the worms learned to contract upon exposure to light alone.

Next, he cut the planaria in half, separating the head from the tail, and then allowed each half to regenerate. His plan was to determine whether the memory of the conditioning would be retained in either of the separated halves. As expected, when the half that contained the head grew itself another tail, the newly formed whole planarian was observed to have retained the memory of the original conditioning. What was unexpected, however, was that when the tail portion grew itself another head, the newly formed whole planarian in that case was also found to have retained the memory of the previous conditioning. Apparently, the physical trace for the conditioned memory was distributed throughout the entire extent of the worm. As McConnell put it:

> We were astounded, then, to discover that the tails not only showed as much retention as did the heads, but in many cases did much better than the heads and showed absolutely no forgetting whatsoever. Obviously memory, in the flatworms, was being stored throughout the animal's body, and as additional proof of this we found that if we cut the worm into three or even more pieces, each section typically showed clear-cut retention of the conditioned response.[19]

McConnell's hypothesis was that the distributed memory trace might consist of a chemical substance located within cells scattered throughout the worm's body. If this were the case, he reasoned, then memory might be an extractable quantity that could be transferred from one worm to another. After several years of abortive attempts to graft or inject portions of one planarian into another, McConnell finally discovered that under the proper conditions, planaria can be induced to engage in cannibalistic feeding on each other. This created the opportunity for memory transfer experiments since planaria contained only a rudimentary digestive tract that could allow ingested memory molecules to reach the brain structurally unaltered. McConnell proceeded to train a group of planaria on the conditioning task and then to kill them, chop them into small pieces, and feed the pieces to a group of untrained planaria. He then tested the untrained cannibals on the conditioning task. The results were startling.

[19] McConnell 1962.

Significant retention of memory was observed in four successive runnings of the experiment. Memory had been transferred from one planarian to another!

McConnell's findings induced a spate of memory transfer experiments by other researchers over the next decade, many of which were published in the most elite scientific journals. The technique even found its way into a high school science fair, as reported by the Washington Post in an article dated March 25, 1962:

> A seventeen-year-old girl's rather startling answer to a rather startling question—"Is Knowledge Edible?"—brought her one of the two top prizes in a Northern Virginia Science Fair yesterday. Tentatively, Ruth Ann Ziegler's answer is "yes."
>
> What Miss Ziegler found was that a worm who eats an educated worm learns things twice as fast as his brother who eats an uneducated worm. Hence her title, "Is Knowledge Edible?" By electrical shocks she taught flatworms to respond to light. An ordinary flatworm needs about 260 shocks before he responds without one. He is then "conditioned." Experiments taught Miss Ziegler that a worm fed the head of an unconditioned worm needs an average of 264 shocks. A worm fed an unconditioned tail needs 269. But a worm fed a conditioned tail takes only 168 shocks and a worm fed a conditioned head a mere 140 shocks.
>
> This experiment was part of Miss Ziegler's effort to see if conditioned learning is affected by chemicals and, if it is, if it can be passed on through regeneration and ingestion. It's apparently "yes" all the way.

In the early planaria experiments, memory transfer was effected by cannibalism, but later the memory transfer was accomplished via injections of brain extracts from donor animals into the abdomens or brains of recipient animals. The behavioral tasks were varied as well, with the simple Pavlovian conditioning techniques of the initial studies being replaced in later experiments by more advanced tasks such as those involving color discrimination and maze running. Over the next dozen years, successful memory transfer was described not only for worms, but also for goldfish, chickens, hamsters, mice, and rats. Evidence for interspecies transfer was also presented, with published reports of memory transfer from hamsters to rats and from rats to mice. By 1974, 150 papers from 35 laboratories had been published that reported successful transfer of memory from one animal to another.[20]

Stimulated by the findings of the memory transfer studies, researchers attempted to determine the exact nature of the memory molecules being transferred. Since recently published work had already indicated that inhibitors of RNA metabolism impaired retention of learning in regenerating planaria, it was proposed that the memory molecules might be composed of RNA. Accordingly, attempts were made to achieve memory transfer by extracting RNA from the brains of trained animals and injecting it into untrained animals. Successful memory transfer in this manner was reported for both planaria and rats by a research group from UCLA in 1965. Later, evidence for an additional possibility, that the transfer chemical might be a protein rather than RNA, was put forward.

By the early 1970s, a full decade of research had accumulated in support of the contention that memory was encoded in the form of memory molecules, not unlike antibodies in the immune system, composed of either RNA or protein, that could be passed from one brain to another to accomplish memory transfer between animals. Yet, within a few short years, this whole program of investigation completely unraveled. The memory transfer research, despite its apparent strength, was found to suffer from the same flaw that has undermined countless other nascent scientific theories throughout history: its popularity was based primarily on a captivating swell of groupthink that could not stand up to the skepticism that inevitably enters the scene. Replication problems first surfaced in 1966, when a paper published in the prestigious journal, *Science*, reported uniformly negative memory transfer results in studies conducted by 23 scientists working in a variety of research laboratories scattered throughout the United States and Canada.[21] Replication difficulties continued to plague the memory research program thereafter. In addition, inadequate attention to controls allowed for the possibility that what was being transferred between the animals was something other than neuronal memories. Indeed, evidence was eventually found indicating that what was likely being transferred in the planaria experiments

[20] Ungar 1974.

[21] Byrne 1966.

was not a memory molecule but a non-specific circulating sensitization factor. While calling such an agent a "memory molecule" might in some sense be valid, the kind of memory involved would be simple and generic, and entirely unsuitable for building a theory of memory in higher animals. Ultimately, the methodological and conceptual problems caught up with the wave of memory transfer experiments and by the mid-1970s the whole idea of memory molecules vanished from the scientific stage.

Coincident with the demise of the memory transfer paradigm came the long-awaited evidence of synaptic memory of the type envisioned by Bain and Hebb. In work beginning in the late 1960s in Oslo, Tim Bliss and Terry Lomo took advantage of newly developed techniques for studying synaptic function to provide the first empirical demonstration that synapses could in fact be modified by activity.[22] Using microelectrodes inserted into the brains of live rabbits to directly measure synaptically induced neuronal activity, Bliss and Lomo were able to find synapses whose efficiency increased for hours following brief intense stimulation. This effect, which came to be called *long-term potentiation* (LTP), provided the first step in validating Hebb's postulate.

Subsequent work would show that LTP depended on the synchronous firing of a weak input with a strong one, as required by Hebb's postulate. Additionally, an inhibitory counterpart for LTP, called long-term depression (LTD), would be identified. The mechanisms underlying LTP and LTD would turn out to consist not of amoeboid protrusions, as Tanzi had suggested, but of a succession of electrical and chemical events that culminate in modifications in synaptic responsivity.[23]

Central to LTP and LTD is the remarkable synaptic receptor protein, N-methyl-D-aspartate (NMDA), which was first implicated in memory processing in the 1980s.[24] The receptor has two glutamate binding sites[25] and a Ca^{++} channel that at rest is blocked by a Mg^{++} ion. The unique property of the NMDA receptor is that it can only be activated when the binding of glutamate molecules is coupled with the presence of a strong

[22] Bliss 1973.

[23] Morris 2013.

[24] Morris 2013; Collingridge 1995.

[25] Polsky 2009.

depolarization of the postsynaptic cell membrane. Under these conditions, the Mg^{++} ion is removed and an influx of Ca^{++} ions floods through the channel. The Ca^{++} influx initiates a chemical sequence that culminates in the forming of new synapses and the strengthening of existing ones. In this way, NMDA receptor activity instantiates Hebb's neurophysiological postulate in physical terms. We will examine the NMDA receptor in more detail in the next chapter.

Neuronal Representations

Representations and Representational Fields

Equipped with the point neuron and integrate-and-fire models, and with a mechanism for laying down memories, we can now look at the means by which neuronal networks process information in the cerebral cortex. A useful way to conceptualize the processing is to equate each layer in the network with a *neuronal representation*, which I will define as *a neuronal activation pattern that arises in response to a stimulus*. In describing representations, note must be taken not only of which neurons are activated but also of which neurons are not. I will refer to the full complement of available neurons for a representation, including both the activated and the non-activated ones, as the *neuronal representational field* for that representation. Representational fields are the landscape upon which representations are inscribed. Sequences of representational fields form the neuronal basis for directed modular pathways.

Neuronal representations and their associated neuronal representational fields should not be confused with a neuron's receptive field. The latter, you will recall from Chap. 3, is the subset of stimulus space to which an individual neuron preferentially responds; the former have to do with the activity patterns of neuronal groups in response to a stimulus. There is a logical connection between neuronal representations and neuronal receptive fields: a neuronal representation associated with a given stimulus consists of activated neurons whose receptive fields correspond to that stimulus. For example, the neuronal representations in V1 produced by a bar of a given orientation and location are formed by the activation of neurons whose receptive fields consist of bars of precisely that orientation and location. In principle, if we knew the receptive field for every neuron in the cortex we would be able, without any additional information, to deduce the neuronal representations associated with any given stimulus.

Density of Neuronal Representations

Neuronal representations are characterized by a number of parameters. First, representations can differ with respect to the fraction of the representational field that becomes activated in response to a stimulus. This fraction is referred to as the *density* of the representation. The density can range from 1/N to 1, where N is the total number of neurons that make up the representational field.

If, in response to a stimulus, many neurons are activated, we say that the representation is *densely distributed.* If only a few neurons are activated, we say the representation is *sparsely distributed.* And if only one neuron is activated, we have *local coding.* Local coding has the advantage of requiring little energy to encode any one stimulus but it has the disadvantage of needing an astronomical number of neurons to potentially code for all possible percepts. Local coding has the additional drawback of being highly susceptible to injury: if the encoding neuron is damaged, the corresponding representation is lost. Dense representations, in contrast, have the advantages of high information processing capacity and resilience in the face of injury but they are costly in terms of energy consumed.

Sparse representations provide an optimal compromise between dense and local representations. Since sparse representations require the activation of only a few neurons to represent a stimulus, little energy is consumed. On the other hand, since information processing capacity goes up factorially with the number of activated neurons, a considerable processing capacity is retained. With face recognition, for example, sparse representations constructed from just 25 cortical neurons can potentially classify three thousand different faces with better than even odds.[26] Both

[26] Koch 2004.

theoretical analyses and experimental studies have shown that only a few percent of cortical neurons are active during perceptual tasks, indicating that sparse representations are in fact the preferred mode of encoding in the cortex.[27]

Dispersion of Neuronal Representations

Neuronal representations can also be classified according to the spatial distribution of the activated neurons. We say that a neuronal representation is spatially *dispersed* if the activated neurons are spread out over a large area and *compact* if they are confined to a small area.

Note that dispersion and density are different notions. For example, representations may be sparsely distributed but spatially dispersed. In such a case, a small number of neurons are activated but they are widely separated from one another. Alternatively, representations may be densely distributed but spatially compact, in which case a large number of neurons are activated but they are all confined to a small area. Compact representations have the advantage of allowing for interneuronal computations to be carried out over shorter distances, thereby reducing energy expenditure. The cortical representations relevant to vr-conscious experience have been observed to exhibit a combination of both compact and dispersed motifs.

Combinative and Holographic Encoding

Density and dispersion describe the physical arrangement of neuronal representations. Neuronal representations can also be described functionally in terms of the receptive fields of their constituent neurons. In particular, they can be graded according to the degree to which the receptive fields of the neurons are overlapping. At one extreme, a neuronal representation may be composed of neurons that have no overlap in their receptive fields. Such a representation would be *combinative*, with each neuron encoding a different aspect of the stimulus. With combinative

[27] Shi 2013; Rolls 2007.

representations, the activated neurons (sometimes called "cardinal cells" to distinguish them from the hypothetical "pontifical cell" of local distributions[28]) are like pieces of a puzzle that reveal the identity of the stimulus only when joined together. Individually, the receptive fields of the activated neurons are narrowly tuned and different from each other, so that the nature of the stimulus cannot be inferred from the activity of any one neuron in the representation. Combinatorial representations facilitate associative operations, such as perceptual completion ("filling-in") and generalization. They are, however, vulnerable to interference from competing representations.

At the other extreme, a neuronal representation may be made up of neurons with almost completely overlapping receptive fields, such that each neuron in the representation has approximately the same receptive field. This would be a *holographic* (also called *coarse coding*) representation. With holographic representations, each of the activated neurons represents the same stimulus feature but does so imprecisely. The joint activation of all the neurons is needed to improve the precision of the representation.[29] Holographic representations are resistant to noise and physical damage, exhibiting graceful degradation in response to injury.[30] With holographic coding, the identity of the stimulus can be discerned, if somewhat indistinctly, through the activity of any one of the participating neurons. As we will see, holographic representations play an important role in the theory I am proposing.

Cortical Maps

Neuronal representations are related to one another via *cortical maps.* These come in two varieties, *functional* and *structural.* Functional cortical maps link stimuli to neuronal representations. Structural cortical maps link neurons of one representation to those of another. As we will see, both types of maps are germane to the theory I am presenting.

---

[28] Koch 2004; Barlow 1972.

[29] Crick 1995.

[30] Bowers 2009.

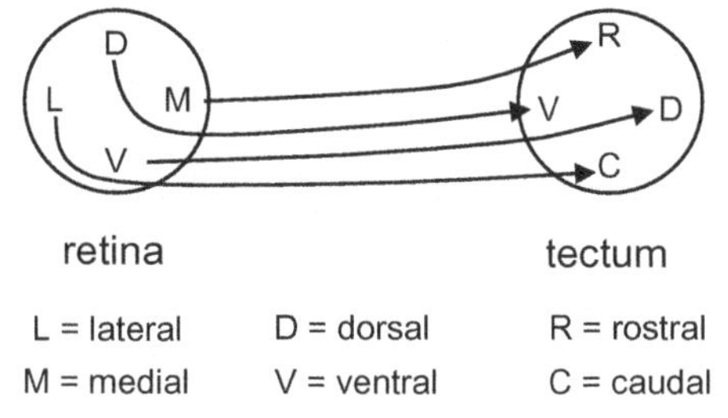

Fig. 8.5 The retinal/tectum structural topographic mapping

A remarkable feature of cortical maps is their spatial patterning. The degree of spatial organization in the cortex is far greater than even the most avid localizationists of the nineteenth century could ever have imagined. The fundamental feature shared by all cortical maps is that they are generally *topographic*, such that neighboring elements in the source set project onto neighboring elements in the target set. This renders cortical maps orderly in a topological sense and distinguishes the arrangement from that in a digital camera, where a pattern recorded on the image sensor is transformed into a digital code that is meaningful to a computer but evinces no topological relationship with the object being imaged.

Structural topographic maps were first identified in the 1940s, when Roger Sperry demonstrated their presence in the axonal projection from the retina to the optic tectum.[31] In the retinal/tectum mapping, receptors in the medial retina project their output to the caudal tectum, while those in the lateral retina project their output to the rostral tectum, those in the dorsal retina project their output to the ventral tectum, and those in the ventral retina project their output to the dorsal tectum (Fig. 8.5).

One might presume that structural topographic maps of this sort arise from simple mechanical forces that maintain parallel positioning of fibers. Such is not the case. The brain actually goes to considerable trouble to institute structural topographic maps. In the case of the retinal/tectum map, the passage of fibers along the optic nerve is initially ordered but quickly gives way to randomness, and only becomes orderly again as the

[31] Sperry 1943.

nerve approaches the tectum.[32] Active processes are involved that utilize guidance by chemoaffinity molecules called *ephrins*.[33] The chemoaffinity mechanism establishes a rough topographic mapping. Hebbian learning then takes care of the final details of the projection.

Research over the last half century has revealed that structural topographic maps abound in the cerebral cortex, and, for that matter, throughout the central nervous system.[34] Examples in the cortex include the projections from the DL-PFC to the parietal,[35] temporal,[36] and cingulate[37] cortices; from the PFC to the mediodorsal nucleus of the thalamus[38]; from the parietal association cortex to the temporal association cortex[39]; from motor to premotor cortex[40]; from the subiculum to both the medial PFC[41] and to the hippocampus[42]; and in the interhemispheric connections that span the corpus callosum.[43] Subcortical examples include projections involving the basal ganglia, the thalamus, the cerebellum, the lateral geniculate nuclei, and the optic tectum.[44]

Functional topographic mapping, like structural topographic mapping, is a recurring theme throughout the central nervous system. Functional topographic maps have been observed in virtually every cortical sensory region that has been examined. In each instance, as stimuli vary continuously over "stimulus space," the positions of the activated neurons in the neuronal representation vary continuously over the cortical surface. Specific examples of such maps include those for orientation

---

[32] Simon 1991.
[33] Sperry 1963.
[34] Tinsley 2009.
[35] Goldman-Rakic 1988.
[36] Ban 1991.
[37] Olson 1992.
[38] Siwek 1991.
[39] Ban 1991.
[40] Matelli 1986.
[41] HIrose 1992.
[42] Tamamaki 1995.
[43] Bock 2013.
[44] Tinsley 2008.

in primary visual cortex,[45] pitch in primary auditory cortex,[46] touch location in primary somatosensory cortex,[47] and memory of place in the hippocampus.[48] Functional topographic maps are found in widely varying species, including crickets,[49] owls,[50] and echolocating bats.[51]

We note that "neighboring" in stimulus space does not necessarily mean "spatially near." It indicates nearness according to the metric specific to the stimulus space, be it "smell space" or "face space" or some other type of stimulus space. Although representations in the primary visual and somatosensory cortices exhibit some topological resemblance to the stimulus, the representations are certainly not veridical renditions of the outside world and they become progressively more distorted and quickly unrecognizable as subsequent modules are traversed. Nonspatial functional topographic mappings have been proposed for the inferior temporal cortex,[52] the VL-PFC,[53] and, in general, for most modules that are distant to the primary sensory cortices.

Spatial Patterns of Cortical Maps

Spurred by the topographic imperative, structural and functional maps take on an organized character.[54] Structural topographic maps may take on elegant forms. The structural topographic map from the retina to V1, for example, is described almost perfectly by a complex logarithmic function (Fig. 8.6).[55]

---

45 Tusa 1978.
46 Schreiner 2007.
47 Whitsel 1978.
48 O'Keefe 1971.
49 Jacobs 2008.
50 Knudsen 1978.
51 Schreiner 2007.
52 Tinsley 2009.
53 Tinsley 2009; Wandell 2007.
54 Yuste 2005.
55 Schwartz 1980.

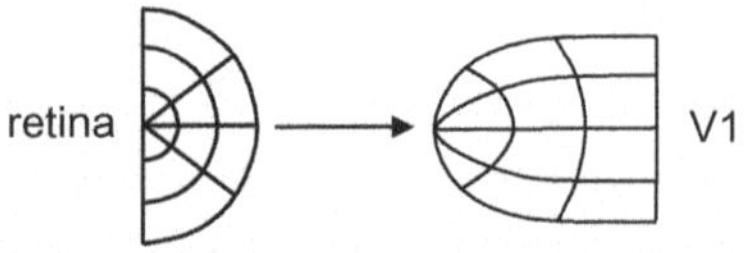

Fig. 8.6 Retinal/cortical structural topographic map is described by a complex logarithmic function

A universal theme for functional topographic maps is a prevalent tendency toward the formation of *clusters*. For form vision in V1, the clusters consist of neurons responsive to varying line orientation that are organized topographically as *pinwheels*. In the fusiform gyrus in the occipito-temporal cortex there are clusters, referred to as *patches*, that are specialized for faces, body parts, places, and recognizable letter strings.[56] In TE, the clustering conforms to abstract stimulus categories.[57] For example, clustering has been observed in both monkeys and humans with respect to whether an object is animate or inanimate. In a study of monkeys by Kiani,[58] activation patterns of more than 600 individual temporal lobe neurons to more than 1000 pictures of natural and artificial objects were examined. Separate neuronal clusters responded to animate and inanimate objects. Clusters in the animate object category were further divided into bodies, hands, and faces, with faces being divided into primate and nonprimate faces and primate faces being further divided into human and monkey faces. In other studies, neurons representing bodies of humans, birds, and four-legged animals clustered together, while those representing fish, reptiles, and insects formed a separate cluster.[59] Supplementing this experimental work have been the clinical assessments of patients who, following damage to their inferior temporal lobes, became deficient in visually recognizing living things but retained the ability to visually recognize non-living things.[60]

[56] Gross 2008.
[57] Huth 2012.
[58] Kiani 2007.
[59] Naseralis 2012.
[60] Warrington 1984.

Recent work has indicated spatial segregation of abstract categories for auditory stimuli.[61]

In a recent combined fMRI and single-cell recording study conducted by Doris Tsao and her colleagues at Harvard University, the researchers used fMRI to identify three patches of cortex located within the fusiform gyrus of monkeys that were selectively activated during a face recognition task. Focusing on the middle patch, they inserted electrodes and recorded from a large sampling of individual neurons in the area. Ninety-seven percent of the visually responsive neurons in the four millimeter diameter area responded selectively to faces, firing at up to 50 times the baseline rate. Only very weak responses were recorded for nonface stimuli that were similar in shape to a face, such as an apple or a clock face.[62]

For color vision in V1, the clusters consist of neurons responsive to colors that are topographically organized as *blobs*. In V2, the clusters take the form of *stripes* and in V4 and onward they take the form of *globs*.[63] The activated neurons within blobs, stripes, and globs are spatially arranged with neurons of similar color preference being positioned near each other.

The spatial patterning of neuronal activation provides the rationale for recent studies that have used functional neuroimaging techniques to discern the content of a subject's vr-conscious experience. In 2001, James Haxby, a psychologist at NIH, used an fMRI technique called *multivariate pattern analysis* to establish that different object categories are associated with different spatial activation patterns in the cortex.[64] He scanned six subjects while they were viewing either faces, cats, five categories of man-made objects (houses, chairs, scissors, shoes, and bottles), and nonsense pictures and found a different response pattern for each stimulus category. Using his technique, he was able to predict with more than 90 percent accuracy which stimulus the subject was viewing at the time of scanning.

---

[61] Giordano 2013.

[62] Tsao 2008.

[63] Conway 2009.

[64] Haxby 2001.

In the years since Haxby's original report, fMRI pattern assessment has been used to infer vr-conscious recognition of line orientation patterns, motion direction patterns, and selective attention patterns in V1. Separate patterns have been found for color, form, and the conjunction of color and form, and for written words. Distinguishable patterns for faces in general and for the identities of individual faces have been reported. Distinct patterns for tools, buildings, animals, and different types of chairs have been observed.

Pattern analysis using fMRI has been applied to the auditory cortex to ascertain the consciously perceived identity of a speaker and, in the case of auditory imagery, the vr-conscious experience of sound in the absence of an external auditory stimulus. Pattern analysis using fMRI has been applied to the somatosensory cortex to distinguish activation patterns corresponding to the vr-conscious perception of tactile stimulation of different fingers, and optical imaging techniques have been used to identify activation patterns in insula cortex corresponding to vr-conscious perception of four of the primary taste modalities (sweet, bitter, salty, and sour). Finally, the use of fMRI pattern analysis has in recent work been extended to natural scenes.

In all, the correspondence between the spatial patterns of cortical neuronal activation and vr-conscious experiences induced by topographic mapping has been nothing short of spectacular, dwarfing the relatively scanty evidence for correlations between temporal activation patterns and vr-conscious experience. This begs the question of why topographic mapping is so prevalent in the brain. The answer comes from natural selection. Topographic maps are efficient because they bring neurons that need to work together into close proximity. This reduces the wire length of the axons and dendrites of interacting neurons that determine sums, differences, and comparisons.[65] It also facilitates lateral inhibition between neurons with slightly different receptive fields, thereby sharpening perceptual boundaries and setting up categorical processing. The minimization of wire length also allows for a smaller brain volume, which lessens communication delays and signal attenuation. Importantly, minimizing wire length lessens energy consumption, the energy demands of

[65] Chklovskii 2004.

action potential propagation being more than a third of total cortical energy consumption.[66] These factors together make topographic mapping inevitable. We will explore the relevance of its presence for mind/brain theorizing in Chap. 10.

Laminar Processing

So far we have confined our review to horizontal information flow from module to module along the cortical surface. There is also a vertical flow to consider, as it has relevance for the theory we are pursuing. Recall from Chap. 2 that the cortical sheet is composed of six layers. Three classes of neurons populate these layers: stellate neurons, pyramidal neurons, and inhibitory interneurons. Stellate and pyramidal neurons make up about 75 percent of these neurons.[67] They use the excitatory neurotransmitter glutamate to communicate with other neurons. Stellate neurons have short axons that connect with other neurons confined to the local neighborhood. The more numerous pyramidal neurons have long axons that traverse distances of 10 centimeters or more, making them the long-distance communicators in the cortex. Inhibitory interneurons are a diverse collection of cells with short axons and that use the inhibitory neurotransmitter gamma-aminobutyric acid (GABA) to communicate with other neurons. The function of the inhibitory interneurons is to enhance and sharpen feedforward information flow and to provide an offset to the excitatory effects of the pyramidal and stellate neurons.[68]

Vertical information flow proceeds from layer to layer in a strict feedforward progression. The flow is confined to *cortical columns*, which are segregated regions made up of neurons with similar receptive fields.[69] The columns are 40–50 microns in diameter and contain 80–100 neurons spanning every cell type.[70] That the primary sensory cortices are segregated

[66] Laughlin 2003.
[67] Bannister 2005.
[68] Lubke 2007.
[69] Wandell 2005.
[70] Buxhoeveden 2002; Mountcastle 1997.

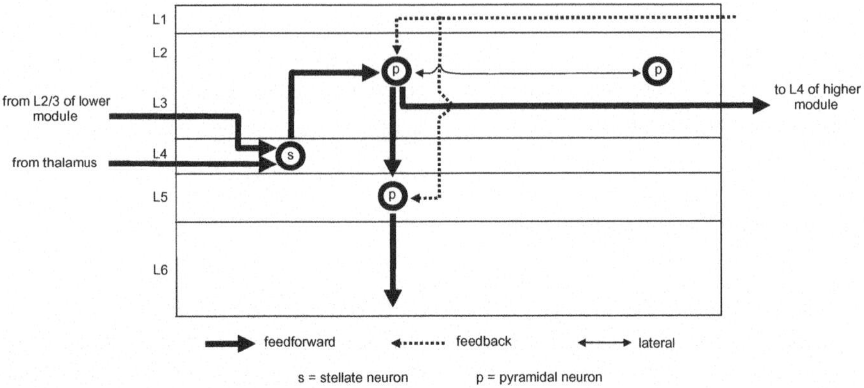

Fig. 8.7 Feedforward progression through the cortical layers

into columns was hypothesized as early as the 1930s[71] but was firmly established by the Johns Hopkins University American neurophysiologist Vernon Mountcastle (1918–) in the 1950s.[72] As Mountcastle recalled it, one day in 1955 he was busily recording the electrical responses to tactile stimuli of cortical neurons in an anesthetized cat. To make his recordings he inserted a microelectrode (a device invented a couple of decades earlier) into the cat's cerebral cortex at various surface locations and at various depths in the cat's somatosensory cortex, listing the neuronal responses on a yellow piece of paper. Suddenly, he became aware that the notations on the paper had taken the form of columns, each column formed by the responses to a different stimulus: cells responsive to touch formed one column, cells responsive to joint position formed another column, and so on.

"That was my 'aha!' experience," he recalled. He remarked that the discovery "was met with disbelief by many neuroanatomists." The idea that the responses of cortical neurons were not randomly distributed but were arrayed in distinct columns "hit neuroanatomists where they lived."

Figure 8.7 illustrates the progression through the layers. Incoming signals originating from the thalamus and from L2/3 layer of the preceding cortical module impinge on the stellate neurons of L4, which is

[71] Lorente de No 1938.

[72] Mountcastle 1957.

the driving layer of the cortex.[73] The L4 stellate neurons are themselves profusely interconnected, which serves to amplify the incoming signals.[74] Information then passes from the stellate neurons in L4 to the pyramidal neurons in L2/3 within the same column.[75] L2/3 is the computational layer. It combines the feedforward signals received from L4 with lateral signals received from distant L2/3 pyramidal neurons and with feedback signals received from L1.[76]

The L2/3 pyramidal neurons then pass feedforward information to L4 stellate neurons in the next cortical module and to L5 pyramidal neurons in the same column, and lateral information to L2/3 pyramidal neurons in other columns within the same cortical module.[77]

L5 is the output layer and, like L2/3, is populated primarily with pyramidal neurons. It sends feedback signals to earlier cortical modules and output to the thalamus and other subcortical structures where it helps dictate the brain's responses to perceived sensory signals.[78] L5 pyramidal neurons also send lateral signals to other L5 pyramidal neurons in the same column. The role of L5 processing is presumably to provide for amplification and improved precision of the messages being exported.

In Which Neurons Are the vr-NCCs Likely Located?

In Chap. 7 I gave reasons for identifying the left VL-PFC as the cortical region in which the vr-NCCs are located. I noted that the left VL-PFC is the recipient of inputs pertaining to the perceptions, memories, internal images, and feelings that comprise conscious experience; that it is activated when vr-conscious experience is present; and that its total destruction eliminates vr-conscious experience.

---

[73] Crick 1998.

[74] Bannister 2005.

[75] Lubke 2007.

[76] Larkum 2004.

[77] Bannister 2005; Thomson 1998.

[78] Thomson 2003; Lubke 2007; Bannister 2005.

In which class of neurons within the VL-PFC might the vr-NCCs reside? Any answer would be speculative but a reasonable guess can be made. For starters, we can rule out the inhibitory interneurons, which lack the well-formed receptive fields that would be expected in neurons containing the vr-NCCs. The general consensus is that the inhibitory interneurons play an adjunctive role in conscious processing by sharpening, modulating, and "sculpting" the feedforward message.[79]

This leaves us with the L4 stellate neurons and the L2/3 and L5 pyramidal neurons as possible loci for the vr-NCCs. Each is squarely within the feedforward information flow but the L4 stellate neurons lack input from either the feedback fibers arriving from L1 or the lateral signals arriving from L2/3. L4 stellate neurons are therefore bereft of attentional and contextual input, both of which are integral components of conscious experience, rendering them unlikely loci for the vr-NCCs.

The L2/3 and L5 pyramidal neurons are the remaining candidates for vr-NCC status. Of the two, there are a number of reasons to favor the L5 neurons, including their "bursty" output composed of rapid repetitive firing.[80] The most decisive reason for choosing the L5 pyramidal neurons, however, may derive from a unique feature of the feedforward input they receive. Unlike the inputs to the dendrites of L4 stellate neurons and L2/3 pyramidal neurons, which are combinatorial in nature, the input to the dendrites of L5 pyramidal neurons is likely holographic in nature. As we will see in Chap. 10, this might allow for the emergence of pyramidal neurons with multiple receptive fields and a possible mechanism by which vr-conscious experience can be specified in these neurons. Before addressing this issue, however, we need to first examine the anatomy and function of individual neurons.

[79] Konstantoudaki 2014; Merchant 2012.

[80] Thomson 2007; Bannister 2005; Crick 1994, 1998.

9

The Single Neuron

Limitation of the Point Neuron Model

Our search for the vr-NCC has led us to the L5 pyramidal neurons in the left VL-PFC. So far, we have regarded these neurons as simple points with no internal structure. Is this way of looking at neurons correct? Is the complexity of the branching dendritic tree irrelevant to neuronal functioning? The answer is not immediately obvious. There are examples throughout nature where potential information processing capacity of this sort is not realized. Take trees in a forest, for example. They have spatially extended limbs and roots but this fact has nothing to do with information processing. The branching patterns of the limbs evolved only to increase the exposure of leaves to sunlight, and that of the roots to increase access to water and nutrients, not to process information. Might it be that the dendritic trees of neurons function likewise, their branching structure having evolved to maximize the surface area available for synaptic inputs and not to increase computational complexity? In support of this possibility, the point neuron model, despite its cartoon-like simplicity, has had a long and productive run and has become the standard tool used by most researchers to study cortical information processing.

S. Sevush, *The Single-Neuron Theory*,
DOI 10.1007/978-3-319-33708-1_9

As it turns out, however, recent experimental work indicates that the spatial extension of the dendritic tree does in fact matter and cannot be ignored. What's more, given its central role in processing information, it is the likely location for the vr-NCC. Accordingly, we now turn to the science of dendritic anatomy and function, starting with their unique electrical nature.

The Brain Is Electrically Active

That nerve cells are electrically active was discovered in 1791 by the Italian physicist, Luigi Galvani (1737–1798). Experimenting on frogs, Galvani demonstrated the presence of internally generated "animal electricity" in neuronal tissue. His discovery brought an end to the ancient belief that nerves conducted "animal spirits," hypothetical entities of unknown nature that were postulated to be present in all living things. What propagated through nerves instead was electricity, a phenomenon whose properties were just beginning to be understood. Galvani was certain he had discovered something fundamental:

> I am attacked by two very opposite sects—the scientists and the know-nothings. Both laugh at me—calling me the frog's dancing-master. Yet I know that I have discovered one of the greatest forces in nature.[1]

Galvani's investigations led to the fanciful conjecture that electricity might even be the central principle of life itself. Galvani's nephew, Giovanni Aldini (1762–1834), intrigued by this possibility, collected fresh human heads at the base of the guillotine and was able to evoke grimaces, jaw movements, and eye openings in the detached heads by passing electrical current through them. And if this was not horrific enough, in 1817 the German physician Karl August Weinhold (1782–1829) removed the brain of a kitten and filled its cranium with an amalgam of zinc and silver, causing a spontaneous flow of electric current. Weinhold described his grizzly experiment:

---

[1] Verkhratsky 2006, p. 233.

> I removed with a small spoon, through an opening at the back of the head, the cerebrum and cerebellum, as well as, by means of a screw probe, the spinal cord. After this, the animal lost all life, all sensory functions, voluntary movement, and eventually its pulse. Afterward, I filled both cavities with the aforementioned amalgam [of zinc and silver]. For almost twenty minutes, the animal got into such a life-tension that it raised its head, opened its eyes, stared for a time, tried to get into a crawling position, sank down again several times, nevertheless finally got up with obvious effort, hopped around, and then sank down exhausted. The heartbeat and the pulse, as well as the circulation were quite active during these observations…Also, body temperature was fully restored.[2]

These observations turned out, we know now, to be entirely artifactual. The concept nevertheless inspired novelist Mary Shelley (1797–1851) to incorporate an electrical basis for life in her novel, Frankenstein, published in 1818, in which a creature was brought back from the dead by injecting it with electricity derived from lightning.

In the more sober arena of rigorous scientific investigation, Galvani's demonstration of animal electricity stimulated subsequent researchers to directly measure internally generated electrical currents within nerve fibers and eventually in the brain itself. As we will see, it is the electrical aspect of brain function, and especially the electrical activity in dendrites and synapses, that is most closely linked to vr-conscious experience.

The Synapse

The electrical activity in neurons accounts for the flow of information through the neuron from the dendritic synapses to the cell body and out via a solitary exiting axon (Fig. 9.1). The discovery of this informational flow was another contribution by Cajal who dubbed it the *law of dynamic polarization.*

The processing begins at the synapses, which are the neuron's main receiving portals. Information flow through the synapse runs from the presynaptic axon terminal to the post synaptic dendrite. Transmission

[2] Finger 2000, p. 115.

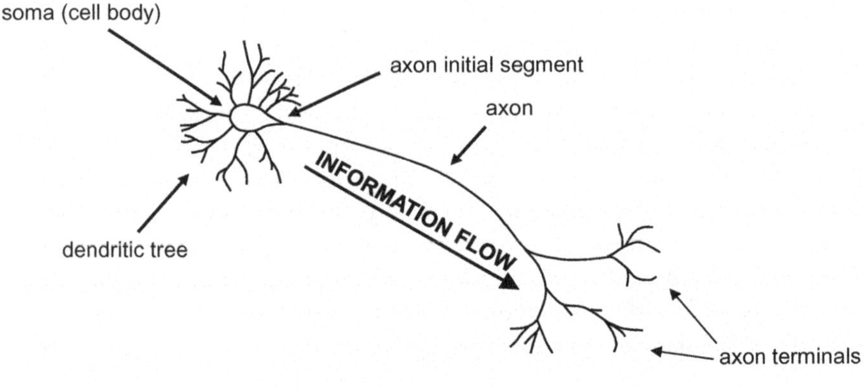

Fig. 9.1 Cajal's law of dynamic polarization: information processing runs from dendrites to axon in feedforward fashion

is initiated when an axonal signal arrives at the presynaptic side of the synaptic gap. Here, hundreds of vesicles in the axon terminal, each laden with thousands of *neurotransmitter molecules*, spill their contents into the synaptic space. The neurotransmitter molecules then diffuse across the synaptic gap, which is 20 to 30 nanometers wide.

On their arrival at the postsynaptic side of the gap, the neurotransmitter molecules engage in lock and key interactions with receptor proteins embedded in the dendrite cell membrane. When a fit occurs, the receptor protein changes its spatial configuration and this opens a channel to one or another type of charged ions, such as Na^+ or K^+. The designated ions pass through the opened gate and enter the intracellular compartment of the dendrite where their presence produces a transient change in electrical potential called the *postsynaptic potential* (PSP). The whole sequence takes about 0.3 to 0.5 milliseconds to complete.

The neurotransmitter molecules are an essential part of the process. The brain uses a large variety of them, although only one type of neurotransmitter is used at any one synapse. By far the most common neurotransmitter is *glutamate*, which is used in 80–90 percent of all cortical synapses, the next most common being GABA, which is used in most of the rest.[3]

[3] Di Maio 2008.

Glutamate synapses are excitatory in that their activation produces a positive PSP called an *excitatory postsynaptic potential* (EPSP). GABA synapses are inhibitory since activation of GABA receptors produces a negative PSP called an *inhibitory postsynaptic potential* (IPSP). As a rule, glutamate synapses transmit feedforward, driving signals, whereas GABA synapses exert primarily feedback and modulatory effects.

What Purpose Do Neurotransmitters Serve?

We note that synaptic transmission inserts a chemical step into what is otherwise a completely electrical affair. This is a feature common to all nervous systems from hydra to humans. An obvious but rarely asked question is, "Why did natural selection favor the intrusion of a chemical step into what would otherwise be a purely electrical process of synaptic transmission?" And further, "Why the need for the many different neurotransmitters that are present in the brain?"

My own thought on the matter is that the insertion of a chemical step provides a way for the brain to participate in a "sympathy" relationship with other parts of the body. Recall from Chap. 2 that in the modern version of the ancient "sympathy" model, chemical factors circulating in the blood mediate a harmonious interaction of the various bodily organs. The brain can be brought into this interaction by virtue of the neurotransmitter step of synaptic transmission, which provides a point of access for circulating enzymes and other chemical factors to gain influence over brain function.

In accord with this perspective, many of the chemicals serving as neurotransmitters in the brain also serve as circulating agents in the blood, the functions being complementary. For example, norepinephrine as a neurotransmitter mediates brain mechanisms of arousal and attentional mechanisms, while as a circulating agent causes the heart to pump faster, the pupils to dilate, and other physical manifestations of arousal to occur. Similarly, cholecystokinin is a neurotransmitter that mediates brain mechanisms of satiety but is also a blood-borne agent that acts on the gall bladder and intestines to facilitate digestion. A particularly compelling example of molecules with dual functions is oxytocin. As a neurotransmitter, oxytocin mediates feelings of love and nurturing, while as a circulating hormone it causes the uterine muscles to contract during childbirth and the breasts to secrete milk during lactation. Comparable dual roles apply for testosterone, estrogen, somatostatin, and a host of other neurotransmitters.

The presence of a chemical intermediary in synaptic transmission offers incidental opportunities for medical interventions. Physicians since antiquity have taken advantage of the chemical component of synaptic transmission by administering medications that selectively modify the effects of one neurotransmitter or another. Most psychiatric medications work in this way. Examples include antidepressants, which target serotonin and norepinephrine synapses; antipsychotics, which target dopamine synapses; and antianxiety agents, which target GABA synapses. Euphoriants can be added to the list: marijuana targets cannabinoid synapses, heroin targets opiate synapses, and cocaine targets dopamine, serotonin, and norepinephrine synapses.

Dendritic Spines

Along each dendritic branch are hundreds of dendritic spines, which are tiny (one micron in length) protrusions that are the site of excitatory synapses.[4] It was Cajal who, in 1911, identified dendritic spines, naming them because of their resemblance to thorns on flower stems.[5] Dendritic spines represent about 40 percent of the dendritic surface area.[6] A large pyramidal neuron will typically contain tens of thousands of spines,[7] indicating that at least that number of excitatory synaptic inputs converge onto it (but not necessarily from as many neurons, since one axon can form multiple synapses with one neuron). Spines increase the connectivity of the dendrites and confer a degree of electrical and chemical isolation to synaptic processing.[8]

---

[4] Koch 2004.

[5] Sidiropoulou 2006.

[6] Azouz 2005.

[7] Grienberger 2015; Koch 2004.

[8] Grienberger 2015; Yuste 2013, 2011.

Why do neurons make tens of thousands of spines to receive excitatory inputs and not simply receive them on the dendritic shaft? Columbia University neuroscientist Rafael Yuste calls this the "spine problem."[9] He points out that, given their large numbers and involvement in almost all excitatory synaptic connections, spines cannot be an accidental design feature. Further experimental probes of spine structure and function will clearly play a role in the final search for the vr-NCC.

The Dendritic Tree

The synapses are scattered along the branches of the dendritic tree. The dendritic branches are sheathed by a 3–4 nm thick lipid membrane that is impermeable to water and most molecules.[10] *Ion channels*, some associated with synapses and others not, permit selected ions to flow freely into the dendrite while keeping other transmission blocked. The efficiency of these channels is enormous, with selected ions flowing 10,000 times more freely than unselected ones.

The responsibility of the dendritic tree is to combine the PSPs generated by individual synapses into a single total potential that is delivered to the soma. The combining is necessary because the individual PSPs are by themselves too weak to induce the firing. The summed total is compared to the threshold for neuronal firing and a decision is made whether or not to issue an axonal action potential.

Due to the large number of synapses distributed across the dendritic tree, dendritic processing is a complex matter. The number of synapses in a typical dendritic tree is staggering, reaching 40,000 for pyramidal neurons in the frontal cortex of humans and more in the cerebellum.[11] An underappreciation of the magnitude of this number is likely one source of the widespread intuition that single neurons are by themselves insufficiently complex to provide a suitable physical substrate for the richness of conscious experience.

[9] Yuste 2011.

[10] Major 2008.

[11] Abeles 1991.

The Soma, the Axon, and Propagating Action Potentials

A defining feature of the axonal action potential is that it is *propagating*, enabling information transmission over long distances. What propagates is a complex electrochemical disturbance that originates at the initial axon segment and moves outward along the length of the axon at a speed of about 10 to 100 meters per second.

The propagating action potential is the universal currency of signal transmission in the nervous system. Its existence was initially intuited in the 1800s but the first real insight into its nature came in 1926 when the British electrophysiologist Lord Edgar Douglas Adrian (1889–1977) became the first to record its presence in single nerve fibers.[12] This effort netted him a Nobel Prize four years later.

What Adrian learned about propagating action potentials was unexpected. The working assumption at the time had been that action potentials came in different shapes and sizes, and could be combined to encode information much as the letters of the alphabet are combined to construct words. To his amazement, however, Adrian found that all action potentials were of the same shape and size and traveled at the same speed. Furthermore, he found the action potentials to be subject to an all-or-none law: each action potential was emitted in its entirety or not at all; no intermediate responses were possible.

The thinking about information transmission along axons clearly had to be revised. If action potentials were indistinguishable on the basis of shape, size, and propagation speed, then all that remained to carry information was the timing of their transmission. In his 1932 book, entitled "The Mechanism of Nervous Action," Adrian reflected upon the results of his experiments on sensory nerves:

> If these records give a true measure of the activity in the sensory nerve fibres it is clear that they transmit their messages to the central nervous system in a very simple way. The message consists merely of a series of brief impulses or waves of activity following one another more or less closely.

[12] Adrian 1926a–d.

> In any one fibre the waves are all of the same form and the message can only be varied by changes in the frequency and duration of the discharge. In fact the sensory messages are scarcely more complex than a succession of dots in the Morse Code.

In further experiments, Adrian was able to discern a mechanism by which action potentials could encode information. Working on frogs and cats, Adrian observed that the average rate of cell firing increased as the strength of the applied sensory stimulus increased. He found this to be true for sensations of touch, pressure, pain, and smell, and it would subsequently be shown to be true for sensory nerves in general. In fact, it applied to motor nerves as well, the rate of motor nerve firing being related to the strength of the contraction of the targeted muscle. The importance of the time-varying firing rate extends to neurons throughout the nervous system and is the basis of the *rate code model* of neuronal interaction that remains relevant in current computational models.

The Hodgkin–Huxley Model

Several decades after Adrian's discoveries, the electrochemical specifics of action potential propagation were worked out. In 1952, in a tour de force of experimental neurophysiology, Alan Lloyd Hodgkin (1914–1998) and Andrew Fielding Huxley (1917–2012) described the processes involved in action potential generation and transmission.[13] Their work garnered them a Nobel Prize in 1963. The details of the Hodgkin–Huxley (H–H) model are a bit complicated but we need to look at them because they illuminate the process by which ions flow into and out of the neuron, not only in axons but also in the dendritic tree. Additionally, they bring into focus a major weakness, the currently prevalent view that vr-conscious experience is mediated by brain wide neuronal network activity.

The H–H model starts with the establishment and maintenance of an intra-axonal *resting potential* (Fig. 9.2). This is accomplished through the combined effects of *Na^+-K^+ ion pumps* and a membrane that is slightly

[13] Hodgkin 1952a–f.

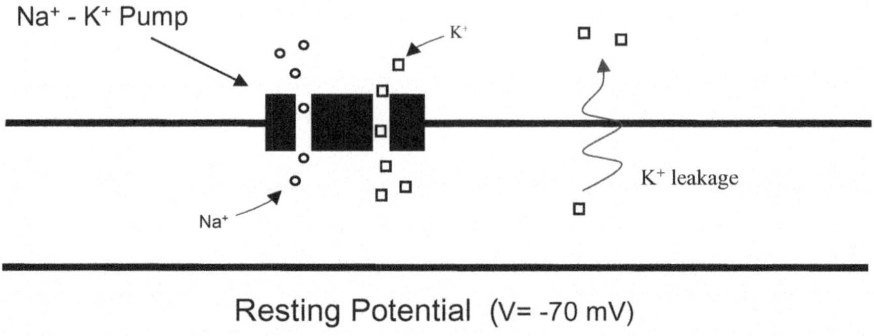

Fig. 9.2 The Hodgkin-Huxley model starts with the establishment and maintenance of an intra-axonal resting potential

permeable to K^+ ions. The Na^+-K^+ ion pumps actively transport K^+ ions into the cell and Na^+ ions out of the cell. This results in an intracellular buildup of K^+ ions, which leak back out of the cell through the slightly permeable membrane. This outward leakage of positive ions causes the intracellular potential to become negative, which tends to draw the K^+ back into the cell. Ultimately, a steady state balance is established between the pumping of K^+ ions into the cell and the leakage of K^+ ions out of the cell. The steady state balance establishes an intracellular resting potential of –70 mV.

The resting potential is the baseline from which propagating action potentials are spawned. Each action potential consists of a brief electrical fluctuation in which there is first a rapid rise and then a rapid fall of the intracellular electrical potential. The process employs *voltage-gated ion channels*, which are channels that are opened or closed depending on the intracellular potential. Two types of voltage-gated ion channels are involved in action potential generation (Fig. 9.3). One, a voltage-gated Na^+ channel, opens when the intracellular potential drops to a threshold value of –55 mV. The other, a voltage-gated K^+ channel, opens when the intracellular potential moves into positive territory. The Na^+ and K^+ voltage-gated ion channels are found in abundance at the initial axon segment, where action potential generation begins.

Action potentials are triggered when the intracellular potential at the initial axonal segment reaches the voltage-gated Na^+ channel threshold

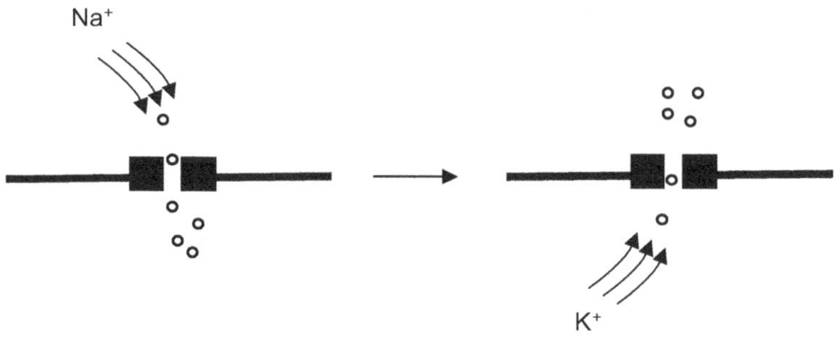

Fig. 9.3 Voltage-gated ion channels

value of –55 mV. When this happens, the Na^+ channel suddenly opens and Na^+ ions begin pouring into the cell along their transmembranal concentration gradient. The influx of the positively charged Na^+ ions makes the intracellular potential less negative, opening still more voltage-gated Na^+ channels. A self-reinforcing feedback cycle eventually takes hold that moves the intracellular potential past zero into positive territory.

The increasingly positive intracellular potential then opens voltage-gated K^+ channels, allowing K^+ ions to spill out into the extracellular space. This causes the intracellular potential to rapidly become markedly negative, overshooting the resting potential. The voltage-gated K^+ and Na^+ channels then close and the intracellular potential returns to the –70 mV resting level, marking the end of the action potential cycle. The duration of the action potential spike is about one millisecond.

Once generated, the axonal action potential propagates outward along the length of the axon. This happens because during the brief positive swing in intracellular potential that occurs during the rising phase of the action potential, the positivity spreads to neighboring sites along the axonal membrane (Fig. 9.4). This causes neighboring sites to reach the threshold for action potential generation and the stereotypical sequence unfolds again at the new sites: the permeability of the membrane for Na^+ increases; Na^+ ions come flooding in; the polarity of the potential reverses; K^+ ions flow out; and the potential resets.

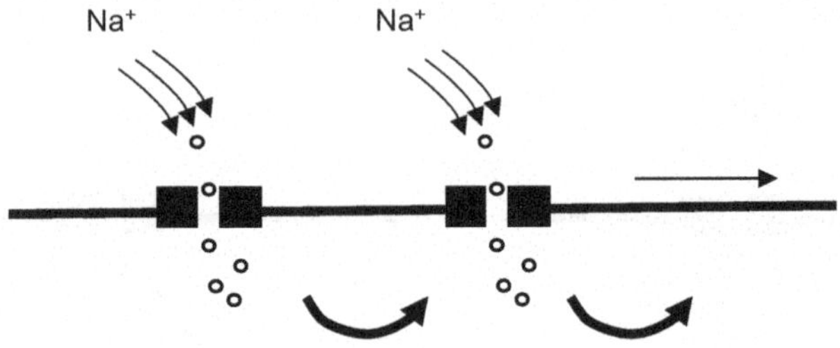

Fig. 9.4 Action potential propagation

Action potentials are generated at successive sites in the direction away from the cell body only. None are generated at sites in the direction back toward the cell body because the action potential sequence just concluded at these sites renders them temporarily refractory to the generation of new action potentials. The end result is that the succession of action potentials at adjacent sites gives the appearance of a single action potential that is propagating along the fiber away from the cell body.

In sum, the H–H model describes a stereotypical process that produces action potentials of the same shape and amplitude that travel along the axon at a fixed velocity, explaining Adrian's findings from several decades earlier. With its generation of action potentials, the initial axon segment functions as an analog to digital converter. This conversion is necessary in order for axonal spikes to be transmitted over long distances, since passive spread of the intracellular potential fluctuations would by themselves attenuate rapidly with distance from their point of origin. The regenerative aspect of the propagating action potential overcomes this attenuation, allowing for long distance signal transmission.

The most important point to extract from the foregoing is that axonal signal transmission is not just a matter of simple current flow through an electrical conductor. Axonal signal transmission consists instead of a complex electrochemical disturbance that propagates along the length of the axonal membrane. The process is intricate and time-consuming, and not at all like the sleek, mercurial flow through a syncytium envisioned by Gerlach and Golgi.

Neuronal Processing and the Binding Problem

Our brief survey of neuronal anatomy and function at the neuronal level has exposed features of microscopic processing that exacerbate the binding problem that already plagues mind/brain theorizing when considered at the macroscopic level. The reader will recall from Chap. 1 that the binding problem is the difficulty of explaining how a spatially dispersed physical substrate could coalesce into a single experiential flow. When considered from a microscopic perspective, the binding difficulties are even more problematic. A distributed vr-NCC would need to traverse synapses and long lengths of axonal wiring, with the physical processes that mediate vr-conscious experience consisting of cumbersome quasi-mechanical movements of ions and molecules. The meandering flow of neurotransmitter molecules across the synaptic gap, one molecule bouncing off another as the group migrates to the postsynaptic receptors, seems more like a crowd of people streaming out of a stadium after a football game than it does a unified correlate for conscious experience. Likewise, the cadre of Na^+ and K^+ ions, banging and bumping their way down concentration gradients during action potential propagation, better resembles a set of billiard balls rolling down a hill than it does a smooth and quick flow of current through a syncytium.

Leibniz captured this sentiment with his famous windmill metaphor:

One is obliged to admit that [conscious] *perception* and what depends upon it is *inexplicable on mechanical principles*, that is, by figures and motions. In imagining that there is a machine whose construction would enable it to think, to sense, and to have perception, one could conceive it enlarged while retaining the same proportions, so that one could enter into it, just like into a windmill. Supposing this, one should, when visiting within it, find only parts pushing one another, and never anything by which to explain a [conscious] perception. Thus it is in the simple substance, and not in the composite or in the machine, that one must look for perception.[14]

Or, as the philosopher John Searle described it, if all that mattered were the functional organization, then conscious experience should, in principle, be achievable with a contraption made of empty beer cans and powered by windmills.

---

[14] Leibniz 1714.

A vr-NCC confined to smaller components within the neuron would have the advantage of lessening the impact of the binding problem. With this in mind, we now examine the information processing that occurs within the confines of individual neurons.

The Apical and Basal Compartments in Pyramidal Neurons

The first feature of intraneuronal processing we will examine is the division of the dendritic tree of pyramidal neurons into separate domains.[15] The separation is facilitated by the pyramidal neuron's long *apical stalk* that partitions the dendritic tree into two distinct compartments: a large *basal compartment* with dendritic branches that arise directly from the cell body,[16] and a sparser *apical compartment* with dendritic branches that come off the long apical stalk (Fig. 9.5).

The two compartments differ in size, with the larger basal compartment receiving two-thirds of all the excitatory inputs to the neuron. The greater size of the basal compartment presumably reflects a greater computational capacity. The basal compartment of L2/3 and L5 pyramidal neurons differ in how they are connected with the neuronal network. In the case of L2/3 pyramidal neurons, the basal compartment resides in L2/3 and is the recipient of feedforward input from L4 stellate neurons[17] and lateral input from other L2/3 pyramidal neurons.[18] In the case of L5 pyramidal neurons, the basal compartment resides in L5 and is the recipient of feedforward input from local L2/3 neurons.[19] The apical compartments of both L2/3 and L5 pyramidal neurons reach up to L1, where feedback information from distant neurons is received.[20]

---

[15] Branco 2009; Larkum 2013; Sidiropoulou 2006; London 2005; Mel 1998.

[16] There are also apical oblique dendrites that sprout from the body of the trunk. I will adopt the common convention of including them in the basal compartment.

[17] Lubke 2007; Thomson 2007; Feldmeyer 2006.

[18] Lubke 2007; Feldmeyer 2006.

[19] Petreanu 2009; Thomson 1998.

[20] Larkum 2013; Douglas 2004.

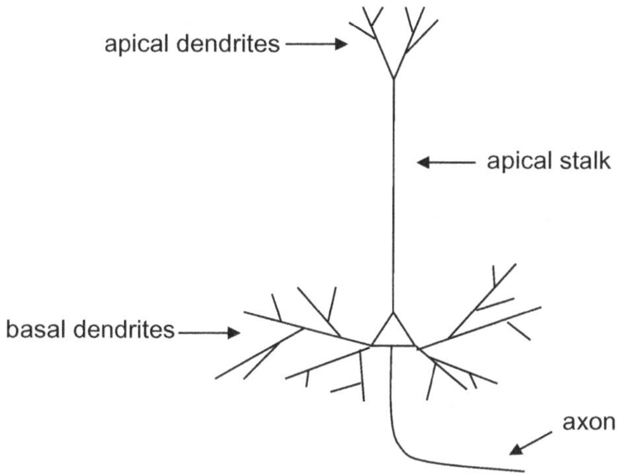

Fig. 9.5 Pyramidal neuron

The anatomical separation of the apical and basal dendritic trees renders them electrically independent.[21] This allows for independent information processing in the two compartments, with the results of the separate computations being combined at the soma. The mechanism by which the two compartments interact is complex and has been discovered to depend on two new kinds of action potentials that have been discovered within the last 20 years (Fig. 9.6). The startling feature of these new action potentials is that they occur in the dendrites, not in the axons. The first of these, the *back-propagating action potential* (BAP), was discovered in the mid-1990s by the Australian neuroscientist Greg Stuart, then a postdoctoral student in Nobel Laureate Bert Sakmann's laboratory at the Max Planck Institute in Germany.[22] The BAP is generated at the same time as the H–H axonal action potential and, like the H–H action potential, it originates in the axonal initial segment and is mediated by voltage-gated Na^+-channel activity. What is novel, however,

[21] Crick 2003.

[22] Stuart 1994.

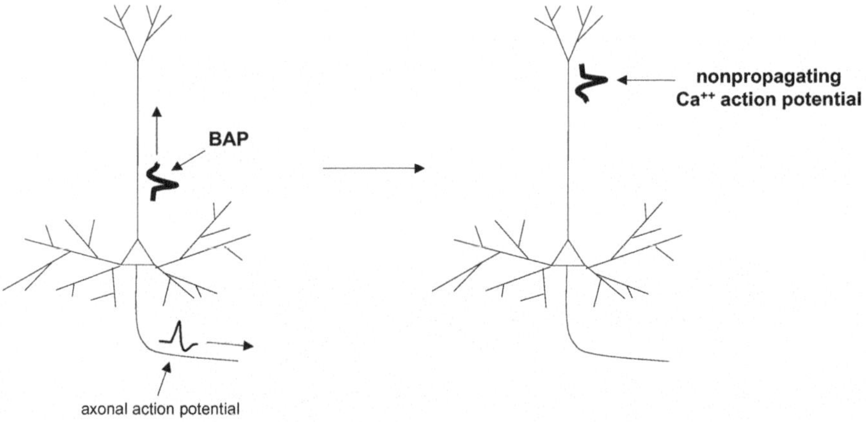

Fig. 9.6 Generation of the BAP and non-propagating Ca^{++} action potentials. Abbreviations: BAP, back-propagating action potential

is that it propagates in the reverse direction back through the soma and into the dendritic tree.[23]

The second newly discovered dendritic action potential arises at the base of the apical dendritic tree located at the far end of the apical stalk.[24] In this case, the action potential is Ca^{++}-mediated and non-propagating. It is generated when a sufficient number of PSPs are synchronously produced in the apical dendritic tree, thus lowering the threshold for the spike initiation.[25] The Ca^{++}-mediated spike produces an electrical effect that spreads to the soma *electrotonically*, which is to say it spreads passively in accord with Coulomb's law, falling off as the square of the distance. At the soma, the Ca^{++} spike interacts with PSPs arriving from the basal dendrites where a decision is made as to whether an outgoing axonal spike is generated.

The interaction of the two dendritic action potentials provides a mechanism by which top-down feedback signals entering the apical tree via L1 can modulate the flow of feedforward activity entering the basal tree via

[23] Larkum 2008; Antic 2003.

[24] Antic 2010; Larkum 2008; Schiller 1997.

[25] Larkum 2004.

L2/3 and L5.[26] If we hypothesize that the vr-NCC is associated specifically with the basal tree (a plausible assumption given the basal tree's size and connectivity), the apical input could be thought of as providing a top-down context for the vr-conscious experiences generated in the basal tree.[27]

NMDA Dendritic Spikes and Cluster Sensitivity

Supposing that the vr-NCC is localized to the basal dendritic tree, it is reasonable to ask whether its spatially extended, branching anatomy needs to be taken into account. Investigations over the past half century indicate that it must.[28] This was first shown by Wilfrid Rall (1922–), a mid-twentieth-century pioneer in computational neuroscience.[29] Rall analyzed the *passive cable model*, which assumes that all electrical interactions occur via passive electrotonic coupling. He examined the effects of dendritic geometry and membrane properties on the spread of electrical potential within the dendritic tree and showed that complex intradendritic computations were possible despite the simplicity of the model.

In the half century since Rall's initial analyses, the passive cable model, while retaining a usefulness as a starting point in dendritic modeling,[30] has had to be modified to incorporate the presence of action potentials.[31] This was made particularly clear by the discovery in 2000 of yet another dendritic action potential, this one arising within the thin distal branches of the dendritic trees.[32] This new action potential was found to be associated with the NMDA receptor protein, which we encountered in the previous chapter in connection with network memory and learning. The generation of an NMDA action potential required that (1) the glutamate binding sites on the NMDA receptor proteins be occupied, (2)

[26] Larkum 2013; 2008.
[27] Larkum 2013.
[28] Hausser 2003.
[29] Rall 1959.
[30] London 2005; Koch 1999.
[31] London 2005; Sidiropoulou 2006.
[32] Schiller 2000.

the membrane be sufficiently depolarized, and (3) the receptor protein occupation and membrane depolarization occur simultaneously at multiple neighboring synapses. If these requirements are met, a regenerative event leading to a dendritic spike takes place: the depolarization of the dendrite causes an influx of Ca^{++} ions, which causes a further depolarization and a further influx of Ca^{++} ions, and so on in a positive feedback loop that results in the production of an NMDA spike. Once generated, the NMDA spike persists for tens to hundreds of milliseconds.[33] NMDA spikes are nonpropagating, so their effect on the soma is solely by direct electrotonic coupling.[34] Their large amplitude (40 to 50 mV), together with their prolonged time course enable them to produce a significant impact on the soma.[35]

A key finding has been that the likelihood of NMDA spike initiation is greatly enhanced by *supralinear summation*[36] of the PSPs produced at neighboring synapses. With supralinear summation, the total depolarization induced by the activated synapses is greater than that predicted by a simple weighted sum.[37] The supralinear enhancement of PSP summation is referred to as *cluster sensitivity*, an effect first demonstrated theoretically in the early 1990s by USC neuroscientist Bartlett Mel, then a postdoctoral fellow under Christof Koch,[38] and subsequently corroborated by numerous computational and empirical studies. In general, cluster sensitivity occurs when about 10–50 NMDA synapses located within 20–40 microns of each other are activated within a 10–20 msec interval.[39]

Cluster sensitivity likely plays an important role in shaping the spatial patterns of synaptic activity during fetal development and beyond, an effect we might call *cluster plasticity*.[40] With cluster plasticity, LTP induction at one synapse decreases the threshold for LTP at nearby syn-

---

[33] Major 2013; Antic 2010; Larkum 2009; Polsky 2004; Schiller 2000.

[34] Polsky 2009; Sidiropoulou 2006; Poirazi 2003a,b.

[35] Branco 2011; Antic 2010; Larkum 2008.

[36] Larkum 2009; Polsky 2004.

[37] Sidiropoulou 2006; London 2005.

[38] Mel 1993.

[39] Wilms 2015; Antic 2010; Polsky 2009, 2004; Major 2008; Sidiropoulou 2006; London 2005; Hausser 2003.

[40] Wilms 2015; Larkum 2008; Hausser 2003.

apses. A number of chemical mechanisms have been proposed for cluster plasticity,[41] with a competition between different candidate synaptic patterns likely involved.[42] It is with respect to cluster sensitivity and cluster plasticity, together with supralinear summation of PSPs, that the single-neuron theory I am proposing has its testable impact. I will expand on this notion in Chap. 11.

As a result of these developments, it has become apparent that the distal dendritic branches may serve as the basic computational units of dendritic processing.[43] With this in mind, we now turn to specific candidates for vr-NCC localized to these distal dendritic branches.

[41] De Roo 2008; Harvey 2007.

[42] Legenstein 2011.

[43] Larkum 2008; Sidiropoulou 2006.

10

The Single-Neuron Theory

On the Plausibility of Single-Neuron Sentience

Our search for the vr-NCC has led us to the left VL-PFC and to the hypothesis that the substrate for vr-conscious experience resides within the dendrites of individual neurons.[1] This hypothesis has, to my knowledge, been put forth by only one other investigator, Jonathan Edwards in England.[2] It is an idea that is usually dismissed on principle, the received wisdom being that a vr-NCC must incorporate a large number of neurons, not just one. This has become an article of faith for most researchers. But, as I have stated, to propose a vr-NCC that is distributed in space and time runs into that eternal bane of mind/brain theorizing, the binding problem. The single neuron alternative offers a way to mitigate this problem and I would suggest for this reason alone it deserves serious consideration. Additionally, the localization of the vr-NCC to individual neurons has the benefit of bringing novel nanophysics into play, and with it the possibility of making headway on the hard problem of consciousness.

[1] Sevush 2006.

[2] Edwards 2005.

S. Sevush, *The Single-Neuron Theory*,
DOI 10.1007/978-3-319-33708-1_10

Accordingly, I will, in this and the next two chapters, explore the plausibility of single neuron vr-NCCs. I will begin in this chapter with an evaluation of the premise that vr-NCCs can be associated with synaptic activation patterns in individual dendritic branches. In Chap. 11, I will then present a specific quantum mechanical model of vr-NCC formation that provides a way of avoiding the binding problem. Then, in Chap. 12, I will consider some implications of the proposed theory.

Hypothesis: VR-NCCs Are Associated with Dendritic Synaptic Patterns

Any candidate theory of single neuron vr-conscious experience has to be considered speculative at this time. Our understanding of the chemistry and physics at the level of thin distal dendrites is still too fragmentary to formulate a specific theory with any confidence. I will in any case present a possible scenario by which single neuron vr-conscious experience might arise in order to make the case that a coherent mechanism can at least be formulated. Research in the next few years will likely bring clarity to the issue.

The crux of my proposal is that the information contained in a vr-conscious experience inheres in spatial activation patterns at the level of neuronal networks and again at the level of dendritic synapses (Fig. 10.1). My contention is that at the neuronal network level, the content of a vr-conscious experience is encoded in the spatial arrangement of activated L2/3 pyramidal neurons in the left VL-PFC, while at the dendritic synapse level it is encoded in the spatial arrangement of activated synapses in the L5 basal dendrites to which the L2/3 pyramidal neurons project.

The idea that the physical substrate for vr-conscious experience might be spatial in character is not new. It was originally put forth by the American experimental psychologist Edwin Boring in 1933 and, as we saw in Chap. 8, there is now considerable evidence for spatial encoding of vr-conscious experience at the cortical network level. The premise that vr-conscious experience is encoded also at the dendritic level has, however, received only scant attention.[3]

[3] Orpwood 1994.

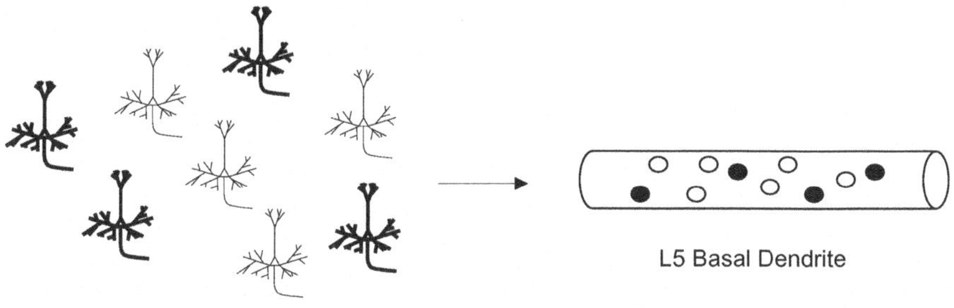

Fig. 10.1 Information content for a vr-conscious experience is expressed in the spatial activation patterns at the neuronal network level and again at dendritic synaptic level

The hypothesis that I am entertaining is based on the assumption that the L2/3-to-L5 network-to-dendrite projection is holographic as opposed to combinative. As I defined it in Chap. 8, with a holographic projection, the entirety of the vr-conscious content is received by each of a pool of recipient dendrites in reduplicative fashion (Fig. 10.2). On the other hand, I am proposing that the L2/3-to-L5 network-to-synapse projection is combinative and conforms to a labeled-line code (also known as an identity code), in which the identities of the individual synapses are preserved by virtue of their specific positions along the dendritic branch. Labeled-line coding uses information more efficiently than does pooled-response coding and is therefore likely to be favored by natural selection.[4]

My proposal actually goes further than just assuming a labeled-line code in that I hypothesize that the network-to-synapse mapping is topographic as well. By this I mean that the information carried in the spatial arrangement of the activated neurons at the level of the L2/3 neuronal network is preserved in the spatial arrangement of the activated synapses in the L5 dendrites. We saw in Chap. 8 that there is abundant evidence for topographic mapping at the cortical network level. By contrast, evidence for topographic mapping at the dendritic level has been scarce.[5]

[4] Reich 2001.

[5] Hopp 2014; Peron 2009; Bollmann 2009; Euler 2002.

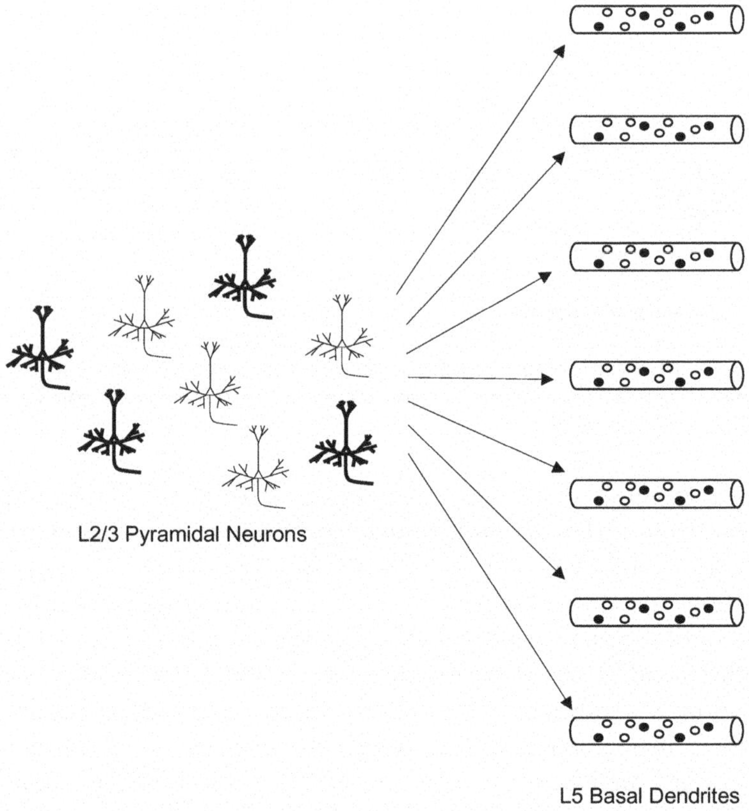

Fig. 10.2 Holographic projection from network to dendrite levels: the entire vr-conscious content is received by each of a pool of recipient dendrites in reduplicative fashion

The specific suggestion that the L2/3-to-L5 network-to-synapse mapping might be topographic was proposed by Erhard Bieberich in a 2002 paper[6] that served as an inspiration for the proposal I am making here.

It is the synaptic activation patterns that arise in the L5 dendrites that I am proposing serve as the basis for the vr-NCCs. With each passing moment, as the L5 dendritic synaptic activation patterns change, so do the vr-conscious experiences associated with them. And remarkably, the vr-conscious experiences are not just microscopic fragments of some

[6] Bieberich 2002.

larger experience but are the entirety of our everyday experiences that we usually attribute to the workings of the brain as a whole.

It is interesting to note in passing that spatial coding is not the only mechanism possible for information processing. Consider the arrangement present in a digital computer, for example. An examination of the spatial distribution of electrical activity on a computer motherboard would be a strange endeavor, since it would offer no insight into the nature of the information processing that is going on. With a digital computer, only the connections that elements make are important; the spatial locations of the activated elements are irrelevant to the content being encoded. This may turn out to be the critical difference between computers and brains with respect to vr-conscious experience.

Output Mechanisms: Generation of Neuronal Spikes

For spatial codes to be useful, there must be a brain mechanism for deciphering them. This is seen by some as a formidable challenge for spatial encoding models.[7] The theory I am advocating takes advantage of the reduplicative nature of the holographic L2/3-to-L5 network-to-dendrite projection to decipher the spatial codes. The mechanism is illustrated in Fig. 10.3. Starting from the left in the figure, we see the pool of L2/3 pyramidal neurons projecting reiteratively to an array of L5 basal dendrites (each dendrite is presumed to be located within a different neuron). Presumably, the spatial pattern of activated synapses evokes an NMDA spike in some cases but not in others (involving a mechanism that will be addressed in the next chapter). Since the NMDA spikes, in turn, contribute to the firing of the pyramidal neurons in which they are contained (for simplicity, we will assume for this discussion that the NMDA spikes are 100 percent effective in eliciting a neuronal action potential), the result is that a spatial pattern of action potential generation is produced in the array of L5 pyramidal neurons that transmits the information contained in the L5 dendrites to the rest of the brain.

[7] Laurent 1999.

In all, information encoded in the spatial patterns formed by synchronously activated cortical neurons at the L2/3 network level maps onto spatial synaptic activation patterns on distal dendritic branches of individual L5 pyramidal neurons, and these then map back up to the L5 neuronal network level, with each of the mappings enacted in an information preserving manner. In neuronal network terms, a distributed pattern of cortical activation in L2/3 has given rise to another distributed cortical pattern in L5, but with a highly nonlinear interaction occurring at the intervening dendritic level. It is worth noting that it is the redundancy invoked by the reduplicative L2/3-to-L5 neuron-to-dendrite projection that manages to avert a massive information loss that might otherwise be expected given the convergence of the large dendritic information content onto an output process in which the neuron either fires or it doesn't.[8] The redundancy also results in the production of multiple copies of the vr-NCC, such that multiples copies of vr-conscious experience are produced, each in a different neuron. Thus, when you, the reader, are training your attention on the words of this sentence, the vr-conscious experience that is being generated is had not by just one neuron but by a pool of neurons, with each neuron having approximately the same experience as all the others.

The Information Capacity of VR-NCCs

For the proposed mechanism to plausibly account for vr-conscious experience, it would have to be the case that the representations instantiated by the dendritic synaptic activation patterns contain the quantity and variety of information that is associated with vr-conscious experience. It is likely that this requirement is satisfied by the basal dendrites of lateral VL-PFC L5 pyramidal neurons. As to the variety of information, we saw in Chap. 7 that left VL-PFC neurons have access to the full variety of sensations, memories, and feelings that make up vr-conscious experience. We can expect, therefore, that the basal dendrites of the L5 pyramidal neurons contained in the left VL-PFC have such access as well.

---

[8] London 2005, p. 505; Crick 1994.

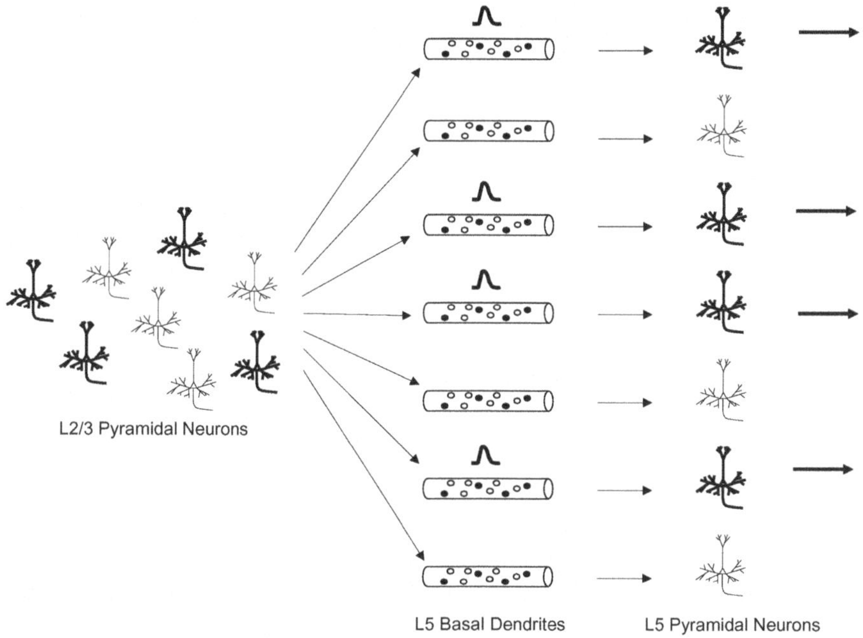

Fig. 10.3 Information encoded in the spatial patterns formed by synchronously activated cortical neurons at the L2/3 network level maps onto spatial synaptic activation patterns on distal dendritic branches of individual L5 pyramidal neurons, and these then map back up to the L5 neuronal network level

As to the quantity of information, it would have to be the case that the basal dendritic activation patterns provide for an amount of information matching that for vr-conscious experience. Whether this requirement is met by the L5 pyramidal basal dendrites will require some discussion. In philosophical circles, this requirement is usually expressed in terms of the concept of *supervenience*. As applied to the L5 pyramidal dendrites, we can say that the vr-conscious experiences supervene on the neural substrate only if for each possible vr-conscious experience there is a different synaptic activation pattern available to encode for it. If, on the other hand, the number of available synaptic activation patterns were in fact smaller than the number of possible vr-conscious experiences, then there would exist vr-conscious experiences that have no associated neuronal substrate, the implication being that vr-conscious experience is beyond the purview of physical science, a situation which it is our desire to avoid.

Is it plausible to assume that vr-conscious experience supervenes on L5 basal dendritic synaptic activation patterns, that the number of synaptic activation patterns is at least as large as the number of possible vr-conscious experiences? At first glance, it would seem not. How could a tiny dendritic branch provide for the astronomical number of different possible vr-conscious experiences? Yet, a careful inspection of the situation suggests that the L5 pyramidal neuron basal dendritic branches might well be up to the task. To see this, we employ a measure of information content introduced in 1948 by the American mathematician and electrical engineer Claude Shannon (1916–2001). Shannon developed his approach during World War II in response to the need to measure the information loss that occurred when messages were sent over transatlantic cables. His formulation provided what has since become the standard way to quantify information.[9] In conceptual terms, Shannon regarded the information contained in a signal to be the decrease in uncertainty the signal provides about the system that has generated it. In practical terms, the decrease in uncertainty is measured in terms of *bits*, the number of bits associated with a given signal being (in simple cases) the average number of efficient "yes/no" questions it would take to extract all the information contained in that signal. Technically, if the reduction in number of available states is N, then the number of bits in the signal is defined as $\log_2 N$.

As applied to synaptic activation patterns, Shannon information would be quantified as the average number of efficient yes/no questions (such as, "Is this particular synapse over here activated?") needed to determine which specific activation pattern is present at a given moment. It can be calculated as follows. Let's for the sake of this calculation assume that (1) a distal dendritic branch 100 microns in length contains 200 synapses, (2) each synapse can be either ON (activated) or OFF (not activated) at any given time, (3) about 20 of these synapses are ON within any several millisecond window, (4) the spatial pattern described by the 20 activated synapses defines the associated vr-conscious experience, and (5) with 20

[9] Shannon 1948.

synapses ON, an NMDA spike is generated 50 percent of the time (we saw the evidence for this estimate in the last chapter). To calculate the amount of Shannon information available for vr-conscious experience for this scenario, we would want to know how many different ways 20 synapses can be selected from the 200 present on the dendrite. If, for example, there were a thousand different ways that this selection could be made, and if we gained knowledge of the specific activation pattern actually present for the 20 synapses at a given moment, our uncertainty regarding the activation state of the dendrite would be reduced a thousand-fold. In fact, there are astronomically more than a thousand ways that 20 synapses can be selected from a dendrite containing 200 synapses. A simple combinatorial calculation yields $\sim 1.6 \times 10^{17}$ as the number of different ways the 20 synapses can be selected from 200 choices. The Shannon information contained in the pattern of 20 activated synapses would be $\log_2(1.6 \times 10^{17}) = \sim 57$ bits.

The Information Capacity of VR-Conscious Experiences

The question we need to ask next is, "Is 57 bits enough informational capacity to account for the information capacity of a vr-conscious experience?" To answer this we need to know how many different vr-conscious experiences are possible. While it might seem intuitively that the number would be extraordinarily large, theoretical arguments and empirical investigations suggest that the number may be smaller than expected.[10] The phenomenon of change blindness, which we met in Chap. 1, highlights this limitation.[11] Recall that change blindness refers to the surprising inability of normal subjects to detect changes between two visual scenes shown in rapid succession if the change occurs during the brief interval during which they refixate their gaze from one point of focus to another.

[10] Huang 2007; Blackmore 2006; Edelman 2000; Cowan 2000; Norretranders 1999.

[11] O'Regan 1999; Rensink 1997; Simons 1997.

Large changes can be made that escape detection, with as much as a fifth of the available scene not being registered. For example, if, while a subject is watching a movie, one actor in a scene is replaced by another actor, most subjects will not notice the change.[12] In one study, subjects failed to notice when two cowboys sitting on a bench exchanged heads. Attention is key in detecting change[13] and there is apparently a severe limitation on the rate with which attention can be shifted.

Another example of our limited attentional capacity is the "invisible gorilla experiment" published in 1999 by Christopher Chabris and Donald Simons. Subjects are shown a one-minute video featuring several basketball players, some in white shirts and some in black shirts, passing a basketball amongst them. The subjects are asked to count the number of passes that are made between players wearing black shirts. Halfway through the video, without warning, an actor wearing a full-body gorilla suit strides into the middle of the screen, waves to the viewer, pounds his chest, and then strides off the screen, the basketball continuing to be passed around the whole while. When the video is over, the viewers are asked whether they saw anything unexpected during the video. Half the subjects are found to have been completely unaware of the gorilla! A "blindness" resulted from the limited attentional resources of the perceptual processing mechanisms.

Estimates of as low as 4 to 7 bits of information per 50 ms frame of conscious experience have been offered,[14] although estimates of upwards of 16 bits are more common. According to one estimation, bits per second for various situations were calculated as 45 for silent reading, 30 for reading aloud, 18 for proofreading, 16 for typewriting, 23 for piano playing, 12 for multiplying and adding two numbers, and 3 for counting objects.[15] These calculations likely underestimate the actual information content of a typical vr-conscious experience, however.[16] Vr-conscious experiences include intangible background elements, including feelings

[12] Simons 2005.

[13] Reddy 2006; Simons 2005.

[14] Edelman 2000.

[15] Norretranders 1999.

[16] Edelman 1989.

and "fringe" experiences,[17] that entail more information processing than these calculations predict. Nevertheless, in round terms, it seems plausible that the information processing capacity of the dendrites is more than able to match that of conscious experience. Clearly, further empirical investigation is needed to resolve this matter.

The Grandmother Cell Conundrum

An important challenge any single-neuron theory must confront is the infamous *grandmother cell* conundrum.[18] A grandmother cell is a hypothetical neuron that represents the epitome of hierarchical processing, responding specifically to the presence of one's grandmother and nothing else. The problem is that if we assume that a separate neuron is needed for every possible vr-conscious experience involving one's grandmother, a separate neuron would be needed for "grandmother smiling," "grandmother weeping," "grandmother sewing," and so on.[19] This, it is argued, would precipitate a *combinatorial explosion*[20] where the number of neurons needed to account for all mental experiences would be wildly out of proportion to the number of neurons actually present in the brain. For example, suppose you had 20 conscious experiences per second nonstop over a 100-year life span. If each conscious experience were encoded by a different neuron, then ~6 billion neurons would be needed to cover the totality of your conscious experiences. This is problematic for a single-neuron theory of consciousness since the cerebral cortex presumably has no more than ~10 to 100 million neurons available for the job. And what's worse, if we consider the number of conscious experiences that could possibly occur rather than just those that actually occur, we would be looking at a number that absolutely dwarfs the number of encoding neurons available. As Crick has put it:

[17] James 1890.

[18] Bowers 2009; Lehar 2003; Gross 2002.

[19] Hubel 1995.

[20] Gold 1999; Tononi 1998b.

> There are an almost infinite number of possible different objects that we are capable of seeing. There cannot be a single neuron, often referred to as a grandmother cell, for each one.[21]

The threat of a combinatorial explosion can in fact be readily handled, however, provided the assumption that neurons have only one preferred stimulus is relaxed. There is empirical evidence that neurons are present in the cortex that have multiple receptive fields,[22] a feature that is particularly prevalent in neurons in the frontal lobes.[23] If we take into account the enormous number of different synaptic activation patterns possible on basal dendritic branches of L5 pyramidal neurons and assume that at least some of these could represent different vr-conscious experiences, it seems reasonable that a combinatorial catastrophe can be avoided.[24]

Persistence Memory and the Generation of vr-NCCs

So far, we have only considered the effect of the incoming signal on the synaptic spatial patterns that develop in the dendritic branches. There is another, complicating factor to consider, which is that the synaptic activation patterns also incorporate the residual effects of immediately preceding synaptic activity. I will refer to this effect as *persistence memory*. It is a type of memory that was alluded to by Alexander Bain back in 1886: "We cannot assign the consciousness due to any present stimulus without taking account of the state of mind previous."[25] Unlike recall memory, in which remembered material is circulated through the neuronal network and returned to a given neuron via its synaptic input, persistence memory is a direct feature of synaptic function itself. It is a factor that must be taken into account in constructing a physical substrate for vr-conscious experience.

---

[21] Crick 1990.

[22] Rishel 2013; Fitzgerald 2011; Viskontas 2008; Steinmetz 2008; Ekstrom 2003.

[23] Miller 2013; Stokes 2013; Cromer 2010; Rao 1997.

[24] Miller 2013, p. 211; Rigotti 2010.

[25] Bain 1886.

If persistence memory were to include residual activity from two or more successive traces, the information could be nested, as with the Russian doll phenomenon: a single large doll contains within it a smaller doll, which in turn contains within it a still smaller doll, and so on. This notion of nested persistence memory would fit well with our intuitive sense of the relationship between successive conscious experiences.

In physiological terms, persistence memory consists of residual synaptic activity from immediately prior synaptic activations. The fading PSP traces from previous activations have a complex effect on newly arriving synaptic inputs,[26] enhancing them if the timing is consistent with LTP and diminishing them if the timing is consistent with LTD. Chemically, glutamate molecules remain bound to the NMDA receptor for hundreds of milliseconds,[27] resulting in interactions between successive synaptic activations. Additionally, the dissipating calcium residue of prior synaptic activations can have persistence memory effects.[28] The substrate for vr-conscious experience may therefore be observable in terms of intradendritic electrical potentials or Ca^{++} concentrations, the two being partially intercorrelated.[29]

Given its contribution to NMDA spike generation,[30] persistence memory provides a rich context for the information processing that occurs in dendrites. Its effects are made still more complex given that NMDA spikes, by virtue of the shunting induced by the massive opening of ion channels, serve to reset the membrane potentials. As a result, dendritic NMDA spikes temporarily inhibit further dendritic spikes in the same dendritic segment,[31] an effect that depends on the location and timing of the NMDA PSPs and spikes.[32]

---

[26] Seong 2014.
[27] Polsky 2009.
[28] Milojkovic 2007.
[29] Milojkovic 2007.
[30] Schiller 2000.
[31] Remy 2009.
[32] Hausser 2001b, p. 138.

Summary

I have presented the first step in a possible model for single-neuron sentience that is localized within the basal dendrites of L5 pyramidal neurons in the left VL-PFC. The model features holographic network-to-dendrite and combinative network-to-synapse mappings from L2/3 to L5 pyramidal neurons, with the vr-NCC being spatial in character. It includes the insertion of persistence memory into the synaptic activation process and the possibility of neurons having multiple receptive fields. In the next chapter we will take on the challenge of defining the vr-NCC in precise physical terms.

11

Quantum Consciousness

Introduction: The Case for Panpsychism

I have so far given a rationale for localizing the vr-NCC to the distal basal dendrites of L5 pyramidal neurons in the left VL-PFC. While this gives us the most explicit neural representation of vr-conscious experience so far, it still falls short of the ultimate goal of explaining how and why these basal dendrites come to be imbued with subjective experience. The philosophical challenges involved in explaining why any physical system would be imbued with subjective experience are considerable. As I noted in Chap. 1, the currently accepted view is that subject/object duality emerges only from complex systems by an undefined process that renders the whole system sentient while its constituent elements are not. But this view fails to explain why complex systems such as the Internet, the global economy, and the population of China are not sentient, yet primitive animals such as worms leave the question of sentience undecided.

An even more critical shortcoming of the currently accepted view is that it fails to offer any criterion for where in the food chain conscious experience first appears. There is nary a hint of consensus on this issue. The noted neuroscientist Edmund Rolls contends that conscious

S. Sevush, *The Single-Neuron Theory*,
DOI 10.1007/978-3-319-33708-1_11

experience is found only in humans and then only during the process of self-reflection.[1] On the other hand, Nobel Laureate Gerald Edelman puts the cutoff at the level of the lobster, while neuroscientist Stuart Hameroff puts it at the level of the paramecium.

The difficulties entailed by attempts to establish a phylogenetic cutoff for sentience were recognized in the nineteenth century by the mathematician and philosopher William Clifford (1845–1879) who wrote:

> We cannot suppose that so enormous a jump from one creature to another should have occurred at any point in the process of evolution as the introduction of a fact entirely different and absolutely separate from the physical fact. It is impossible for anybody to point out the particular place in the line of descent where that event can be supposed to have taken place.[2]

Equally lacking is any consensus regarding when sentience arises during a baby's development. Is the fetus aware in the third trimester? The second? The first? Nor is there a consensus concerning the point at which brain damage removes sentience from an adult human. Are language-impaired patients sentient? How about those in a vegetative state who have lost all higher function but retain the ability to respond at a low level to external stimuli?

Also unresolved is the question of machine awareness. What would it take to make computers sentient beings? And what about the thought experiment of replacing neurons in a human brain with silicon chips one by one.[3] At what point does sentience go away? Or does it ever go away?

In sum, the accepted idea that subjectivity emerges from complex systems fails to explain either how conscious experience emerges from nonsentient constituents or why it emerges in some systems but not in others. If we are to find a mechanism by which activity in dendritic trees gives rise to vr-conscious experience, we will need to consider alternatives to the received wisdom. The alternative that I wish to propose and defend is the possibility that conscious experience "goes all the way down," that

---

[1] Rolls 2013.

[2] Clifford 1874, p. 38.

[3] Chalmers 1996; Pylyshyn 1980.

it is present in the basic elements of the universe. This is the panpsychist view, the conception that mentality is fundamental and ubiquitous. With *panpsychism* there are no "vacuous" elements, no islands bereft of the stuff of conscious experience. The need to account for cutoffs between conscious and nonconscious things is obviated, and the impulse to postulate new physics in order to explain radically emergent phenomena is quelled.

In what follows, I will try to make the case that a coherent theory of conscious experience can be forged within a panpsychist framework. Before proceeding, it is important that we distinguish between two very different forms of panpsychism, only one of which I believe is relevant to the mind/brain problem. The first form is "atomistic panpsychism," according to which conscious experience is attributed only to the elemental units of physical reality, with no implication that aggregates of these elemental units achieve some sort of combined sentience. The alternative form is "holistic panpsychism," which attributes sentience not only to elemental units but also to aggregates of these units as well.

It is atomistic, not holistic, panpsychism that I am suggesting has relevance for the mind/brain problem. I am not, for instance, attributing sentience to plants, thermostats, or loaves of bread. Nor am I suggesting that the universe as a whole is sentient. Indeed, to do so would invite a "panpsychic explosion" in which experience would be associated not only with all individual elements in nature but with all possible combinations of these elements as well. Instead, I am contending that a parsimonious mind/brain theory can be forged on the premise that the fundamental elements of reality are each independently sentient, and that there is no joining of these independent experiential foci into any sort of aggregate experiences.

Panpsychism in its general form is an ancient doctrine. It was already present in pre-Socratic Greece, as for example in Anaxagoras' (c. 500–425 BC) view that "everything is in everything." In its atomistic form, panpsychism dates back to Leibniz who, in the early eighteenth century, proposed that the world was composed of experiential units called "monads" from which all was constituted. Panpsychist theorizing flourished in the nineteenth century when it was noted that emergence theories clashed with the spirit of the newly formulated theory of evolution. William Clifford noted that "if we accept the doctrine of evolution at all, [then] even in the very lowest organism, even in the Amoeba which swims about in our own blood, there is something or other, inconceivably simple to us, which is of the same nature with our own consciousness.".[4]

In the early twentieth century, the chief exponent of panpsychist theorizing was Alfred North Whitehead (1861–1947) who, like Leibniz, assumed that experiential events made up the world. Aside from the writings of Whitehead, however, little interest was directed toward panpsychism for most of the twentieth century, the rise of behaviorism eclipsing theorizing about conscious experience altogether during the early part of the century.

Panpsychist ideas have made a modest comeback in recent years but, to be clear, it remains at present a minority view and even at times an object of ridicule. The esteemed philosopher John Searle describes panpsychism as an "absurd view" and goes on to write: "There is not the slightest reason to adopt panpsychism, the view that everything in the universe is conscious. Consciousness is above all a biological phenomenon and is as restricted in its biology as the secretion of bile or the digestion of carbohydrates." The philosopher Colin McGinn concurs, calling panpsychism "ludicrous," "a complete myth, a comforting piece of utter balderdash." The philosopher Georges Rey[5] follows suit, quipping that panpsychism "seems about as plausible as a claim that all energy involves lactation, or that quarks are a kind of mammal."

But these are not refutations of panpsychism, they are merely assertions that it is counterintuitive and seemingly implausible. Yet, do we really expect a solution to the mind/brain problem to be otherwise? Science has been built on ideas that seem at first to be counterintuitive and implausible, which is precisely why such ideas are so difficult to uncover. Panpsychism may well be one of these ideas.

Panpsychism nevertheless faces a significant hurdle if it is to help unravel the hard problem of consciousness. It must effectively address the question, "What is it that goes all the way down?" What would it mean to say an electron has conscious experience and what kind of experience would it be? Here again there has been mockery and declarations of

---

[4] Clifford 1874, p. 38.

[5] Rey 2006, p. 110.

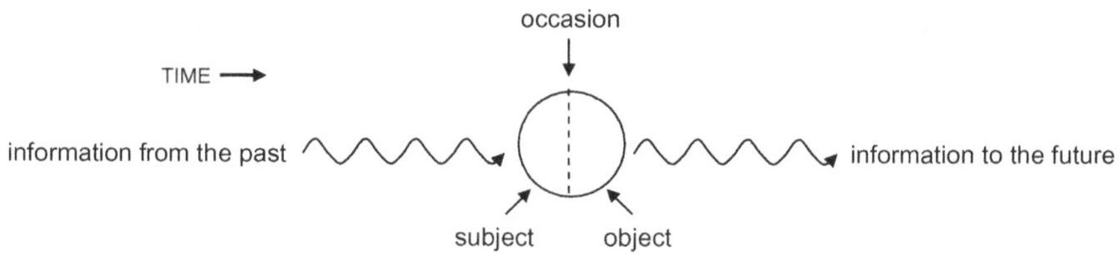

Fig. 11.1 Whitehead's subject/object framework

implausibility. The philosopher William Lycan opines: "If every ultimate particle has mental properties, what sort of mental properties in particular do the particles have? It seems ludicrous to think that a photon has either sensory experience or intentional states. (It does not even have mass.) How could it see, hear or smell anything? And if it has experiential properties, then presumably it also has rudimentary propositional attitudes. What would be the contents of its beliefs or desires? Perhaps it wishes it were a μ quark."[6] Similarly, the philosopher David Rosenthal writes: "The ultimates that physics describes seem in any case poorly suited to be bearers of experiential features, however primitive or elemental. Indeed, it is arguably harder to see how such ultimates could have intrinsically experiential features than to see, even at our current stage of empirical and theoretical knowledge, how ordinary conscious experiences might emerge from neurophysiological function.".[7]

In response, I offer the specific thesis that what "goes all the way down" is subject/object duality. This was Whitehead's view (Fig. 11.1).[8] The universe, according to Whitehead, is composed entirely of sentient "occasions" and their interrelations, with each sentient occasion constituting a single "throb" of conscious experience. Sentient occasions are both subjects and objects, the difference depending on the relationship being considered. In relation to the past, a sentient occasion is a subject that, in effect, "observes," "perceives," or, in Whitehead's terminology, "prehends" information from previous sentient occasions. In relation to the future,

[6] Lycan 2006, p. 70.
[7] Rosenthal 2006, p. 123.
[8] Klose 2007; Whitehead 1933.

a sentient occasion is an object that emits information to be "observed" or "perceived" by future sentient occasions. When defined in this way, subject/object duality becomes a coherent notion that could potentially apply all the way up and all the way down.

Quantum Mechanics and the Hard Problem

How can we apply these philosophical considerations to the neuroscience of single neurons? To answer this question, we need to take the additional step of identifying a scientific correlate to Whitehead's panpsychic formulation. To do this, we will need to employ science that is up to date. Since panpsychism is a theory that "goes all the way down," we will need science that likewise "goes all the way down." This means that we must move past Newtonian physics, which is valid only at macroscopic scales, and look to quantum mechanics, which is valid at all scales. Accordingly, we now embark on a brief sojourn into the quantum world.

Before proceeding, it is only fair to explain to the reader that our endeavor will not be looked upon favorably by the current scientific establishment. The suggestion that quantum mechanics is needed to explain conscious experience in scientific terms in fact usually evokes a smirk or a sneer from many in the field, particularly from philosophical emergentists who contend that sentience is strictly a macroscopic affair. The expectation held by this group is that conscious experience will eventually be explained wholly in terms of macroscopic processes obeying Newton's laws, and that "fancy" quantum effects are irrelevant.[9] They contend that arguments in favor of quantum mechanical involvement amount to no more than metaphorical invocations of quantum oddities such as entanglement and wave particle duality, without a substantive theory to back them up. Efforts to link consciousness to quantum mechanics, they sardonically opine, are merely attempts to "explain one mystery in terms of another" or, as David Chalmers' puts it, to satisfy the "law of minimization of mystery."

[9] Pessoa 2001; Crick 1990.

Actually, I have no quibble with this latter indictment, only I would call it the "law of parsimony" rather than the law of minimization of mystery. Quantum mind theories do try to find unitary explanations for multiple phenomena, and this is not necessarily a bad thing. It was precisely this maneuver that Newton applied when he linked celestial motion with the proverbial falling of an apple from a tree, explaining both in terms of the mystery of gravity. Einstein used the same maneuver to develop general relativity when he invoked his "equivalency principle," linking noninertial motion with gravity by interpreting both in terms of the mysterious curvature of space-time.

I would suggest that this maneuver may prove profitable once again, this time by equating subjective experience to a central aspect of quantum theory. To see how this might work, we start with a rudimentary synopsis of quantum theory.

Schroedinger's Equation and the Collapse Postulate

In 1687, long before the dawn of quantum theory, Isaac Newton (1643–1727) published his Philosophiae Naturalis Principia Mathematica, in which he proposed a set of principles that dominated the scientific worldview for two centuries. At the center of the theory were Newton's laws, which described the evolution of physical systems over time. In the Newtonian world, if you know the state of a system of particles (that is, if you know the position and momentum of each particle in the system) at one point in time, and if you also know the forces to which the system of particles is subject, then you can use Newton's laws (supplemented by Maxwell's equations) to calculate the precise state of the system at any other point in time, both past and future.

The Newtonian framework was straightforward and provided what seemed to be a satisfactory model of the physical world. The framework began to unravel, however, when in the early twentieth century several observed phenomena (the ultraviolet catastrophe, the discrete nature of spectral lines, and the photoelectric effect) were found to be inconsistent with the Newtonian picture. A breakthrough occurred when it was recognized by Max Plank (1858–1947), Albert Einstein (1859–1955), and Niels Bohr (1885–1962), that by making one simple, yet entirely unexpected assumption, all the problematic phenomena could be accounted for mathematically. The simple assumption was that energy could only be emitted or absorbed in discrete amounts, which they called quanta. Why this was so was unknown at that point. And another problem had arisen as well: the enigmatic observation that light sometimes acted like a wave and at other times it acted like a particle.

It took two decades for a mathematical formulation to be developed by Erwin Schroedinger (1887–1961), Werner Heisenberg (1901–1976), and others that could account for both the quantization of energy exchange and the wave/particle duality of light. This new mathematical formulation was called quantum mechanics. In a nutshell, a two-step procedure was proposed:

1. *Schroedinger's Equation*: In the first step, an equation devised by Schroedinger is used to follow the evolution of a system over time. The way this works is that you feed the system's initial values into Schroedinger's equation, then add in the forces acting on the system, and what you get back is a *wavefunction* that specifies the state of the system at any previous or subsequent time.

The procedure is similar to the one used in Newtonian physics but with one huge difference. Whereas Newton's laws produce an output that specifies a unique state of the system at each moment in time, Schroedinger's equation produces an output that specifies only a "menu of possibilities" for the system at each moment in time, with a probability weighting assigned to each possibility.

For example, suppose you know the location of a particle at one moment in time and you want to know what its location will be at some later time. You would proceed by plugging the initial location into Schroedinger's equation, add in the forces to which the particle is subject, and use the equation to calculate the particle's location at the later time. What you would get at the later time is not the designation of a specific location of the particle, as you would with Newton's laws, but a menu of possible locations where the particle might be found, together with a probability weighting assigned to each possible location.

2. *The Collapse Postulate*: A vital issue remains. If Schroedinger's equation yields only a menu of possibilities, it can offer only an incomplete rendering of reality. After all, we live in a world where specific things actually happen, not in a world where possibilities abound but nothing actually occurs.

To make quantum mechanics complete, it is necessary to postulate that a second process, called *the collapse of the wavefunction*, operates on the menu of possibilities with the result that one of the possibilities is selected and the rest are discarded. This second process operates under laws that are separate from Schroedinger's equation and are deemed unknowable and inherently unpredictable. Any and all attempts to understand why one possibility is chosen over another always yields the same conclusion: the choice, beyond the probability weightings, is inherently random.

This two-step procedure resolved the problems that had plagued Newtonian physics. For one thing, the solutions to Schroedinger's equation displayed exactly the kind of quantized behavior intuited by Plank, Einstein, and Bohr. Additionally, the collapse postulate explained why entities acted like a wave in some ways and like a particle in others: wave-like behavior was evident in the mathematics of Schroedinger's equation, while particle-like behavior was manifest in the collapse of the wavefunction.

Quantum mechanics has been a spectacularly successful theory, one that has handled all new observations that have come its way and has done so with unparalleled precision. The interpretation of quantum mechanics is another matter, with the meanings of the two steps being a matter of dispute. Particularly vexing has been the second step, the collapse postulate, which has unknowability and unpredictability at its core. It was precisely this step that irked Einstein, prompting him to famously quip, "God doesn't play dice." Heroic efforts have been directed towards trying to improve on the second step or even eliminating it altogether, so far to no avail.

Quantum Collapse and Reality: The Whitehead/Heisenberg Picture

Given these quantum mechanics basics, we now look at the possible relevance of the theory to the mind/brain problem. The key is in the act of observation. In the earliest and still most widely accepted interpretation of quantum mechanics, the *Copenhagen interpretation* put forth by Bohr, Heisenberg, and others in the 1920s, observation is central to the theory. Put simply, it is the act of observation itself that collapses the wavefunction. In Heisenberg's version of the Copenhagen interpretation, Schroedinger's equation yields only "potentialities" while acts of observation yield "actualities," or *quantum events*. Quantum events are taken to be the actual things in nature and collectively account for the full extent of reality.[10] Thus, if the proverbial tree were to fall in the forest without anyone there to hear it, the falling would not be observed and it therefore could not be said to have really occurred.

At the microscopic scale, the Heisenberg picture joins seamlessly with Whitehead's panpsychist subject/object philosophy.[11] Heisenberg's quantum events can be equated with Whitehead's sentient occasions, each quantum event being construed as either a subject or an object depending on its relationship with other quantum events: it is a subject with respect to prior quantum events but an object with respect to subsequent quantum events. The content of each sentient quantum event is determined by the two-step quantum mechanical procedure: a menu of possibilities is offered by Schroedinger's equation; wavefunction collapse selects one of the possibilities and discards the rest. The resulting framework weaves conscious experience directly into the causal chain of real events.

Figure 11.2 illustrates the causal relationships of successive events in the Whitehead/Heisenberg picture. We see that quantum event A (produced by a previous wavefunction collapse, not shown) creates a Schroedinger menu of possibilities (menu A) that emanates forward in time (as prescribed by Schroedinger's equation). Quantum event B is created by a

[10] Stapp 1993.

[11] Klose 2007; Haag 2004; Shimony 1997; Stapp 1993.

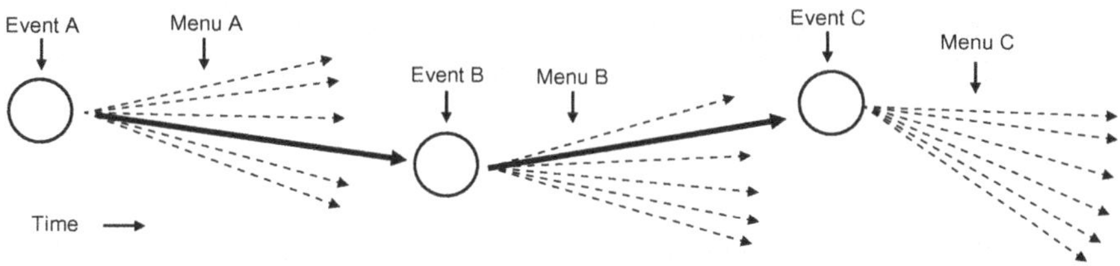

Fig. 11.2 Whitehead/Heisenberg framework

collapse of menu A, yielding a new menu of possibilities (menu B) that emanates forward in time. Quantum event C is then created by a collapse of menu B, and so on. If we focus on quantum event B, the duality of conscious experience is laid bare: quantum event B serves as a conscious subject relative to quantum event A but as a physical object relative to quantum event C.

The Whitehead/Heisenberg worldview gives an accounting of reality in which subject/object duality is entwined within its very fabric. Indeed, if all we were concerned about was explaining the workings of the universe at the microscopic level, the deed would be done. An obstacle remains, however. An explanation must still be given for how microscopic sentient quantum events might combine to yield macroscopic sentient entities, such as human brains.

The Combination Problem

The difficulty of accounting for macroscopic conscious experience on the basis of microscopic sentient units has been dubbed the "*combination problem*" by William Seager who rates it as the most serious problem facing any atomistic panpsychist theory of consciousness.[12] The trouble stems from the lack of any known mechanism by which independent sentient units might merge. William James addressed this issue more than a century ago with his well-known metaphor:

---

[12] Seager 2001.

> Take a sentence of a dozen words, and take twelve men and tell to each one word. Then stand the men in a row or jam them in a bunch, and let each think of his word intently as he will; nowhere will there be a consciousness of the whole sentence.[13]

James regarded the suggestion that units of experience might merge into higher forms of experience as "logically unintelligible." Many others have voiced a similar opinion.[14] For microscopic sentient events to combine and form macroscopic sentient events, they argue, some new kind of physics would be needed, but none is on offer, not even in principle.

Alternatively, one could propose that gigantic brain-wide quantum events are responsible for macroscopic conscious experience. This is the approach taken by theoretical physicist Roger Penrose and neuroscientist Stuart Hameroff in formulating their "Orchestrated Objective Reduction" theory of consciousness. Proponents of this approach must, however, overcome the objection that brain-wide quantum events are exceedingly implausible because, except under exceptional conditions not likely to be present in the brain, such gigantic quantum events are quite unlikely to form.

This leaves us in a quandary. If we decide against the possibility that the human brain incorporates gigantic quantum events into its functioning, and also reject the possibility of microscopic quantum events combining into larger quantum events, we are left with no apparent means of dealing with the combination problem. And without a solution to the combination problem, atomistic panpsychism is no better than emergentism in accounting for macroscopic conscious experience.

Which leads us to the approach I am advocating in this book, an approach that eliminates the need for postulating gigantic quantum events or for supposing that small quantum events combine into larger ones. To illustrate how this approach would work, I will now briefly present a specific, albeit speculative, quantum mechanical mechanism by which vr-conscious experience might arise in dendrites. After presenting the model, I will show how it can serve to alleviate the combination problem.

---

[13] James 1890.

[14] Goff 2006; Carruthers 2006; Macpherson 2006; McGinn 2006.

Quantum Mechanics and Dendritic Processing

Evidence of quantum mechanical involvement in biological processes has proliferated in recent years. Quantum mechanisms have been proposed for photosynthesis,[15] avian magnetoreception,[16] and olfactory perception.[17] Instances of quantum coherence,[18] in which particles act like waves, has taken the form of quantum tunneling,[19] quantum beating,[20] and other like phenomena.[21]

The involvement of quantum mechanics in conscious experience remains more tentative. The most discussed possibility is that quantum consciousness may arise in microtubules,[22] which are cylindrical transport channels found in all cells. Hameroff and Penrose have spearheaded a research effort aimed at uncovering a microtubule-based quantum mechanical process that could underlie conscious experience.[23] As I have noted, however, their formulation invokes vr-NCCs spanning distances beyond the usual quantum mechanical domain. Additionally, they have not offered a clear accounting of how the quantum mechanical effects would interface with the known neurobiology of cortical and subcortical brain function.

Here, I explore an alternative possibility that quantum mechanical effects relevant to vr-NCCs might inhere in synaptic activation patterns in the basal dendrites of L5 pyramidal neurons in the left VL-PFC. This mechanism, which has been advocated independently by Jonathan Edwards,[24] focuses specifically on vibratory activity present in dendritic membranes. I will provide only a sketch of the mechanism, which must be considered tentative given the primitive state of our current nanophysics knowledge.

---

[15] Chenu 2015.

[16] Gauger 2011.

[17] Brookes 2012.

[18] Salari 2011.

[19] Nagel 2010.

[20] Engel 2007.

[21] Fleming 2011.

[22] Johnson 2012.

[23] Hameroff 2014.

[24] Edwards 2005.

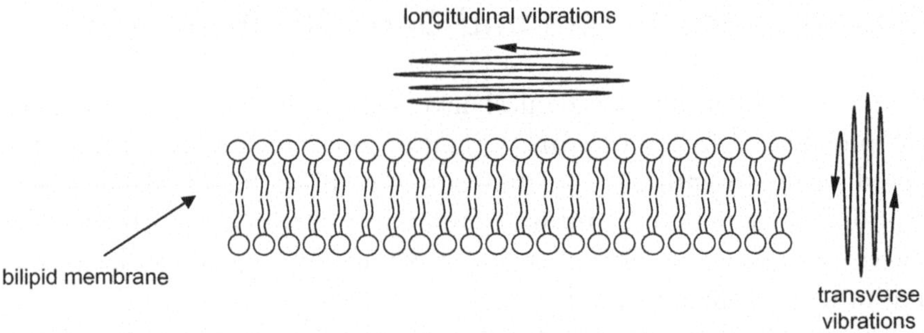

Fig. 11.3 High energy transverse vibratory modes and low energy longitudinal vibratory modes in the dendritic bilipid membrane

The endeavor will, however, illustrate the form a single-neuron quantum mechanical model might take.

The scheme derives from a suggestion made in 1968 by the German-born theoretical solid-state physicist Herbert Frohlich (1905–1991), one of the pioneers in the study of superconductivity.[25] In his analysis, Frohlich focused on vibratory activity in biologic membranes. As illustrated in Fig. 11.3, biologic membranes are composed of well-organized lipid layers. Like all molecular structures, the membranes are in constant oscillatory motion. These consist of 10^{11} cycles/second vibrations in two modes: a high energy transverse mode driven by transmembrane electrical forces and a low energy longitudinal mode driven by long-range intermolecular forces. As applied to dendrites, Frohlich's theory supposes an energy transfer from activated membrane receptor proteins to the two membrane vibratory modes—first into the high energy transverse modes and then into the low energy longitudinal modes.

Frohlich modeled the vibratory activity of the membranes quantum mechanically with the energy being quantized into discrete levels. His analysis indicated that all of the vibratory activity in the membrane would coalesce into a single low energy longitudinal vibratory mode, rather than being dispersed into the surrounding random heat bath of the membrane.[26] He suggested that this coalescence would be similar to

[25] Frohlich 1968.

[26] Lockwood 1989; Bolterauer 1989.

a phenomenon first proposed by Bose and Einstein in 1924 and referred to as *Bose-Einstein condensation* (BEC). With BEC, large numbers of particles in a single quantum state act coherently as a single unit. BEC is the basis for superconductivity and superfluidity, which occur only at temperatures near absolute zero, and also for lasers, which operate at room temperature. Frohlich's proposal involved a BEC-like condensation similar to that in lasers.

Frohlich's proposal has been actively debated, with its validity still not certain.[27] If we assume for the sake of argument that it is valid, a mechanism can be envisioned in which quantum events corresponding to vr-conscious experience are produced. The key to the proposed mechanism is the emission of electromagnetic energy from the membranes in the form of photons (quanta of electromagnetic energy) that are perfectly in phase and that would have a wavelength of 10–100 microns. This wavelength would be just the right size for the photons to extend across a pool of synapses in a dendritic branch. The photons would thereby instantiate spatial patterns that reflect the synaptic activation patterns in the dendritic branch. The BEC-like phenomenon would serve as a biological amplifier, converting otherwise weak signals into powerful coherent ones.[28] The entire mechanism would be expected to contribute to the supralinear summation of EPSPs needed to generate NMDA spikes in distal dendritic branches, making it a favored target for natural selection.

In sum, this adaptation of Frohlich's model provides for a specific, although hypothetical, mechanism by which vr-NCCs take the form of photons emitted by the vibrating membranes. The emergence of each photon would constitute a quantum event that would serve as a vr-NCC for a vr-conscious experience, with the spatial pattern of the quantum event correlating precisely with the content of a vr-conscious experience. Of course, the sketch presented here would need to be fleshed out, with attention paid to the mechanism of energy transfer from proteins to the membranes, to the plausibility of BEC-like condensation, and to the exact nature and impact of photonic emissions. Importantly, it is likely that the model will be testable in the coming years as our understanding

[27] Acbas 2014; Reimers 2014.

[28] Marshall 1989; Lockwood 1989.

of supralinear summation of dendritic PSPs matures. In any event, the proposal provides an illustrative example of how quantum events might serve as the physical substrate for vr-conscious experiences.

Frohlich vs. Routine Quantum Events

Given this proposed quantum mechanical mechanism, we can now revisit the combination problem. The solution to the combination problem that becomes possible with the single-neuron theory is based on the proposition that all that exists are individual quantum events that do not combine. The impression that they do combine is an illusion that is perpetrated by the exquisite organization to which the individual quantum events are subject.

To see how this works, we start with the overall picture of a universe populated entirely by quantum events that are both subjects and objects and are therefore sentient. Each quantum event is uniquely characterized by its informational content. For most quantum events, such as those associated with electrons and quarks and other particles that make up the universe, the information content is extremely limited, reflecting only the happenings in the immediate environment: the pull of a nucleus, the repulsion of a neighboring electron, and so on. On the other hand, for certain quantum events in the dendrites of neurons, let's call them *Frohlich events*, the information content reflects not the local environment but the happenings in the far off macroscopic world. The Frohlich events are rare, comprising only a miniscule fraction of the quantum events that make up the dendrites, but their coordinated behavior is able to impact the macroscopic world to a far greater degree than their numbers would suggest. On the input side, the brain acts like a funnel that channels incoming stimuli from the macroscopic world into the dendrites of individual neurons and then into sentient Frohlich events. On the output side, the brain acts like a megaphone, amplifying the effects of the sentient Frohlich events, leading ultimately to observable behavior in the macroscopic world.

The reason that brains are considered conscious while other objects are not is due to the manner in which the individual quantum events are assembled. In general, two types of assembly are possible. The first type, *random assembly*, is that which produces completely nonsentient macroscopic objects, such as plants and chairs. With such assemblies, the constituent quantum events are arrayed haphazardly, the information associated with individual events being averaged out over the large spatial scales. The experiences and actions of constituent quantum events reflect only the goings-on in their immediate microscopic neighborhoods.

The second type of assembly, *coherent assembly*, is uniquely present in brains. Here an exquisite arrangement renders the experiences and actions of the Frohlich events linked not to the local neighborhood but to the larger world. The Frohlich events, although small in number, are able, through amplification provided by Bose–Einstein-like condensation, supralinear summation, NMDA spikes, and redundant activity across populations of neurons, to measurably affect macroscopic behavior. Coherent assemblies appear to be sentient, although in fact they are not. I will refer to their status as *pseudosentient*. According to this formulation, the distinction between "conscious" and "nonconscious" macroscopic objects is the difference between pseudosentience and absence of pseudosentience, not the difference between conscious experience and the absence of conscious experience. And by eliminating the need to explain macroscopic sentience, Seager's combination problem is averted.

The distinction between nonsentient and pseudosentient assemblies also provides a basis for responding to a question posed by Francis Crick (1998a, p. 97):

> We can state bluntly the major question that neuroscience must first answer. It is probable that at any moment some active neuronal processes in your head correlate with consciousness, while others do not: *what is the difference between them*?

With the approach I am advocating, Crick's question is reformulated as, how are neuronal processes that are pseudosentient different from those that are nonsentient? The answer we arrive at is that the difference between the two processes is one of organization, not of the presence or absence of conscious experience.

An objection I often encounter is how is it possible that a pool of neurons, each independently having the same experience, can coordinate their outputs so as to produce coherent macroscopic behavior without merging their experiences and without communicating their intentions to each other. I offer the following analogy to illustrate how this can happen. In 1999, an event was staged in which Gary Kasparov, the then reigning world chess champion, played a game of chess with "the world" over the Internet. Thousands of chessplayers participated. Each player was hooked into a central node through which they each received Kasparov's moves and were each able to submit their own replies. Moves selected by the largest number of respondents were chosen as "the world's" replies. The resulting game (which Kasparov won) was of unexpectedly high quality. From Kasparov's point of view, he was playing a single strong opponent whose moves included both short-term tactical and long-term strategic motifs. In fact, he was playing a population of chessplayers, each individually and separately perceiving the chess position and each individually and separately issuing responses. We note that in this setup, the outputs were summed but the individual experiences did not merge nor did the chess players coordinate their responses with one another.

Pseudosentience Associated with Verbal Report

In the analysis so far I have restricted the focus to vr-conscious experience and vr-pseudosentience. The focus has, accordingly, been on the activities of dendrites and neurons in the left ventrolateral PFC. We now broaden the discussion to include forms of pseudosentience that are not of the verbally reportable variety. There are at least two such forms of pseudosentience in human brains. First, there is the pseudosentience present in the right hemisphere. The dendrites of L5 pyramidal neurons in right VL-PFC presumably contain Frohlich events that function the same way as their colleagues in the left VL-PFC do, the important difference being that they are not directly connected to language mechanisms. These Frohlich events would lead to a nonverbal form of pseudosentience characteristic of the right hemispheres of split-brain patients.

Second, there is the pseudosentience present in subcortical brain regions. The type of pseudosentience in these regions is what Damasio calls "core consciousness"[29] and what Edelman calls "primary consciousness."[30] It is characterized by a primitive awareness of the self and its environment, in conjunction with a simple form of short-term memory. It is the type of pseudosentience that characterizes low-level non-human species, is evident in human infants, and is observable in human adults following extensive damage to the cerebral cortices. The theory I have presented readily incorporates these forms of "consciousness" within the rubric of pseudosentience.

In summary, then, we have seen in this chapter that a coherent theory of conscious experience can be fashioned around a panpsychist philosophy and a quantum mechanical mechanism for sentience at the microscopic level. In the next chapter, we will explore some of the implications of this theory.

[29] Damasio 1998.

[30] Edelman 2003.

12

Reflections and Ramifications

Duality

Having laid out the panpsychic argument that conscious experience "goes all the way down," we can now ponder some of its implications. For one thing, there is the simplification made possible by the fact that the mental/physical duality is pervasive. With the received view, the situation is complex, with the existence of entities that are subject/object dyads as well as entities that are just objects. With the panpsychic view, the situation is simple, with all entities being subject/object dyads. This raises the question: What is the nature of the two components? On the mental side we have our phenomenal experiences, referred to as "qualia." These consist of the colors, sounds, smells, and other experiences that fill up our lives. But what of the physical world on the other side of the duality? What is its nature? Arguably, it is ultimately mathematical,[1] no more and no less. This is Roger Penrose's view:

> What substance does this "reality" that we see about us actually have? What, after all, is the real table that I am now sitting at actually composed of? It is made of wood, yes, but what is wood made of? Well, fibres that were

[1] Penrose 2006.

S. Sevush, *The Single-Neuron Theory*,
DOI 10.1007/978-3-319-33708-1_12

> once living cells. And these? Molecules that are composed of individual atoms. And the atoms? They have their nuclei, built from protons and neutrons and glued together by strong nuclear forces; these nuclei are orbited by electrons, held in by the considerably weaker electromagnetic forces. Going deeper, protons and neutrons are to be thought of as composed of more elementary ingredients, quarks, held together by further entities called gluons. Just what are electrons, quarks and so on, though? The best we can do at this stage is simply to refer to the mathematical equations that they satisfy, which for electrons and quarks would be the Dirac equation. What distinguishes a quark from an electron would be their very different masses and the fact that quarks indulge in interactions—namely the "strong" interactions—that electrons are blind to. What, then, are gluons? They are "gauge" particles that mediate the strong force—which is again a notion that can only be understood in terms of the mathematics used to describe them.[2]

In any case, the remarkable feature of the two poles of the mental/physical duality is that they are in tight correspondence. The relationship in fact appears to take the form of an *isomorphism*. As applied to mental/physical duality, an isomorphism is a mapping with the properties that: (1) for each mental event there is exactly one physical event; (2) for each physical event there is exactly one mental event; and (3) the structure of the set of mental events matches the structure of the set of physical events. We note that what makes the isomorphic relationship plausible is the ubiquity of mental/physical duality. If there were entities in existence that were either only mental or only physical, then the notion of an isomorphic relationship would not be applicable.

If the mental/physical connection is in fact an isomorphism, we can anticipate that we will someday be able to construct a "mind/brain codebook" by which we could translate every mental event into a physical event and vice versa. Would this mean that we might be able to answer the age-old question: "Is the blue that I see the same as the blue that you see?" Perhaps not. Psychologist Stephen Palmer proposes that there is an "isomorphic constraint"[3] present in the mental/physical connection that puts a limit on

[2] Penrose 2006, p. 4.

[3] Palmer 1999.

what is included in the relationship. The isomorphic nature of the connection stipulates only that patterns in the mental world match patterns in the physical world. It does not speak to the absolute nature of the mental and the physical worlds themselves. Thus, a "subjectivity barrier" would remain that would deny us insight into the nature of the events themselves. To know how a bat sees the world would still require that we be a bat.

Choice

What about choice ("free will")? Choice can be considered as a second "hard problem" that supplements the hard problem of subjective experience. Is choice even possible? In 1814, the French physicist and mathematician Pierre-Simon Laplace famously asserted that it was not:

"We may regard the present state of the universe as the effect of its past and the cause of its future. An intellect which at any given moment knew all of the forces that animate nature and the mutual positions of the beings that compose it, if this intellect were vast enough to submit the data to analysis, could condense into a single formula the movement of the greatest bodies of the universe and that of the lightest atom; for such an intellect nothing could be uncertain and the future just like the past would be present before its eyes".

Laplace was expressing an opinion steeped in a Newtonian worldview. Since the advent of quantum mechanics the situation has changed. Quantum mechanics incorporates an indeterminate component into the universe that could conceivably allow for the presence of true choice. Quantum mechanics is, however, usually rejected as a way out of determinism in the everyday macroscopic world because quantum mechanical phenomena are thought to be "washed out" at macroscopic time and distance scales.[4] If, however, the single-neuron theory is right, we as sentient beings reside not in the macroscopic world but in the microscopic world in which quantum uncertainty prevails. It is quantum mechanical choice that in fact gives rise to our very existence as quantum events. It is sobering to reflect that the act of choice that determines our existence

[4] Grush 1995.

is beyond any known law of nature, other than conforming to a probability distribution dictated by Schroedinger's equation. Our existence as sentient beings is therefore the product of a process of which we can have no knowledge, a conclusion with a curiously spiritual feel.

The Self

The theory I am proposing has implications for who and what we are. First of all, we are very tiny and don't exist for very long. Our small size is counterintuitive, given that our common sense portrays us as unequivocally macroscopic. The idea that we are no more than quantum events arising within dendritic branches seems preposterous. But recall that until the ancient Greeks opined on the matter, common sense led people to believe that their conscious self was associated with their whole body. It took a conceptual leap by the ancient Greeks to hypothesize that sentience was localized to the brain. What is needed now is another leap, a big one perhaps, but no different in principle from the one made by the ancient Greeks.

As for the duration of our existence, the single-neuron theory as presented would have us existing only as long as the quantum event to which we are attached exists, which is a very short duration indeed. The idea that we live for only a quantum moment is somewhat jarring. It is not a new idea, however, nor is it unique to the single-neuron theory. The opinion that we exist as a sequence of consecutive selves, each existing for only a short interval, is, for example, a tenet of Buddhism. And in the eighteenth century, David Hume famously opined that conscious experience is discontinuous over time. His contention was that the mind was "nothing but a bundle or collection of different perceptions, which succeed each other with an inconceivable rapidity, and are in perpetual flux and movement."[5] While the issue remains in debate, most people who have written on the subject over the years have favored the view that conscious experiences are temporally discrete.[6]

The duration of an episode of conscious experience is at this time a matter of conjecture but is likely to be at least shorter than 50 ms since

[5] Hume 1739.

[6] Hameroff 2014; Bodovitz 2008; Crick 2003; Garver 1880; Spence 1879.

we are able to distinguish events in real time that are separated by the "flicker fusion frequency" of about 20/second. The actual duration of our existence is likely of much shorter duration. Packed into this short interval would have to be all the perceptions, memories, and feelings that go into a given conscious experience, with individual conscious experiences lined up like a string of pearls. The world would, in effect, be experienced as a series of snap shots.

An interesting implication of the single-neuron theory is that, while it makes a fundamental distinction between our microscopic sentient selves and the macroscopic pseudosentient self to which they give rise, there really is no logical justification for favoring our pseudosentient self over any other nonsentient entity. As William James put it:

> *In its widest possible sense*, however, *a man's Self is the sum total of all that he* CAN *call his*, not only his body and his psychic powers, but his clothes and his house, his wife and children, his ancestors and friends, his reputation and works, his lands and horses, and yacht and bank-account. All these things give him the same emotions. If they wax and prosper, he feels triumphant; if they dwindle and die away, he feels cast down,—not necessarily in the same degree for each thing, but in much the same way for all.[7]

We note that there is a limit on how well we can know our own sentient self. Because of the physics of the situation, any attempts to directly observe one's sentient self will consistently be met with failure. The best we can do is observe our sentient self from a moment ago and then only as an object in the past. Similarly, perception of the present moment is not possible. James captured the frustration of trying to perceive the present moment when he wrote:

> Let any one try, I will not say to arrest, but to notice or attend to, the present moment of time. One of the most baffling experiences occurs. Where is it, this present? It has melted in our grasp, fled ere we could touch it, gone in the instant of becoming...Reflection leads us to the conclusion that it must exist, but that it does exist can never be a fact of our immediate experience.[8]

[7] James 1890, p. 292.

[8] James 1890, p. 608.

Instead of observation of the present moment, all we have is a vision of its lingering echo, what ER Clay called the "specious present."

If we cannot perceive the present moment, then memory becomes central to who we are. Suppose memory were not present in the system. What would be the implication? As James noted, if each moment of sentience were totally independent of all others, "our consciousness would be like a glow-worm spark, illuminating the point it immediately covered, but leaving all beyond in total darkness."

Implications for Physics

There are some intriguing implications of the single-neuron theory for physics. One has to do with string theory and a phenomenon called T-duality. In string theory, which is currently a prevalent theory in physics, the elemental units of reality are strings. The strings are unfathomably tiny cylindrical structures of radius 10^{-34} meters. What, we may ask, are strings made of? What is inside of the cylinder? A stunning finding is that what is inside of the cylinder is no more and no less than what is outside the cylinder. That is, if you approach a string from the outside, reach its surface, and then pass inside, what you find is that the mathematics of the world inside the string is precisely the same as the mathematics of the world outside the string. This is known as T-duality. An interesting side point is that all of the information present in the world outside the string, or all of the information present in the world inside the string, can be encoded in its entirety on the surface of the string. As a result, reality can be economically described as an information surface with two perspectives, one inside and the other outside.

T-duality raises interesting possibilities in relation to the single-neuron theory. Specifically, in view of the plausibly isomorphic nature of the mental/physical relationship, it becomes possible to regard mental/physical duality as a form of T-duality. That is, we can regard the mathematics of the world outside a quantum event as the physical world and the mathematics of the world inside a quantum event as the mental world, with an exact correspondence between the two. Intriguingly, the information content of either of these worlds would be contained on the surface that separates the inside of the quantum event from the outside. And if you want to really stretch your imagination, try considering that the inside and outside perspectives can trade places with no change in the mathematics. So we can think of ourselves equally well as either inside or outside! Clearly, something is wrong with our simplistic conceptions of spatial dimensions, a point that is central to string theory.

Another implication for physics of the single-neuron theory has to do with general relativity. If every quantum event is an instance of conscious experience, then Einstein's "equivalency principle" might be profitably applied. In developing his theory of relativity, Einstein argued that, since Maxwell's laws of electromagnetism (the mathematics of which includes the speed of light) appear to remain valid regardless of reference frame, then the speed of light must be a constant and space and time must be relative. Along the same lines, an equivalency principle might apply in the mind/brain arena. Specifically, might we invoke an equivalency principle that insists that mental experiences, together with their corresponding quantum events, remain invariant, regardless of the reference frame from which they are observed?

Space, time, quantum events, and mental experiences—what strange bedfellows! Sprinkle in a little quantum gravity and who knows?

So Where Is the Red?

Our mind/brain odyssey has taken us from the macroscopic to the ultramicroscopic in our search for the NCC. Along the way we have identified features of brain function that weave together to form a logical theory of conscious experience. Let's review what we have gleaned from the journey. We began with the philosophical argument that there is a mind/brain duality present and that aspect dualism is the only way to reconcile the dualism with modern science. We then embarked on a search for the physical component of the duality, the NCC. At the macroscopic level, we addressed the question of whether a directed modular pathway model most effectively captured the nature of cortical functioning. Although the alternative, that cortical function is fundamentally omnidirectional, would have lent itself to single-neuron modeling just as well as directed modular pathways do, it appears that natural selection has favored the directed modular pathway arrangement.

We then reviewed the evidence gained from the split-brain research paradigm that pointed to the presence of at least two separate experiential domains, one in the left hemisphere and one in the right. In view of this multiplicity of conscious experiences, we adopted a strategy of focusing on vr-conscious experience, the kind of conscious experience that is mediated by the left hemisphere and that is involved in philosophical discussions of the mind/brain problem. We then reviewed evidence that favored the VL-PFC as the locus of vr-conscious experience within the left hemisphere.

Next, we shifted the discussion from the macroscopic to the microscopic domain. We examined neuronal networks and neuronal representations, observing that vr-conscious experience is represented repeatedly along directed modular pathways with ever increasing explicitness. We noted that the representations for vr-conscious experience are sparse and at certain points holographically distributed. We then reviewed the arguments favoring a localization of the vr-NCC to the basal dendrites of L5 pyramidal neurons in the left VL-PFC. At this point, I offered the hypothesis that the content of vr-conscious experience correlates with the spatial patterns of synaptic activation in the basal dendrites of L5 pyramidal neurons. I reviewed the evidence that the complexity and variety of synaptic activation patterns can comfortably match that of vr-conscious experience. Additionally, I presented a mechanism by which the information contained in the spatial synaptic activation patterns could, without degradation, be projected back out to the neuronal network. The mechanism involved supralinear summation of synaptic PSPs, NMDA dendritic spike generation, recruitment of multiple output neurons that redundantly process the same information, and the presence of persistence memory in the synapses of the dendrites.

Finally, I presented a sketch of a quantum mechanical mechanism involving membrane vibrations, BE-like condensation, and photon emissions that constitute quantum events that could serve as the direct neural correlate for vr-conscious experience. I presented the sketch in the context of a panpsychist framework in which every quantum event making up the universe is both a subject and an object, and in which quantum events can aggregate but cannot combine. I then drew the distinction between true sentience at the quantum level and pseudosentience at the macroscopic level formed from coherent aggregates of sentient quantum events. I drew the distinction, as well, between left hemisphere pseudosentience, right hemisphere pseudosentience, and the vegetative pseudosentience associated subcortical structures.

What a journey! The search for a mind/brain theory has taken us through multiple spatial domains and several scientific disciplines. I've dubbed the overarching conjecture the "single-neuron theory" to emphasize the localization of the NCC to within individual neurons. It should be understood, however, that the single neurons come in multiple copies and that the NCC is confined to the basal dendrites within the neurons, not the neurons as a whole. No doubt, the theory stands in opposition to the conception of holistic macroscopic sentience invoked by the received view that the brain as a whole is sentient, and by the Eastern view that the universe as a whole is sentient. The theory is nevertheless testable with technology that is currently available or that will be so in the coming years.[9]

And so we return to the question with which we began: When you gaze at a red rose, where is the red? If the theory I am advocating is correct, the red is localized within the basal dendrites of certain pyramidal neurons and there are many such neurons having the same "red" experience. The simultaneous action of these neurons affects macroscopic behavior and gives the illusion of a single conscious experience of red being had by the whole brain.

This is only part of the answer, however. The full response brings us to the quantum sphere, where the hard problem of consciousness corresponds to certain hard problems of contemporary physics. The question of where the red is located begs the question of where any quantum event is located, and this is not completely known at this time. Nor is the answer to the question of whether the collapse of the wavefunction is a real process that may require new physics yet to be discovered.[10] And, importantly,

---

[9] Chen 2011a.

[10] Penrose 1989.

there is the unanswered question of whether collapse is truly a matter of chance, or is merely reflective of our current ignorance of a deeper theory.

My own preference is to regard the incorporation of chance into quantum mechanics as inherent to the system. I feel comfortable considering it a final limitation on what we can know, cast in mathematical terms. The way I see it, my own journey of self discovery has led me to the edge of the known world, beyond which is rank uncertainty. I know what Schroedinger's equation allows but I accept that the rest is intrinsically unknowable. And after a lifetime spent in pursuit of truth, I feel strangely at ease with this conclusion.

Bibliography

Abeles M. Corticonics: neural circuits of the cerebral cortex. Cambridge: Cambridge University Press; 1991.

Absher JR, Benson DF. Disconnection syndromes: an overview of Geschwind's contributions. Neurology. 1993;43:862–7.

Acbas G, Niessen KA, Snell EH, Markelz AG. Optical measurements of long-range protein vibrations. Nat Commun. 2014;5:3076 1–7.

Ackerly SS, Benton AL. Report of a case of bilateral frontal lobe defect. Res Publ Assoc Res Nerv Ment Dis. 1948;27:479–504.

Adrian ED. The impulses produced by sensory nerve endings. Part 1. J Phys. 1926a;61:49–72.

Adrian ED. The impulses produced by sensory nerve endings. Part 4. Impulses from pain receptors. J Phys. 1926b;62:33–51.

Adrian ED, Zotterman Y. The impulses produced by sensory nerve endings. Part 2. The response of a single end-organ. J Phys. 1926a;61:151–71.

Adrian ED, Zotterman Y. The impulses produced by sensory nerve endings. Part 3. Impulses set up by touch and pressure. J Phys. 1926b;61:465–83.

Akelaitis AJ. Studies on the corpus callosum. IV. Diagnostic dyspraxia in epileptics following partial and complete section of the corpus callosum. Am J Psychiatry. 1945;101:594–9.

Antic SD. Action potentials in basal and oblique dendrites o rat neocortical pyramidal neurons. J Physiol. 2003;550:35–50.

Antic SD, Zhou WL, Moore AR, Short SM, Ikonomu KD. The decade of the dendritic NMDA spike. J Neurosci Res. 2010;88:2991–3001.

S. Sevush, *The Single-Neuron Theory*,
DOI 10.1007/978-3-319-33708-1

Ardito RB. Dreaming as an active construction of meaning. Commentary on Hobson 2000. Behav Brain Sci. 2000;23:907–8.

Azouz R. Dynamic spatiotemporal synaptic integration in cortical neurons: neuronal gain, revisited. J Neurophysiol. 2005;94:2785–96.

Baars BJ. Global workspace theory of consciousness: toward a cognitive neuroscience of human experience. Prog Brain Res. 2005;150:45–53.

Baddeley AD, Hitch GJ. In Recent Advances in Learning and Motivation. Bower GA, editor. New York: Academic Press; 1974. p. 47–89.

Bain A. Mind and body. The theories of their relation. London: Henry S. King and Co; 1873.

Bain A. Mr. James Ward's 'Psychology'. Mind. 1886;44:31-457–71.

Ban T, Shiwa T, Kawamura K. Cortico-cortical projections from the prefrontal cortex to the superior temporal sulcal area (STs) in the monkey studied by means of HRP method. Arch Ital Biol. 1991;129:250–72.

Bannister AP. Inter- and intra-laminar connections of pyramidal cells in the neocortex. Neurosci Res. 2005;53:95–103.

Barbas H. Proceedings of the human cerebral cortex: from gene to structure and function connections underlying the synthesis of cognition, memory, and emotion in primate prefrontal cortices. Brain Res Bull. 2000;52:319–30.

Barlow HB. Single units and sensation: a neuron doctrine for perceptual psychology? Perception. 1972;1:371–94.

Bartlett FC. Remembering: A study in experimental and social psychology. Cambridge: Cambridge University Press; 1932.

Bartolomei F, Barbeau E, Gavaret M, Guye M, McGonigal A, Regis J, Chauvel P. Cortical stimulation study of the role of rhinal cortex in deja vu and reminiscence of memories. Neurology. 2004;63:858–64.

Benson DF, Djenderedjian A, Miller BL, Pachana NA, Chang L, Itti L, Eng GE, Mena I. Neural basis of confabulation. Neurology. 1996;46:1239–43.

Benson DF, Gardner H, Meadows JC. Reduplicative paramnesia. Neurology. 1976;26:147–51.

Berridge KC. Pleasures of the brain. Brain Cognition. 2003;52:106–28.

Berridge KC, Kringelbach ML. Neuroscience of affect: brain mechanisms of pleasure and displeasure. Curr Opin Neurobiol. 2013;23:294–303.

Bieberich E. Recurrent fractal neural networks: a strategy for the exchange of local and global information processing in the brain. Biosystems. 2002;6:145–64.

Blackmore S. Conversations on consciousness: What the best minds think about the brain, free will, and what it means to be human. USA: Oxford University Press; 2006.

Bliss TV, Lomo T. Long-lasting potentiation of synaptic transmission in the dentate area of the anaesthetized rabbit following stimulation of the perforant path. J Physiol. 1973;232:331–56.

Block N. Consciousness, accessibility, and the mesh between psychology and neuroscience. Behav Brain Sci. 2007;30:481–548.

Blumenfeld RS, Ranganath C. Dorsolateral prefrontal cortex promotes long-term memory formation through its role in working memory organization. J Neurosci. 2006;26:916–25.

Bock AS, Saenz M, Tungaraza R, Boynton GM, Bridge H, Fine I. Visual callosal topography in the absence of retinal input. Neuroimage. 2013;81:325–34.

Bodovitz S. Consciousness disintegrates without conscious vectors. Med Hypotheses. 2008;70:8–11.

Bogen JE. The neurosurgeon's interest in the corpus callosum. Chapter 24. In: Greenblatt SH, Dagi TF, Epstein MH, editors. A history of neurosurgery. Park Ridge, IL: Am Assoc Neurol Surg; 1997. p. 489–98.

Bollmann JH, Engert F. Subcellular topography of visually driven dendritic activity in the vertebrate visual system. Neuron. 2009;61:895–905.

Bolterauer H, Tuszynski JA. Frohlich's condensation in a biological membrane viewed as a Davydov soliton. J Biol Phys. 1989;17:41–59.

Bowers JS. On the biological plausibility of grandmother cells: implications for neural network theories in psychology and neuroscience. Psychol Rev. 2009;116:220–51.

Bradshaw J. Interview with Robyn Williams, Radio National, Ockhams's Razor, 10/1/1999.

Branco T, Hausser M. The selfish spike: local and global resets of dendritic excitability. Neuron. 2009;61:815–7.

Branco T, Hausser M. Synaptic integration gradients in single cortical pyramidal cell dendrites. Neuron. 2011;69:885–992.

Brancucci A, Franciotti R, D'Anselmo A, Della Penna S, Tommasi L. The sound of consciousness: neural underpinnings of auditory perception. J Neurosci. 2011;31:16611–8.

Brickner RM. Bilateral frontal lobectomy: follow-up report of a case. Arch Neurol Psychiatry. 1939;41:580–5.

Broadbent DE. Perception and communication. London: Pergamon Press; 1958.

Broca PP. Loss of speech, chronic softening and partial destruction of the anterior left lobe of the brain. Bulletin De La Société Anthropologique. 1861;2:235–8.

Brookes JC, Horsfield AP, Stoneham AM. The swipe card model of odorant recognition. Sensors. 2012;12:15709–49. doi:10.3390/s121115709.

Bruce C, Desimone R, Gross CG. Visual properties of neurons in a polysensory area in superior temporal sulcus of the macaque. J Neurophysiol. 1981;46:369–84.

Buxhoeveden DP, Casanova MF. The minicolumn hypothesis in neuroscience. Brain. 2002;125:935–51.

Byrne WL, Samuel D, Bennett EL, Rosenzweig MR, Wasserman E, Wagner AR, Gardner F, Galambos R, Berger BD, Margules DL, Fenichel RL, Stein L, Corson JA, Enesco HE, Chorover SL, Holt CE, Schiller PH, Chiappetta L, Jarvik ME, Leaf RC, Dutcher JD, Horovitz ZP, Carlson PL. Memory transfer. Science. 1966;153:658–9.

Cajal SR. Recollections of my life. 1937. Translated by Craigie EH and Cano J. Philadelphia: MIT Press; 1989.

Capgras J, Reboul-Lachaux J. L'illusion des "sosies" dans un delire systematize chronique. Bulletin de la Societe Clinique de Medecine Mentale. 1923;2:6–16.

Carmichael L. Sir Charles Bell: A contribution to the history of physiological psychology. Psychol Rev. 1926;25:188–217.

Carruthers P, Schechter E. Can panpsychism bridge the gap? J Conscious Stud. 2006;13:32–9.

Chalmers DJ. The conscious mind. In search of a fundamental theory. Oxford University Press. 1996.

Chalmers DJ. Consciousness and the philosophers: an exchange. Reply by Searle JR. N Y Rev Books. 1997;44:1–8.

Chalmers DJ. How can we construct a science of consciousness? Ann N Y Acad Sci. 2013;1303:25–35.

Chen X, Gabitto M, Peng Y, Ryba NJP, Zuker CS. A gustotopic map of taste qualities in the mammalian brain. Science. 2011;333:1262–6.

Chen X, Leischner U, Rochefort NL, Nelken I, Konnerth A. Functional mapping of single spines in cortical neurons in vivo. Nature. 2011;475:501–5.

Chenu A, Scholes GD. Coherence in energy transfer and photosynthesis. Annu Rev Phys Chem. 2015;66:69–96.

Chklovskii DB, Koulakov AA. Maps in the brain: what can we learn from them? Annu Rev Neurosci. 2004;27:369–92.

Clarke E, Jacyna LS. Nineteenth-century origins of neuroscientific concepts. Berkeley: University of California Press; 1987.

Clifford WK. Body and mind. Fortnightly Review 1874 (Reprinted in Lectures and Essays ed. Stephen L, Pollock F. London: Macmillan; 1879.

Collingridge GL. Memories of NMDA receptors and LTP. TINS. 1995;18:54–6.

Conway BR, Tsao DY. Color-tuned neurons are spatially clustered according to color preference within alert macaque posterior inferior temporal cortex. Proc Natl Acad Sci U S A. 2009;106:18034–9.

Conway BR, Chatterjee S, Field GD, Horwitz GD, Johnson EN, Koida K. Mancuso: Advances in color science: from retina to behavior. J Neurosci. 2010;30:14955–63.

Conway BR, Moeller S, Tsao DY. Specialized color modules in macaque extrastriate cortex. Neuron. 2007;56:560–73.

Corkin S. What's new with the amnesic patient H.M.? Nat Rev Neurosci. 2002;3:153–60.

Cowan N. The magical number 4 in short-term memory: a reconsideration of mental storage capacity. Behav Brain Sci. 2000;24:87–114.

Craig AD. How do you feel? Interoception: the sense of the physiological condition of the body. Nat Rev Neurosci. 2002;3:655–66.

Craig AD. How do you feel–now? The anterior insula and human awareness. Nat Rev Neurosci. 2009;1:59–70.

Craig AD. Significance of the insula for the evolution of human awareness of feelings from the body. Ann N Y Acad Sci. 2011;1225:72–82.

Crick F. The astonishing hypothesis. New York: Charles Scribner's Sons; 1994.

Crick F, Koch C. Towards a neurobiological theory of consciousness. Semin Neurosci. 1990;2:263–75.

Crick F, Koch C. Are we aware of neural activity in primary visual cortex? Nature. 1995;375:121–3.

Crick F, Koch C. Consciousness and Neuroscience. Cerebral Cortex. 1998;8:97–107.

Crick F, Koch C. A framework for consciousness. Nat Neurosci. 2003;6:119–26.

Crick F, Koch C, Kreiman G, Fried Y. Consciousness and neurosurgery. Neurosurgery. 2004;55:273–82.

Critchley HD, Harrison NA. Visceral influences on brain and behavior. Neuron. 2013;77:624–38.

Cromer JA, Roy JE, Miller EK. Representation of multiple, independent categories in the primate prefrontal cortex. Neuron. 2010;66:796–807.

Damasio A. Descartes' error. Emotion, reason, and the human brain. New York: Avon Books; 1994.

Damasio A. The feeling of what happens. Body and emotion in the making of consciousness. New York: Harcourt Brace & Company; 1999.

Damasio AR. Time-locked multiregional retroactivation: a systems-level proposal for the neural substrates of recall and recognition. Cognition. 1989;33:25–62.
Damasio AR. Investigating the biology of consciousness. Phil Trans R Soc Lond B. 1998;353:1879–82.
Damasio AR, Anderson SW: The frontal lobes. In: Clinical neuropsychology, 3rd edition (Heilman KM, Valenstein E, eds) pp 409–460, Oxford: Oxford University Press, 1993.
Damasio AR, Graff-Radford NR, Eslinger PJ, Damasio H, Kassell N. Amnesia following basal forebrain lesions. Arch Neurol. 1985;42:263–71.
Dandy WE. Operative experience in cases of pineal tumor. Arch Surg. 1936;33:19–46.
Dandy WE. The location of the conscious center in the brain—the corpus striatum. Bull Johns Hopkins Hosp. 1946;79:34–58.
De Graaf TA, Hsieh PJ, Sack AT. The 'correlates' in neural correlates of consciousness. Neurosci Biobehav Rev. 2012;36:191–7.
De Roo M, Klauser P, Muller D. LTP promotes a selective long-term stabilization and clustering of dendritic spines. PLoS Biol. 1850–1860;6(e219):2008.
Dehaene S. The cognitive neuroscience of consciousness. MIT Press; Elsevier. 2001.
Dehaene S, Kerszberg M, Changeux JP. A neuronal model of a global workspace in effortful cognitive tasks. Proc Natl Acad Sci U S A. 1998;95:14529–34.
Deiters O. Untersuchungen über Gehirn und Rückenmark des Menschen und der Säugethiere. (edited by Max Schultze). Braunschweig: Vieweg; 1865.
Denk W, Strickler JH, Webb WW. Two-photon laser scanning fluorescence microscopy. Science. 1990;248:73–6.
Dennett DC. Consciousness explained. Boston: Little, Brown and Company; 1991.
Dennis C. The sweet smell of success. Nature. 2004;428:362–4.
Destexhe A. Dendrites do it in sequences. Science. 2010;329:1611–2.
Di Maio V. Regulation of information passing by synaptic transmission: a short review. Brain Res. 2008;1225:26–38.
Douglas RJ, Martin KAC. Neuronal circuits of the neocortex. Annu Rev Neurosci. 2004;27:419–51.
Dudai Y. The neurobiology of consolidations, or, how stable is the engram? Ann Rev Psychol. 2004;55:51–86.
Eccles JC. The brain and the unity of conscious experience. The 19th Arthur Stanley Eddington Memorial Lecture. 1965.
Edelman G. The remembered present. New York: Basic Books; 1989.

Edelman GM. Building a picture of the brain. Ann N Y Acad Sci. 1999;882: 68–89.

Edelman GM. Naturalizing consciousness: a theoretical framework. Proc Natl Acad Sci U S A. 2003;100:5520–4.

Edelman GM, Tononi G. A universe of consciousness. New York: Basic Books; 2000.

Edwards JCW. Is consciousness only a property of individual cells? J Conscious Stud. 2005;12(4/5):60–76.

Eichenbaum H, Sauvage M, Fortin N, Komorowski R, Lipton P. Towards a functional organization of episodic memory in the medial temporal lobe. Neurosci Biobehav Rev. 2012;36:1597–608.

Ekstrom AD, Kahana MJ, Caplan JB, Fields TA, Isham EA, Newman EL, Fried I. Cellular networks underlying human spatial navigation. Nature. 2003;425:184–7.

Ekstrom LB, Roelfsema PR, Arsenault JT, Bonmassar G, Vanduffel W. Bottom-up dependent gating of frontal signals in early visual cortex. Science. 2008; 321:414–7.

Ellenberg L, Sperry RW. Lateralized division of attention in the commissurotomized and intact brain. Neuropsychologia. 1980;18:411–8.

Elston GN. Cortex, cognition and the cell: new insights into the pyramidal neuron and prefrontal function. Cerebral Cortex. 2003;13:1124–38.

Engel GS, Calhoun TR, Read EL, Ahn TK, Mancal T, Cheng YC, Blankenship RE, Fleming GR. Evidence for wavelike energy transfer through quantum coherence in photosynthetic systems. Nature. 2007;446:782–6.

Eskenasy ACC, Clarke S. Hierarchy within human SI: supporting data from cytochrome oxidase, acetylcholinesterase and NADPH-diaphorase staining patterns. Somatosens Motor Res. 2000;17:123–32.

Euler T, Detwiler PB, Denk W. Directionally selective calcium signals in dendrites of starburst amacrine cells. Nature. 2002;418:845–52.

Feldmeyer D, Lubke J, Sakmann B. Efficacy and connectivity of intracolumnar pairs of layer 2/3 pyramidal cells in the barrel cortex of juvenile rats. J Physiol. 2006;575:583–602.

Felleman DJ, Van Essen DC. Distributed hierarchical processing in the primate cerebral cortex. Cerebral Cortex. 1991;1:1–47.

Ferster D, Miller KD. Neural mechanisms of orientation selectivity in the visual cortex. Annu Rev Neurosci. 2000;23:441–71.

Finger S. Minds behind the brain. A history of the pioneers and their discoveries. New York: Oxford University Press; 2000.

Flechsig PE. Anatommie des menschlichen Gehirns und Rudkenmarks auf myelogenetischer Grundlage, I. Leipzig: Thieme; 1920 (in Clarke E, O'Malley CD. The human brain and spinal cord. 2nd ed. Norman Publishing: San Francisco. 1996, p. 552).

Fleming GR, Huelga SF, Plenio MB. Focus on quantum effects and noise in biomolecules. New J Phys. 2011; 11500213:1–5.

Fletcher PC, Henson RNA. Frontal lobes and human memory. Insights from functional neuroimaging. Brain. 2001;124:849–81.

Freeman J, Ziemba CM, Heeger DJ, Simoncelli EP, Movshon JA. A functional and perceptual signature of the second visual area in primates. Nat Neurosci. 2013;16:974–81.

Freud S. The interpretation of dreams. 1999.

Frey S, Mackey S, Petrides M. Cortico-cortical connections of areas 44 and 45B in the macaque monkey. Brain Lang. 2014;131:36–55.

Frith CD. The role of dorsolateral prefrontal cortex in the selection of action as revealed by functional imaging. In: Monsell S, Driver J, editors. Control of cognitive processes: Attention and performance XVIII. Cambridge: MIT Press; 2000. p. 549–65.

Frohlich H. Long-range coherence and energy storage in biological systems. Int J Quantum Chem. 1968;2:641–9.

Fuster J, Alexander G. Neuron activity related to short-term memory. Science. 1971;173:652–4.

Fuster JM. Memory in the cerebral cortex. Cambridge: MIT Press; 1999.

Gabrieli JDE, Cohen NJ, Corkin S. The impaired learning of semantic knowledge following bilateral medial temporal-lobe resection. Brain Cognition. 1988;7:157–77.

Garver MM. The periodic character of voluntary nervous action. Am J Sci. 1880;20:189–93.

Gasquoine PG. Localization of function in anterior cingulate cortex: From psychosurgery to functional neuroimaging. Neurosci Biobehav Rev. 2013;37:340–8.

Gauger EM, Rieper E, Morton JJL, Benjamin SC, Vedral B. Sustained quantum coherence and entanglement in the avian compass. http://arxiv.org/pdf/0906.3725v5.pdf

Gazzaniga MS. The bisected brain. New York: Appleton-Century Crofts; 1970.

Gazzaniga MS. Forty-five years of split-brain research and still going strong. Nat Rev Neurosci. 2005;6:653–9.

Gazzaniga MS. Shifting gears: seeking new approaches for mind/brain mechanisms. Annu Rev Psychol. 2013;64:1–20.

Gazzaniga MS, Sperry RW. Language after section of the cerebral commissures. Brain. 1967;90:131–48.

Gazzaniga MS, Bogen JE, Sperry RW. Some functional effects of sectioning the cerebral commissures in man. Proc Natl Acad Sci U S A. 1962;48:1765–9.

Gegenfurtner KR. Cortical mechanism of colour vision. Nat Rev Neurosci. 2003;4:563–72.

Gegenfurtner KR, Kiper DC. Color vision. Annu Rev Neurosci. 2003;26:181–206.

Geschwind N. Disconnexion syndromes in animals and man. Part 1. Brain. 1965a;88:237–94.

Geschwind N. Disconnexion syndromes in animals and man. Part 2. Brain. 1965b;88:585–644.

Geschwind N. The perverseness of the right hemisphere. Behav Brain Sci. 1981;4:106–7.

Geschwind N, Kaplan E. A human cerebral deconnection syndrome: a preliminary report. Neurology. 1962;12:675–85.

Giordano B, McAdams S, Zatorre RJ, Kriegeskorte N, Belin P. Abstract encoding of auditory objects in cortical activity patterns. Cerebral Cortex. 2013;23:2025–37.

Goff P. Experiences don't sum. J Conscious Stud. 2006;13:535–61.

Gold I. Does 40-Hz oscillation play a role in visual consciousness. Consciousness Cognition. 1999;8:186–95.

Goldman-Rakic PS. Topography of cognition: parallel distributed networks in primate association cortex. Annu Rev Neurosci. 1988;11:137–56.

Gordon HW, Sperry RW. Lateralization of olfactory perception in the surgically separated hemispheres of man. Neuropsychologia. 1969;7:111–20.

Grabenhorst F, Rolls ET. Value, pleasure and choice in the ventral prefrontal cortex. Trends Cognitive Sci. 2011;15:56–67.

Gross CG. Genealogy of the "grandmother cell". Neuroscientist. 2002;3:512–8.

Gross CG. Single neuron studies of inferior temporal cortex. Neuropsychologia. 2008;46:841–52.

Gross CG, Bender DB, Rocha-Miranda CE. Visual receptive fields of neurons in inferotemporal cortex of the monkey. Science. 1969;166:1303–6.

Grush R, Churchland PS. Gaps in Penrose's Toilings. J Conscious Stud. 1995;2:10–29.

Haag R. Quantum theory and the division of the world. Mind Matter. 2004;2:53–66.

Hackett TA. Information flow in the auditory cortical network. Hear Res. 2011; 271:133–46.

Hameroff S, Penrose R. Consciousness in the universe. A review of the 'Orch OR' theory. Phys Life Rev. 2014;11:39–78.

Hartline HK. The response of single optic nerve fibers of the vertebrate eye to illumination of the retina. Am J Physiol. 1938;121:400–15.

Harvey CD, Svoboda K. Locally dynamic synaptic learning rules in pyramidal neuron dendrites. Nature. 2007;450:1195–200.

Hausser M, Mel B. Dendrites: bug or feature? Curr Opin Neurobiol. 2003;13: 372–83.

Hausser M, Spruston N, Stuart GJ. Diversity and dynamics of dendritic signaling. Science. 2000;290:739–44.

Heath RG. Electrical self-stimulation of the brain in man. Am J Psychiatry. 1963;120:571–7.

Hebb DO. Organization of behavior. New York: John Wiley and Sons; 1949.

Hebb DO, Penfield W. Human behavior after extensive bilateral removals from the frontal lobes. Arch Neurol Psychiatry. 1950;44:421–38.

Heil J. Comment on Kosslyn. Behav Brain Sci. 1979;2:554–5.

Heilman KM. Aphasia and the diagram makers revisited: an update of information processing models. J Clin Neurol. 2006;2:1490–162.

Hering E. Outlines of a theory of the light sense. Originally published in 1872; Re-published in 1964 by Harvard University Press, Cambridge.

Hirose S, Tadashi L, Takada M, Kimura J, Akiguchi I, Noboru M. Topographic projections from the subiculum to the limbic regions of the medial frontal cortex in the cat. Neurosci Lett. 1992;139:61–4.

Hodgkin AL, Huxley AF. Propagation of electrical signals along giant nerve fibres. Proc R Soc Lond B Biol Sci. 1952a;140:177–83.

Hodgkin AL, Huxley AF. Currents carried by sodium and potassium ions through the membrane of the giant axon of Loligo. J Physiol. 1952b;116: 449–72.

Hodgkin AL, Huxley AF. The components of membrane conductance in the giant axon of Loligo. J Physiol. 1952c;116:473–96.

Hodgkin AL, Huxley AF. The dual effect of membrane potential on sodium conductance in the giant axon of Loligo. J Physiol. 1952d;116:497–506.

Hodgkin AL, Huxley AF. A quantitative description of membrane current and its application to conduction and excitation in nerve. J Physiol. 1952e;117: 500–44.

Hodgkin AL, Huxley AF, Katz B. Measurement of current-voltage relations in the membrane of the giant axon of Loligo. J Physiol. 1952;116:424–48.

Hoffman KL, McNaughton BL. Coordinated reactivation of distributed memory traces in primate neocortex. Science. 2002;297:2070–3.

Hopp E, Borst A, Haag J. Subcellular mapping of dendritic activity in optic flow processing neurons. J Comp Physiol A. 2014;200:359–70.

Huang L, Treisman A, Pashler H. Characterizing the limits of human visual awareness. Science. 2007;317:823–5.

Hubel DH. Eye, brain, and vision. WH Freeman. 1995.

Hubel DH, Wiesel TN. Receptive fields, binocular interaction and functional architecture in the cat's visual cortex. J Phys. 1962;160:106–54.

Hubel DH, Wiesel TN. Early exploration of the visual cortex. Cortex. 1998;20: 401–12.

Hume D. A treatise of human nature. Oxford: Clarendon Press; 1739/1978.

Huth AG, Nishimoto S, Vu AT, Gallant JL. A continuous semantic space describes the representation of thousands of object and action categories across the human brain. Neuron. 2012;76:1210–24.

Huxley TH. Presidential address at the British association: Biogenesis and abiogenesis. 1870.

Jacobs GA, Miller JP, Aldworth Z. Computational mechanisms of mechanosensory processing in the cricket. J Exp Biol. 2008;211:1819–28.

Jacobsen CF. Functions of the frontal association area in primates. Arch Neurol Psychiatry. 1935;33:558–69.

James W. What is an emotion? Mind. 1884;9:188–205.

James W. The principles of psychology. New York: Holt; 1890.

James W. The physical basis of emotion. Psychol Rev. 1894;1:516–29.

John ER. A field theory of consciousness. Conscious Cognition. 2001;10: 184–213.

Johnson DMG, Illig KR, Behan M, Haberty LB. New features of connectivity in piriform cortex visualized by intracellular injection of pyramidal cells suggest that "primary" olfactory cortex functions like "association" cortex in other sensory systems. J Neurosci. 2000;20:6974–82.

Johnson K. Terahertz vibrational properties of water nanoclusters relevant to biology. J Biol Phys. 2012;38:85–95.

Jonides J, Lewis RL, Nee DE, Lustig CA, Berman MG, Moore KS. The mind and brain of short-term memory. Annu Rev Psychol. 2008;59:193–224.

Judkewitz B. Dendritic enlightenment: using patterned two-photon uncaging to reveal the secrets of the brain's smallest dendrites. Neuron. 2006;50: 180–3.

Kaas JH, Hackett TA. Subdivisions of auditory cortex and processing streams in primates. Proc Natl Acad Sci U S A. 2000;97:11793–9.

Kanizsa G. Margini quasi-percettivi in campi con stimulazioni omogeana. Revista di Psicologia. 1955;49:7–30.

Kay RB, Meyer EA, Illig KR, Brunjes PC. Spatial distribution of neural activity in the anterior olfactory nucleus evoked by odor and electrical stimulation. J Comp Neurol. 2011;519:277–89.

Keane MM, Gabrieli JDE, Mapstone HC, Johnson KA, Corkin S. Double dissociation of memory capacities after bilateral occipital-lobe or medial temporal-lobe lesions. Brain. 1995;118:1129–48.

Kerr JND, Greenberg D, Helmchen F. Imaging input and output of neocortical networks in vivo. Proc Natl Acad Sci U S A. 2005;102:14063–8.

Kiani R, Esteky H, Mirpour K, Tanaka K. Object category structure in response patterns of neuronal population in monkey inferior temporal cortex. J Neurophysiol. 2007;97:4296–309.

Kiebel SJ, Friston KJ. Free energy and dendritic self-organization. Front Syst Neurosci. 2011;5:1–13.

Klose J. Process ontology from Whitehead to quantum physics. ("submitted") 1–21. 2007.

Kluver H, Bucy P. Preliminary analysis of functions if the temporal lobes in monkeys. Arch Neurol Psychiatry. 1939;42:979–1000.

Knudsen EI, Konishi M. A neural map of auditory space in the owl. Science. 1978;200:795–7.

Koch C. The quest for consciousness: a neurobiological approach. Englewood: Roberts and Company Publishers; 2004.

Koch C. A theory of consciousness. Sci Am Mind. July/August 2009; 16–9.

Koechlin E, Hyafil A. Anterior prefrontal function and the limits of human decision-making. Science. 2007;318:594–8.

Koelsch S, Siebel WA. Towards a neural basis of music perception. Trends Cognitive Sci. 2005;9:578–84.

Komatsu H, Kinoshita M, Murakami I. Neural responses in the retinotopic representation of the blind spot in the macaque V1 to stimuli for perceptual filling-in. J Neurosci. 2000;20:9310–9.

Konstantoudaki X, Papoutsi A, Chalkiadaki K, Poirazi P, Sidiropoulou K. Modulatory effects of inhibition on persistent activity in a cortical microcircuit model. Front Neural Circuitry. 2014; [8:7. doi:10.3389/fncir.2014.00007]8: 1–15.

Kriegeskorte N, Kiev RA. Representational geometry: integrating cognition, computation, and the brain. Trends Cognitive Sci. 2013;17:401–12.

Kuffler SW. Discharge patterns and functional organization of mammalian retina. J Neurophysiol. 1953;16:37–68.

Kurt G. Zur Lehre von der motorischen Apraxie. J fur Psychol und Neurol. 1908;11:169–187, 270–83.

Lamme VAF. Neural mechanisms of visual awareness: a linking proposition. Brain Mind. 2000;1:385–406.

Lange CG. Om sindsbevaegelser: et psyko-fysiologisk studie [On emotions: a psycho-physiological study], Kjbenhavn: Jacob Lunds. 1885. Reprinted in The emotions. Lange CG and James W, editors, Haupt IA (trans.). Baltimore, Williams & Wilkins Company; 1922.

Lanteaume L, Khalfa S, Regis J, Marquis P, Chauvel P, Bartolomei F. Emotion induction after direct intracerebral stimulations of human amygdala. Cerebral Cortex. 2007;17:1307–13.

Lapicque L. Recherches quantitatives sur l'excitation electrique des nerfs traitee comme une polarization. J Physiol Pathol Gen. 1907;9:620–35.

Larkum M. A cellular mechanism for cortical associations: an organizing principle for the cerebral cortex. Trends Neurosci. 2013;36:141–51.

Larkum ME, Nevian T. Synaptic clustering by dendritic signaling mechanisms. Curr Opin Neurobiol. 2008;18:1–11.

Larkum ME, Senn W, Luscher HR. Top-down dendritic input increases the gain of layer 5 pyramidal neurons. Cerebral Cortex. 2004;14:1059–70.

Lashley KS. In search of the engram. Symp Soc Exp Biol. 1950;4:454–82.

Laughlin SB, Sejnowski TJ. Communication in neuronal networks. Science. 2003;301:1870–4.

Laurent G. A systems perspective on early olfactory coding. Science. 1999;286: 723–8.

Legenstein R, Maass W. Branch-specific plasticity enables self-organization of nonlinear computation in single neurons. J Neurosci. 2011;31:10787–802.

Lehar S. Gestalt isomorphism and the primacy of subjective conscious experience: a Gestalt bubble model. Behav Brain Sci. 2003;26:375–444.

Leibnitz WG. Monadology. 1714.

Leopold DA, Logothetis NK. Activity changes in early visual cortex reflect monkeys' percepts during binocular rivalry. Nature. 1996;379:549–63.

Levy J, Nebes RD, Sperry RW. Expressive language in the surgically separated minor hemisphere. Cortex. 1971;7:49–58.

Liang M, Mouraux A, Iannetti GD. Parallel processing of nociceptive and non-nociceptive somatosensory information in the human primary and secondary somatosensory cortices: evidence from dynamic causal modeling of functional magnetic resonance imaging data. J Neurosci. 2011;31:8976–85.

Libet B. Mind time. Boston: First Harvard University Press; 2004.

Llinas R, Ribary U, Contreras D, Pedroarena C. The neuronal basis for consciousness. Phil Trans R Soc Lond B. 1998;353:1841–9.

Lockwood M. Mind, brain, and the quantum. Oxford: Blackwell; 1989.

Loftus EF. Creating false memories. Sci Am. 1997;277:70–5.

Logothetis NK. Single units and conscious vision. Phil Trans R Soc Lond B. 1998;353:1801–18.

Logothetis NK. Vision: a window into consciousness. Sci Am. 1999;281: 66–75.

London M, Hausser M. Dendritic computation. Annu Rev Neurosci. 2005;28: 503–32.

Lorente de No R. The cerebral cortex: architecture, intracortical connections, motor projections. In: Fulton JF, editor. Physiology of the nervous system. Oxford University Press; 1938. p. 274–301.

Losonczy A, Magee JC. Integrative properties of radial oblique dendrites in hippocampal CA1 pyramidal neurons. Neuron. 2006;50:291–307.

Lubke J, Feldmeyer D. Excitatory signal flow and connectivity in a cortical column: focus on barrel cortex. Brain Struct Func. 2007;212:3–17.

Lycan WG. Resisting ?-ism. J Conscious Stud. 2006;13:65–71.

Macpherson F. Property dualism and the merits of solutions to the mind-body problem. A reply to Strawson. J Conscious Stud. 2006;13:72–89.

Maia TV, Cleeremans A. Consciousness: converging insights from connectionist modeling and neuroscience. Trends Cognitive Sci. 2005;9:397–404.

Major G, Larkum ME, Schiller J. Active properties of neocortical pyramidal neuron dendrites. Annu Rev Neurosci. 2013;36:1–24.

Major G, Polsky A, Denk W, Schiller J, Tank DW. Spatiotemporally graded NMDA spike/plateau potentials in basal dendrites of neocortical pyramidal neurons. J Neurophysiol. 2008;99:2584–601.

Maquet P, Ruby P, Maudoux A, Albouy GV, Sterpenich V, Dang-Vu T, Desseilles M, Boly M, Perrin F, Peigneux P, Laureys S. Human cognition during REM sleep and the activity profile within frontal and parietal cortices: a reappraisal of functional neuroimaging data. Prog Brain Res. 2005;150:219–27.

Markowitsch HJ, Kessler J. Massive impairment in executive functions with partial preservation of other cognitive functions: the case of a young patient with severe degeneration of the prefrontal cortex. Exp Brain Res. 2000; 133:94–102.

Marshall IN. Consciousness and Bose-Einstein condensates. New Ideas Psychol. 1989;7:53–83.

Martin KAC. Microcircuits in visual cortex. Curr Opin Neurobiol. 2002;12: 418–25.

Mataro M, Jurado A, Garcia-Sanchez C, Barraquer L, Costa-Jussa FR, Junque C. Long-term effects of bilateral frontal brain lesion. 60 years after injury with an iron bar. Arch Neurol. 2001;58:1139–42.

Matelli M, Camarda R, Glickstein M, Rizzolatti G. Afferent and efferent projections of the inferior area 6 in the macaque monkey. J Comp Neurol. 1986; 251:281–96.

Matsumoto M, Komatsu H. Neural responses in the macaque V1 to bar stimuli with various lengths presented on the blind spot. J Neurophysiol. 2005;93: 2374–87.

Maury LFA: Le sommeil et les rêves. Chapitre 5. 1865.

Maxwell JC. On colour vision. Proc R Inst Gr Br. 1872;6:260–71.

McClelland JL, McNaughton BL, O'Reilly RC. Why there are complementary learning systems in the hippocampus and neocortex: insights from the successes and failures of connectionist models of learning and memory. Psychol Rev. 1995;102:419–57.

McConnell JV. Memory transfer through cannibalism in planarians. J Neuropsychiatry. 1962;3:S42–8.

McCulloch W, Pitts W. A logical calculus of the ideas immanent in nervous activity. Bull Math Biophys. 1943;5:115–33.

McGinn C. Can we solve the mind/body problem? Mind. 1989;98:349–66.

McGinn C. Hard questions: comments on Galen Strawson. J Conscious Stud. 2006;13:90–9.

Mel BW. Synaptic integration in an excitable dendritic tree. J Neurophysiol. 1993;70:1086–93.

Mel BW, Ruderman DL, Archie KA. Translation-invariant orientation tuning in visual "complex" cells could derive from intradendritic computations. J Neurosci. 1998;18:4325–34.

Meng M, Remus DA, Tong F. Filling-in of visual phantoms in the human brain. Nat Neurosci. 2005;8:1248–54.

Merchant H, Lafuente VD, Pena-Ortega F, Larriva-Sahd J. Functional impact of interneuronal inhibition in the cerebral cortex of behaving animals. Prog Neurobiol. 2012;99:163–78.

Meunier D, Lambiotte R, Bullmore E. Modular and hierarchically modular organization of brain networks. Front Neurosci. 2010;4:1–11.

Miller EK, Cohen JD. An integrative theory of prefrontal cortex function. Annu Rev Neurosci. 2001;24:167–202.

Miller EK, Fusi S. Limber neurons for a nimble mind. Neuron. 2013;78: 211–3.

Miller G. Sweet here, salty there: evidence for a taste map in the mammalian brain. Science. 2011;333:1213.

Miller SM. Closing in on the constitution of consciousness. Front Psychol. 2014;5:1–18.

Milner AD, Goodale MA. The visual Brain in action. Oxford: Oxford University Press; 1995.

Milner B. Amnesia following operations on the temporal lobes. In: Zangwill OL, editor. Amnesia (Whitty CWM). London: Butterworth; 1966.

Milojkovic BA, Zhou WL, Antic SD. Voltage and calcium transients in basal dendrites of the rat prefrontal cortex. J Physiol. 2007;585:447–68.

Morin A. Right hemispheric self-awareness: a critical assessment. Conscious Cognition. 2002;11:396–401.

Morris RGM. NMDA receptors and memory encoding. Neuropharmacology. 2013;74:32–40.

Mountcastle VB. Modality and topographic properties of single neurons of cat's somatic sensory cortex. J Neurophysiol. 1957;20:408–34.

Mountcastle VB. The columnar organization of the neocortex. Brain. 1997;120:701–22.

Nagel T. What is it like to be a bat? Philos Rev. 1974;83:435–50.

Nagel T. Mortal questions. Cambridge: Cambridge University Press; 1979.

Nagel ZD, Klinman JP. Update 1 of: tunneling and dynamics in enzymatic hydride transfer. Chem Rev. 2010;110:PR41–67.

Naselaris T, Kay KN, Hishimoto S, Gallant JL. Encoding and decoding in fMRI. Neuroimage. 2012;56:400–10.

Naselaris T, Olman CA, Stansbury DE, Ugurbil K, Gallant JL. A voxel-wise encoding model for early visual areas decodes mental images of remembered scenes. Neuroimage. 2015;105:215–28.

Nauta WJH. The problem of the frontal lobe: a reinterpretation. J Psychiatr Res. 1971;8:167–87.

Neisser U. Cognitive psychology. New York: Appleton-Century-Crofts; 1967.

Newton I. Opticks: A treatise of the reflections, refractions, inflections and colours of light. 1730.

Nir Y, Tononi G. Dreaming and the brain: from phenomenology to neurophysiology. Trends Cognitive Sci. 2010;14:88–100.

Norretranders T. The user illusion. 1991. (Translation by Jonathan Sydenham. Penguin Books: New York; 1999.)

O'Keefe J, Drovtosky J. The hippocampus as a spatial map. Preliminary evidence from unit activity in the freely-moving rat. Brain Res. 1971;34: 171–5.

O'Regan JK, Rensink RA, Clark JJ. Change-blindness as a result of "mud-splashes.". Nature. 1999;398:34.
Olds J. Self-stimulation of the brain. Science. 1958;127:315–24.
Olson CR, Musil SY. Topographic organization of cortical and subcortical projections to posterior cingulate cortex in the cat: evidence for somatic, ocular, and complex subregions. J Comp Neurol. 1992;324:237–60.
Orpwood RD. A possible neural mechanism underlying consciousness based on the pattern processing capabilities of pyramidal neurons in the cerebral cortex. J Theor Biol. 1994;169:403–18.
Palmer SE. Color, consciousness, and the isomorphism constraint. Behav Brain Sci. 1999;22:923–89.
Pasternak T, Greenlee MW. Working memory in primate sensory systems. Nat Rev Neurosci. 2005;6:97–107.
Penfield W. The cerebral cortex in man. I. The cerebral cortex and consciousness. Arch Neurol Psychiatry. 1938; (The Harvey Lecture, given at the New York Academy of Medicine, New York, Oct 15, 1936)40:417–42.
Penfield W. Ferrier lecture. Some observations on the cerebral cortex of man. Proc R Soc Ser B. 1947;134:329–47.
Penrose R. The emperor's new mind. Oxford University Press; 1989.
Penrose R. What is reality? New scientist. November 15, 2006.
Peron SP, Jones PW, Gabbiani F. Precise subcellular input retinotopy and its computational consequences in an identified visual interneuron. Neuron. 2009;63:830–42.
Pessoa O. What is an essentially quantum mechanical effect? Revista Eletrônica Informação e Cognição. 2001;3(1):1–13.
Petreanu L, Mao T, Sternson SM, Svoboda K. The subcellular organization of neocortical excitatory connections. Nature. 2009;457:1142–6.
Phillips ML, Drevets WC, Rauch SL, Lane R. Neurobiology of emotion perception I: The neural basis of normal emotion perception. Biol Psychiatry. 2003;54:504–14.
Poirazi P, Brannon T, Mel BW. Arithmetic of subthreshold synaptic summation in a model CA1 pyramidal cell. Neuron. 2003a;37:977–87.
Poirazi P, Brannon T, Mel BW. Pyramidal neuron as two-later neural network. Neuron. 2003b;37:989–99.
Polsky A, Mel BW, Schiller J. Computational subunits in thin dendrites of pyramidal cells. Nat Neurosci. 2004;7:621–7.
Polsky A, Mel BW, Schiller J. Encoding and decoding bursts by NMDA spikes in basal dendrites of layer 5 pyramidal neurons. J Neurosci. 2009;29:11891–903.

Price JL. Prefrontal cortical networks related to visceral function and mood. Ann N Y Acad Sci. 1999;877:383–96.

Pylyshyn ZW. Computation and cognition: issues in the foundation of cognitive science. Behav Brain Sci. 1980;3:111–32.

Quian Quiroga R, Reddy L, Kreiman G, Koch C, Fried I. Invariant visual representation by single neurons in the human brain. Nature. 2005;435: 1102–7.

Raichle ME. Two views of brain function. Trends Cognitive Sci. 2010;14: 180–90.

Rall W. Branching dendritic trees and motoneuron membrane resistivity. Exp Neurol. 1959;1:491–527.

Rao SC, Rainer G, Miller EK. Integration of what and where in the primate prefrontal cortex. Science. 1997;276:821–4.

Rauschecker JP, Scott SK. Maps and streams in the auditory cortex: nonhuman primates illuminate human speech processing. Nat Neurosci. 2009;12: 718–24.

Reddy L, Quian Quiroga R, Wilken P, Koch C, Fried I. A single-neuron correlate of change detection and change blindness in the human medial temporal lobe. Curr Biol. 2006;16:2066–72.

Rees G, Kreiman G, Koch C. Neural correlates of consciousness in humans. Nat Rev Neurosci. 2002;3:261–70.

Reich DS, Mechler F, Victor JD. Independent and redundant information in nearby cortical neurons. Science. 2001;294:2566–8.

Reimers JR, McKemmish LK, McKenzie RH, Mark AE, Hush NS. The revised Penrose-Hameroff orchestrated objective-reduction proposal for human consciousness is not scientifically justified. Comment on "Consciousness in the universe. A review of the 'Orch OR' theory" by Hameroff and Penrose. Phys Life Rev. 2014;11:101–3.

Rensink RA, O'Regan JK, Clark JJ. To see or not to see: the need for attention to perceive changes in scenes. Psychol Sci. 1997;8:368–73.

Rey G. Better to study human than world psychology. Comment on Strawson. J Conscious Stud. 2006;13:110–6.

Ribot T. Les maladies de la mémoire. Paris: Germer-Ballière; 1881.

Richmond BJ, Wurtz RH, Sato T. Visual responses of inferior temporal neurons in awake rhesus monkey. J Neurophysiol. 1983;50:1415–32.

Rigotti M, Rubin DBD, Wang XJ, Fusi S. Internal representation of task rules by recurrent dynamics: the importance of the diversity of neural responses. Front Comput Neurosci. 2010;4:1–29.

Rishel CA, Huang G, Freedman DJ. Independent category and spatial encoding in parietal cortex. Neuron. 2013;77:969–79.

Rockland KS. Visual cortical organization at the single axon level: a beginning. Neurosci Res. 2002;42:150–66.

Roe AW, Chelazzi L, Connor CE, Conway BR, Fujita I, Gallant JL, Lu H, Vanduff W. Toward a unified theory of visual area V4. Neuron. 2012;74: 12–29.

Rolls ET. Memory systems in the brain. Annu Rev Psychol. 2000a;51: 599–630.

Rolls ET. Précis of the brain and emotion. Behav Brain Sci. 2000b;23: 177–234.

Rolls ET. Emotion explained. Oxford: Oxford University Press; 2005.

Rolls ET. The representation of information about faces in the temporal and frontal lobes. Neuropsychologia. 2007;45:124–43.

Rolls ET. A computational theory of episodic memory formation in the hippocampus. Beh Brain Res. 2010;215:180–96.

Rolls ET. On the relation between the mind and the brain: a neuroscience perspective. Philosophia Scientiæ. 2013;17:31–70.

Rolls ET, O'Dohery J, Kringelbach MI, Francis S, Bowtell R, McGlone F. Representations of pleasant and painful touch in the human orbitofrontal and cingulate cortices. Cerebral Cortex. 2003;13:308–17.

Romanski LM. Representation and integration of auditory and visual stimuli in the primate ventral lateral prefrontal cortex. Cerebral Cortex. 2007;17: 161–9.

Rosen GM, Sageman M, Loftus E. A historical note on false traumatic memories. J Clin Psychol. 2004;60:137–9.

Rosenthal DM. Experience and the physical. J Conscious Stud. 2006;13: 117–28.

Rumelhart DE, McClelland JL, the PDP Research Group, editors. Parallel distributed processing, vol 1: Foundations. Cambridge: MIT Press; 1986.

Rushworth MFS. Intention, choice, and the medial frontal cortex. Ann N Y Acad Sci. 2008;1124:181–207.

Rushworth MFS, Behrens TEJ, Rudebeck PH, Walton ME. Contrasting roles for cingulate and orbitofrontal cortex in decisions and social behaviour. Trends Cognitive Sci. 2007;11:168–76.

Russell B. Human knowledge. Its scope and limits. London: Allen & Unwin; 1948.

Russell JA. Core affect and the psychological construction of emotion. Psychol Rev. 2003;110:145–72.

Ryle G. The concept of mind. London: Hutchinson; 1949.

Salari V, Tuszynski J, Rahnama M, Bernroider G. Plausibility of quantum coherent states in biological systems. J Phys Conf Series. 2011;306:1–10, 012075.

Schiller J, Major G, Koester HJ, Schiller Y. NMDA spikes in basal dendrites of cortical pyramidal neurons. Nature. 2000;404:285–9.

Schnider A. Spontaneous confabulation and the adaptation of thought to ongoing reality. Nat Rev Neurosci. 2003;4:662–71.

Schreiner CE, Winer JA. Auditory cortex mapmaking: principles, projections, and plasticity. Neuron. 2007;56:356–65.

Schwartz EL. Computational anatomy and functional architecture of striate cortex: a spatial mapping approach to perceptual coding. Vision Res. 1980;20:645–69.

Scoville WB, Milner B. Loss of recent memory after bilateral hippocampal lesions. J Neurol Neurosurg Psychiatry. 1957;20:11–21.

Seager W. Consciousness, information and panpsychism. J Conscious Stud. 1995;2:272–88.

Seager W. Panpsychism. Stanford Encyclopedia of Philosophy. 2001.

Seong HJ, Behnia R, Carter AG. The impact of subthreshold membrane potential on synaptic responses at dendritic spines of layer 5 pyramidal neurons in the prefrontal cortex. J Neurophysiol. 2014;111:1960–72.

Seth AK, Baars BJ. Neural Darwinsim and consciousness. Conscious Cognition. 2005;14:140–68.

Sevush S. A case of literal alexia: evidence for a disconnection syndrome. Brain Lang. 1984;22:92–108.

Sevush S. Single-neuron theory of consciousness. J Theor Biol. 2006;238:704–25.

Shannon C. The mathematical theory of communication. Bell Syst Tech J. 1948;27:379–423.

Sherman SM, Guillery RW. On the actions that one nerve cell can have on another: distinguishing "drivers" from "modulators.". Proc Natl Acad Sci U S A. 1998;95:7121–6.

Shi JV, Wielaard J, Smith RT, Sajda P. Perceptual decision making "through the eyes" of a large-scale neural model of V1. Front Psychol. 2013;4:1–12.

Shimony A. On mentality, quantum mechanics and the actualization of potentialities. In: Penrose R, editor. The large, the small and the human mind; Chapter 4. Cambridge University Press; 1997. p. 144–60.

Sidiropoulou K, Pissadaki EK, Poirazi P. Inside the brain of a neuron. EMBO Rep. 2006;7:886–92.

Simon DK, O'Leary DDM. Relationship of retinotopic ordering of axons in the optic pathway to the formation of visual maps in central targets. J Comp Neurol. 1991;307:393–404.

Simons DJ, Levin DT. Change blindness. Trends Cognitive Sci. 1997;1: 261–7.

Simons DJ, Rensink RA. Change blindness: past, present, and future. Trends Cognitive Sci. 2005;9:16–20.

Siwek DF, Pandya DN. Prefrontal projections to the mediodorsal nucleus of the thalamus in the rhesus monkey. J Comp Neurol. 1991;312:509–24.

Skinner BF. The behavior of organisms: An experimental analysis. Cambridge: Massachusetts; 1938.

Skinner BF. Science and human behavior. New York: The Free Press; 1965.

Smith SL, Hausser M. Parallel processing of visual space by neighboring neurons in mouse visual cortex. Nat Neurosci. 2010;13:1144–9.

Smith EH. Temporal processing in the auditory core: transformation or segregation? J Neurophysiol. 2011;106:2791–3.

Spence P. Time and space considered as negations. J Speculative Philos. 1879; 13:4–13.

Sperry RW. Visuomotor coordination in the newt (Triturus viridescens) after regeneration of the optic nerve. J Comp Neurol. 1943;79:33–55.

Sperry RW. Some general aspects of interhemispheric integration. In: Mountcastle VB, editor. Interhemispheric relations and cerebral dominance. The Johns Hopkins Press: Baltimore; 1961.

Sperry RW. Chemoaffinity in the orderly growth of nerve fiber patterns and connections. Proc Natl Acad Sci U S A. 1963;50:703–10.

Sperry RW. Brain bisection and mechanisms of consciousness. In: Eccles JC, editor. Brain and conscious experience. Springer-Verlag: New York; 1966a.

Sperry RW. Mental unity following surgical disconnection of the cerebral hemispheres. Harvey Lect Ser. 1966b;62:293–323.

Sperry RW, Gazzaniga MS, Bogen JE. Inter hemispheric relationships: the neocortical commissures; syndromes of hemisphere disconnection. In: Vinken PJ, Bruyn GW, editors. Handbook of clinical neurology, vol. 4. Amsterdam: North Holland Publishing Company; 1969. p. 273–90.

Sperry R. Some effects of disconnecting the cerebral hemispheres. (Nobel Lecture December 8, 1981). Science. 1982;217:1223–6.

Sperry R. Consciousness, personal identity and the divided brain (Public Lecture Presented at the Smithsonian Institute, December 1977). Neuropsychologia. 1984;22:661–73.

Staddon J. The new behaviorism. New York: Psychology Press; 2014.

Stapp HP. Mind, matter, and quantum mechanics. Berlin: Springer-Verlag; 1993.

Steinmetz PN. Alternate task inhibits single-neuron category-selective responses in the human hippocampus while preserving selectivity in the amygdala. J Cognitive Neurosci. 2008;21:347–58.

Stokes MG, Kusunoki M, Sigala N, Nili H, Gaffan D, Duncan J. Neuron. 2013;78:364–75.

Stoughton CM, Conway BR. Neural basis for unique hues. Curr Biol. 2008; 18:R698–9.

Stuart GJ, Sakmann B. Active propagation of somatic action potentials into neocortical pyramidal cell dendrites. Nature. 1994;367:69–72.

Stuss DT, Alexander MP, Lieberman A, Levine H. An extraordinary form of confabulation. Neurology. 1978;28:1166–72.

Stuss DT, Gow CA, Hetherington CR. "No longer Gage:" frontal lobe dysfunction and emotional changes. J Consult Clin Psychol. 1992;60:349–59.

Swanson LW. Brain architecture. New York: Oxford University Press; 2003.

Swindale NV. Cortical cartography: what's in a map? Curr Biol. 2001;11: R730–3.

Tamamaki N, Nojyo Y. Preservation of topography in the connections between the subiculum, field CAl, and the entorhinal cortex in rats. J Comp Neurol. 1995;353:379–90.

Terzian H, Ore GD. Syndrome of Klüver and Bucy; reproduced in man by bilateral removal of the temporal lobes. Neurology. 1955;5:373–80.

Thompson RF. James Olds, a biographical memoir. Natl Acad Sci. 1999;77.

Thomson AM, Bannister AP. Postsynaptic pyramidal target selection by descending layer III pyramidal axons: dual intracellular recordings and biocytin filling in slices of rat neocortex. Neuroscience. 1998;84:669–83.

Thomson AM, Bannister AP. Interlaminar connections in the neocortex. Cerebral Cortex. 2003;13:5–14.

Thomas N. Are theories of imagery theories of imagination? An active perception approach to conscious mental content. Cognitive Sci. 1999;23:207–45.

Thomson AM, Larry C. Functional maps of neocortical local circuitry. Front Neurosci. 2007;1:19–42.

Tinsley CJ. Coding of distributed, topographic and non-specific representations within the brain. Biosystems. 2008;92:159–67.

Tinsley CJ. Creating abstract topographic representations: implications for coding, learning and reasoning. Biosystems. 2009;96:251–8.

Tononi G, Edelman GM, Sporns O. Complexity and coherency: integrating information in the brain. Trends Cognitive Sci. 1998;2:474–84.

Tononi G, Koch C. The neural correlates of consciousness. An update. Ann NY Acad Sci. 2008;1124:239–61.

Tononi G, Koch C. Consciousness: here, there and everywhere? Philos Trans R Soc B. 2015;370:1–18.

Trevarthan C. In: Gregory RL, Zangwill OL, editors. The Oxford companion to the mind. Oxford: Oxford University Press; 1987.

Treves A. Computational constraints that may have favoured the lamination of sensory cortex. J Comp Neurol. 2003;14:271–82.

Tsao DY, Livingstone MS. Mechanisms of face perception. Annu Rev Neurosci. 2008;31:411–37.

Tulving E. Episodic and semantic memory. In: Tulving E, Donaldson W, editors. Organization of memory. New York: Academic Press; 1972. p. 381–403.

Tusa RJ, Palmer LA, Rosenquist AC. The retinotopic organization of area 17 (striate cortex) in the cat. J Comp Neurol. 1978;177:213–36.

Tyndall, John. Fragments of science. 1871. p. 86–7.

Ungar G. Molecular coding of memory. Life Sci. 1974;14:595–604.

Ungerleider LG, Bell AH. Uncovering the visual "alphabet": advances in our understanding of object perception. Vision Res. 2011;51:782–99.

Van Wagenen WP, Herren RY. Surgical division of commissural pathways in the corpus callosum: relation to spread of an epileptic attack. Arch NeurPsych. 1940;44:740–59.

Verkhratsky A, Krishtal OA, Peters OH. From Galvani to patch clamp: the development of electrophysiology. Pflugers Arch—Eur J Physiol. 2006; 453:233–47.

Viskontas IV. Advances in memory research: single-neuron recordings from the human medial temporal lobe aid our understanding of declarative memory. Curr Opin Neurobiol. 2008;21:662–8.

Wandell BA, Brewer AA, Dougherty RF. Visual field map clusters in human cortex. Philos Trans R Soc B. 2005;360:693–707.

Wandell BA, Dumoulin SO, Brewer AA. Visual field maps in human cortex. Neuron. 2007;56:366–83.

Watson JB. Psychology as the behaviorist views it. Psychol Rev. 1913;20: 158–77.

Watson JB. Behaviorism. New York: W.W. Norton & Company; 1925.

Warrington EK, Shallice T. Word-form dyslexia. Brain. 1980;103:99–112.

Warrington EK, Shallice T. Category specific semantic impairments. Brain. 1984;107:829–54.

Westheimer G. Center-surround antagonism in spatial vision: retinal or cortical locus? Visual Res. 2004;44:2457–65.

Whitehead AN. Adventures of ideas. New York: The Free Press; 1933.

Whitsel BL, Rustioni A, Dreyer DA, Loe PR, Allen EE, Metz CB. Thalamic projections to SI in macaque monkey. J Comp Neurol. 1978;178:385–410.

Wilms CD, Hausser M. Reading out a spatiotemporal population code by imaging neighbouring parallel fibre axons in vivo. Nat Commun 9. 2015;6:6464.

Winocur G, Moscovitch M. Memory transformation and systems consolidation. J Int Neuropsychol Soc. 2011;17:766–80.

Yuste R, MacLean JN, Smith H, Lansner A. The cortex as a central pattern generator. Nat Rev Neurosci. 2005;6:477–83.

Yuste R. Dendritic spines and distributed circuits. Neuron. 2011;772–81.

Yuste R. Electrical compartmentalization in dendritic spines. Annu Rev Neurosci. 2013;36:429–49.

Yuste R. From the neuron doctrine to neural networks. Nat Rev Neurosci. 2015;16:487–97.

Zaidel E. Unilateral auditory language comprehension on the Token Test following cerebral commissurotomy and hemispherectomy. Neuropsychologia. 1977;15:1–18.

Zeki S, Aglioti S, McKeefry D, Berlucchi G. The neurological basis of conscious color perception in a blind patient. Proc Natl Acad Sci U S A. 1999;96:14124–9.

Zhan C, Luo M. Diverse patterns of odor representation by neurons in the anterior piriform cortex of awake mice. J Neurosci. 2010;30:16662–72.

Zola SM. The neurobiology of recovered memory. J Neuropsychiatry Clin Neurosci. 1997;9:449–59.

Index

A

Abeles, Moshe, 204n11
ablation paradigm, 158–60, 163, 164
ablation paradigm fallacy, 158, 164
action potential. *See* spike
activation paradigm, 164–6
activation paradigm fallacy, 164
Adrian, Edgar Douglas, 204, 204n12, 205
aggression, 121, 122
Akelaitis, Andrew, 125, 128, 141
alien hand, 134
Alzheimer's disease, 95, 99, 122
amnesia
  anterograde, 84, 97–9
  retrograde, 84, 97–9
amygdala, 94, 113, 120–2, 157
anaxagoras, 233
ancient greeks, 10, 254
animal spirits, 198
anterior cingulate cortex (ACC). *See* cortex, cerebral
anterior commissure, 127
anterograde amnesia. *See* amnesia
antidepressants, 202
antipsychotics, 202
apical compartment, 210, 211
apical stalk, 210, 212
apical tree, 213
Aristotle, 21, 22
aspect dualism, 13–14, 257
assembly
  coherent, 247
  random, 247
automaton, 137, 140
axon, 51, 52, 124, 170, 171, 176, 177, 192, 193, 199, 200, 203–8, 212

S. Sevush, *The Single-Neuron Theory*,
DOI 10.1007/978-3-319-33708-1

B

Bain, Alexander, 174–8, 182, 228, 228n25
BEC-like condensation, 245
behaviorism, 37–40, 234
behaviorist manifesto, 38
Bell–Magendie law, 33, 34
Berkeley, Bishop George, 9
Berridge, Kent, 116, 116n17, 117, 117n20, 117n21, 118n22
binding problem, 16, 209–10, 217, 218
binocular rivalry, 73, 74
blind spot, 79–81, 143
blob, 71, 191
Block, Ned, 141n34
Bogen, Joseph, 124, 124n1, 126, 127, 127n9, 128
Bohr, Niels, 238–40
Bose-Einstein condensations (BEC), 245
brain
  brainstem, 19, 75, 112
  cerebellum, 19
  cerebral cortex (*see* cortex, cerebral)
  cerebral ventricles, 23
  cerebrum, 19, 20
  diencephalon, 19
  hypothalamus, 112
  thalamus, 75
bridge locus, 16
Broca, Paul, 26, 28, 156n17
Broca's area, 35, 156, 157, 160, 161
brodmann area, 30
bursty output, 196

C

Cajal. *See* Ramon y Cajal, Santiago
Capgras syndrome, 95
cardinal cells, 185–6
cascade model of PO-PFC functioning, 166
catastrophic interference, 90
cell
  amacrine, 51
  bipolar, 51
  bistratified, 68, 69, 71
  ganglion, 51, 56–8, 63, 68–72
  horizontal, 51
  koniocellular, 71
  magnocellular, 71
  midget, 68, 69, 71
  parasol, 68–71
  parvocellular, 71
cell body (soma), 171, 199, 208, 210
center-surround arrangement, 57
central executive, 88, 89, 155
Chalmers, David, 4, 12n7, 14, 16n11, 22, 22n3, 232n3, 236
chemoaffinity mechanism, 188
chimeric figure, 144
choice, 1, 13, 21, 61, 129, 133, 145, 225, 239, 253–4
cingulotomy, 119
Clifford, William, 232, 232n2, 233, 234n4
clinico/anatomical correlation, 28
cluster plasticity, 215
cluster sensitivity, 213–15
coarse coding, 186, 219
cochlea, 75
cognitive revolution, 40, 44

cognitive therapy, 120
collapse of the wavefunction, 239, 260
collapse postulate, 237–9
color
  achromatic, 68–71
  cardinal axes, 70
  chromatic, 68–72
  constancy, 72–3
  opponent pairs, 68, 69, 72
color space, 66, 70
combination problem, 241–2, 246, 247
combinatorial explosion, 227, 228
commissurotomy. *See* split-brain surgery
complexity, 15, 23, 37, 38, 60, 112, 171, 172, 175, 197, 258
computer assisted tomographic (CAT) scan, 28
concussion, 97
conditioning
  classical (Pavlovian), 40, 121
  operant (Skinnerian), 39–40, 47
cones
  L-cones, 65, 67
  M-cones, 65
  S-cones, 65
confabulation, 103–6, 145, 146
connections
  afferent, 155–7
  bilateral, 121
  convergent, 59, 71, 174
  divergent, 71, 174
  efferent, 155–7
  feedback, 43, 52
  feedforward, 42, 45, 51, 52, 174
  input, 157
  lateral, 43, 45, 71
  output, 174
  reentrant, 43
conscious awareness, 6, 140
conscious computer, 3
conscious experience (conscious awareness)
  abnormalities of, 161
  absence of, 247, 248
  anatomy of, 83
  categories of, 48, 49, 108
  complexity of, 258
  components of, 77
  content of, 10, 219, 220, 227, 245, 258
  cortical substrate for, 48, 123
  definition of, 5, 15
  duration of, 255
  emergence of, 15
  existence of, 1, 11, 12
  generation of, 50
  ineffability of, 5, 6, 68
  localization of, 22
  multiplicity of, 258
  neural substrate for, 48, 123
  non-verbally reportable (nvr-), 140
  pathway for, 258
  physical substrate for, 78, 218, 229, 246
  separate spheres of, 137, 147
  simplest instances of, 152
  sparing of, 163
  spatial encoding of, 218, 221
  subjective nature of, 5
  two centers of, 146
  two streams of, 148

conscious experience (*cont.*)
  verbally reportable (vr-), 140, 152–67, 185, 191, 192, 195, 196, 199, 206, 209, 213, 217–29, 231, 232, 242, 245, 246, 248, 259
consciousness
  access, 141
  core, 249
  dual, 136–49
  easy problems of, 4, 6
  hard problem of, 4, 6, 217, 234, 259
  neural correlate of (NCC), 16–18
  neuronal correlate of, 228
  phenomenal, 141
  primary, 249
  quantum, 231–49
  single-neuron theory of, 227
  verbally reportable neural correlate of (vr-NCC), 151
conscious perception, 2, 8, 22, 23, 50, 55, 58, 68, 72, 74, 77–9, 89, 97, 102, 107, 108, 175, 209, 210
consolidation, memory
  synaptic, 96–8
  systems, 98–9
contralateral, 131, 132
contrast detection, 57
convergence zone, 151, 153
copenhagen interpretation, 240
corpus callosum, 124–8, 131, 133, 134, 136, 144, 146–8, 188
cortex, cerebral
  anterior cingulate (ACC), 118–19, 154, 157
  anterior temporal, 121
  association, 188
  auditory, 189, 192
  entorhinal, 90–2
  frontal, 37, 52, 77, 87, 89, 103, 153
  gustatory, 76
  inferior temporal, 60, 61, 74, 92, 189
  insular, 110–13
  interoceptive, 112
  motor, 36, 37, 188
  occipital, 153
  olfactory, 76
  orbitofrontal (*see* prefrontal)
  parahippocampal, 90–2
  parietal, 153
  perirhinal, 90–2
  posterior, 37, 43, 47, 89, 106
  prefrontal (*see* prefrontal cortex)
  premotor, 36, 37, 188
  pyriform, 76
  sensory, 36, 37, 75, 189, 193
  somatosensory, 75, 76, 189, 192, 194
  tactile, 36
  temporal, 35, 52, 60, 61, 64, 74, 92, 112, 121, 153, 189
  visual, 52, 54, 57–60, 71, 75, 189
cortical column, 193
cortical functions
  reading, 17
  smell, 70
  speaking, 19, 53, 140
  taste, 70
  vision, 4
  writing, 110

cortical layers
L1, 195, 196, 211, 213
L2/3, 194–6, 210, 211, 213, 218–23, 230
L4, 194–6, 211
L5, 195, 197, 210, 211, 213, 220–4, 228, 230, 231, 243, 248, 258
Craig, Bud, 112, 112n6
Crick, Francis, 6, 16n11, 19, 62n22, 151, 153n7, 154n9, 160n23, 164n34, 171n9, 186n29, 194n73, 196n80, 211n21, 222n8, 228n21, 236, 247, 254n6
cross-cueing, 142, 148

D

Damasio, Antonio, 6n4, 104n41, 113n12, 113n13, 119, 119n24, 119n25, 151–3, 156n13, 159n21, 160, 160n25, 160n26, 164n33, 249, 249n29
Dandy, Walter, 124, 125n3, 160, 163
Darwin, Sir Francis,
deja vu, 94–5
democritus, 10
dendrite
apical, 210–12
basal, 211, 213, 218, 221, 228, 230, 231, 243, 258, 259
dendritic spine, 202–3
Dennett, Daniel, 10, 11, 77, 78, 78n55, 151n2
depression, 32
Descartes, Rene, 8, 9, 11, 32–345
digital camera, 65, 79, 187
digit span, 86
directed modular pathway, 43, 45, 47–52, 56, 60, 77, 81, 83, 110, 122, 123, 152, 155, 157, 169, 183, 258
directional cortical pathways, 35, 41, 43
dominance
mixed, 123, 149
reversed, 123
dorsal stream, 52–4, 71
dreams
conscious experience during, 107
REM sleep and, 165
drug addiction, 118
duality
mind/brain, 3, 10, 14, 257
object/object, 14–15
subject/object, 14–15
wave/particle, 238

E

eating disorder, 118
Edelman, Gerald, 6, 19, 225n10, 226n14, 227n16, 232, 249, 249n30
Edwards, Jonathan, 217, 243
egyptians, 21, 22, 104
Einstein, Albert, 13, 237–9, 245, 257
electrical stimulation studies, 26, 95
electrotonic spread, 213
eliminative materialism, 10–13

emergence, 14, 15, 17, 48, 196, 233, 245
emotion, 6, 53, 109–11, 113–14, 120, 156
energy consumption, 192, 193
ephrins, 188
epilepsy, 62, 84, 125, 128
equipotentiality, 24, 27
equivalency principle, 237, 257
euphoriants, 202
events, 3, 7, 13, 28, 84, 85, 92, 98–102, 104, 106, 108, 110, 127, 145, 152, 165, 166, 182, 234, 240–2, 245–9, 252–5, 257, 259
excitatory postsynaptic potential (EPSP), 201

F

face cell, 61, 62
face identity cell, 62
false memories, 101
Fechner, Theodore, 13, 14
feelings
  associated with drives, 110, 114, 122
  cognitive, 96, 110
  emotional, 120, 156
  of familiarity, 108, 156
  of fear, 120
  hunger, 110, 112
  interoceptive, 112
  of knowing, 95–6, 108, 110
  pain, 156
  pleasure, 156
  thirst, 110, 112
filling-in (fill-in), 79, 81, 143, 144, 148
fireworks, 17
flicker fusion frequency, 255
free will. *See* choice
Freud, Sigmund, 39, 100, 100n32, 102
Frohlich events, 246–9
Frohlich, Herbert, 244, 245
frontal lobe damage, 46, 103–6, 159, 161–4
frontocentric theory, 153
functionalism, 10
functional MRI (fMRI), 28, 74, 81, 87, 164, 191, 192
functional neuroimaging, 87, 122, 152, 165, 191

G

gamma-amino-butyric acid (GABA). *See* neurotransmitter
Gage, Phineas, 159, 160
Galen, 21–3
Gall, Franz Joseph, 24–6
Galvani, Luigi, 198, 199
ganglion cell, 51, 56–8, 63, 68–72
Gazzaniga, Michael, 29n6, 127n10, 128–30, 134, 135n15, 135n16, 137, 138n22, 138n23, 142n39, 143n41, 144n45, 145, 145n46, 145n48, 146n49
generation problem, 15–18
geniculate (geniculate nucleus)
  lateral, 51, 57, 59, 73, 188
  medial, 75
Gerlach, Joseph von, 170, 209
Geschwind, Norman, 40, 41, 41n21, 126, 126n9, 134, 134n14, 142, 142n40

glob, 71, 72, 191
glutamate binding sites, 182, 214
Goblot's conjecture, 164–6
God, 9, 13, 239
Golgi, Camillo, 170, 171, 209
graceful degradation, 186
grandmother cell, 227, 228
grandmother cell conundrum, 227–8
gray matter, 20, 23, 24
Gross, Charles, 23n4, 24n5, 60, 60n19, 61, 141, 190n56, 227n18
guillotine dream, 165

H

Haller, Albrecht von, 23, 24
hallucination, 65, 107
hand cell, 61
Hebb, Donald, 161, 161n28, 176, 176n18, 177, 178, 182
hebbian learning, 90, 177, 188
Heilman, Kenneth, 36n13, 55, 158
Heisenberg, Werner, 238
hemisphere
  dominant, 135
  left, 123, 127, 131–3, 135–40, 142–5, 147, 148, 151, 163, 258, 259
  mute, 139, 140
  right, 127, 131, 133, 135–41, 143, 144, 145, 147, 163, 248, 249, 259
  speaking, 140
hierarchical modular processing, 64
hierarchical pathway, 73, 75, 77, 81, 112
high energy transverse modes, 244
hippocampus
  CA1, 90, 91
  CA3, 90, 91
  dentate gyrus, 90, 91
  subiculum, 90, 91
hippocrates, 21, 31
HM, 83–6, 90, 99, 107
Hodgkin–Huxley (H–H) model, 205–9
homunculus, 77, 78
humoral theory, 31
Huxley, Thomas, 171, 171n6
hyperorality, 121
hypersexuality, 121

I

idealism, 9–10, 13
identity code, 219
identity thesis, 13
illusion, 9, 12, 22, 79, 80, 143–6, 246, 259
  visual, 143
imagery, 107–9, 192
impulse control, 113
incentive, 113, 121
ineffability, 5, 6, 68
information
  bits of, 226
  capacity, 184, 197, 224, 225, 227
  information flow, 47, 48, 51, 92, 118, 130, 152, 193, 196, 199
  Shannon information, 224, 225
information processing model, 35, 44

information processing pathway, 44
inhibitory interneuron, 193, 196
inhibitory postsynaptic potential (IPSP), 201
input-output pathway, 24, 31, 34
instinct, 22, 113
integrate-and-fire, 173, 183
intelligence, 23, 29, 135
interleaving, 90
interoception, 110–13
interpreter, 146
intractable pain, 119
invisible gorilla experiment, 226
ion channels
  Ca^{++}, 182, 183, 214
  K^+, 200, 206–9
  Na^+, 200, 206–9, 212
ipsilateral, 131, 135
IQ, 84
isomorphic constraint, 252
isomorphism, 252

J

jamais vu, 95
James-Lange theory, 111
James, William, 34, 35n12, 79, 93, 96, 110, 111, 241, 255

K

Kanizsa triangle, 79, 80
Kluver–Bucy syndrome, 121, 122
Koch, Christof, 6, 6n4, 16, 16n11, 60n15, 81n62, 140n33, 154, 162, 184, 186n26, 186n28, 202n4, 202n7, 213n30, 214

L

labeled-line code, 219
Lashley, Karl, 26–7, 29, 30, 83, 83n1, 84, 85, 125, 176, 176n17
lateral inhibition, 192
law of dynamic polarization, 199, 200
law of parsimony, 237
Leibniz, Gottfried, 209, 210n14, 233, 234
  windmill metaphor, 209
light
  infrared, 67
  ultraviolet, 67
  visible, 67
liking, 116–18
local coding, 184
localization, 22, 24, 26–8, 30, 47, 71, 75, 83, 84, 153, 154, 162, 163, 187, 217, 258, 259
localization principle, 24
lock and key interaction, 200
long-term depression (LTD), 182, 229
long-term memory (LTM), 86, 89–93, 97–9, 106–8, 155, 156, 157
long-term potentiation (LTP), 182, 215, 229
low energy longitudinal modes, 244
luminance, 68, 73

M

mantis shrimp, 66
Maury, Louis Ferdinand, 166, 166n36
Maxwell, James Clark, 64, 64n26

Maxwell's equations, 237
McConnell, James, 178, 179, 179n19, 180
McGinn, Colin, 4, 4n2, 234, 242n14
medial temporal lobe (MTL), 84
mediodorsal nucleus of the thalamus, 118, 188
memory
 auditory, 4, 5, 35, 36, 75, 87, 89, 94, 143, 155, 175, 189, 191, 192
 childhood, 100
 episodic, 98, 99, 100
 familiarity, 93, 94
 procedural, 107–8
 recall, 93, 228
 recent, 99
 recognition, 93, 110
 recollection, 93, 95
 reconstructive nature of, 100
 remote, 94, 99, 104
 semantic, 98, 99
 visual, 88, 104
memory molecules, 178, 179, 181, 182
memory retrieval, 86, 92, 100, 102, 107, 175
memory trace, 83, 84, 89, 90, 92, 93, 96, 98, 100, 175, 177, 179
memory transfer experiments, 178, 179, 180, 182
menu of possibilities, 238, 239, 240
Meyers, Ron, 126
microelectrodes, 182
microtubules, 243
mind, 3, 6–9, 10, 14, 21, 23–31, 34, 37, 43, 50, 65, 86, 96, 97, 111, 119, 133, 136, 147, 154, 167, 170, 210, 215, 228, 237, 254
mind/brain interaction, 8, 9, 10
mind/brain problem, 1–18, 136, 158, 233, 234, 240, 258
mirror-reflected words, 107, 108
modular arrangement, 29, 30, 31, 44
monads, 233
monochromats, 66
Morse code, 205
MRI scan, 28, 162
MTL. *See* medial temporal lobe (MTL)
multifocality, 24
multivariate pattern analysis, 191

N

Nagel, Thomas, 4, 4n3, 5, 67, 142n36, 243n19
Na+-K+ ion pump, 206
nanophysics, 217, 243
natural selection, 31, 40, 66, 72, 113, 192, 201, 219, 245, 258
Nauta, Walle, 153, 153n6
nerves
 motor, 33, 171, 205
 sensory, 33, 112, 113, 171, 205
network, neuronal, 169–96, 206, 210, 218, 219, 222, 223, 228, 258
network-to-dendrite mapping, 220

neuron, 6, 16, 17, 18, 19, 20, 22, 30, 41, 45, 52, 57, 58, 59, 60, 61, 62, 63, 64, 70, 71, 72, 73, 74, 76, 81, 87, 90, 154, 166, 169–72, 172, 173, 174, 175, 177, 178, 183, 184, 185, 186, 188, 190, 191, 192, 193, 194, 195, 196, 197–215, 217, 218, 219, 221, 222, 223, 224, 227, 228, 229, 231, 232, 243, 246, 247, 248, 258, 259
neuronal representation, 183– 185, 186, 188, 258
neuronal representational field, 183, 186
neuron doctrine, 169–72
neurons with multiple receptive fields, 196
neurophysiological postulate, 176, 183
neuropsychological testing, 141, 162
neurotransmitter
  cholecystokinin, 202
  dopamine, 117, 202
  estrogen, 202
  excitatory, 193
  gamma-aminobutyric acid (GABA), 193, 201, 202
  glutamate, 182, 193, 200, 201, 214, 229
  inhibitory, 193
  norepinephrine, 201, 202
  oxytocin, 202
  somatostatin, 202
  testosterone, 202
neutral monism, 13
Newtonian physics, 8, 236, 238, 239
Newton, Isaac, 64, 64n25, 237
Newton's laws, 236, 237, 238
N-methyl-D-aspartate (NMDA), 182, 183, 213–15, 221, 225, 229, 245, 247, 258
  NMDA receptor, 182, 183, 214, 229
  NMDA spike, 214, 221, 222, 225, 229, 245, 247
Nobel prize, 37, 58, 128, 137, 171, 204, 205

O

OFC. *See* prefrontal cortex (PFC)
olfactory pathways, 132
omnidirectional pathway, 31, 32, 45, 50, 152, 258
opiates, 118, 202
  heroine, 118, 202
  morphine, 118
optic chiasm, 51
optic nerve, 51, 52, 80, 187
optic tectum, 187, 188
optic tract, 51
orbitofrontal cortex (OFC), 113, 114, 118, 120, 154, 155, 157, 159, 164, 166
orchestrated objective reduction, 242
organology, 25

P

panpsychism, panpsychist
  atomistic panpsychism, 233, 242
  holistic panpsychism, 233
  panpsychic explosion, 233

parallel distributed processing (PDP), 173
passive cable model, 213
patches, 58, 190, 191
pathway
feedback, 40, 42, 43, 45, 46, 47, 52, 118, 195, 196, 201, 207, 211, 213, 214
feedforward, 120
lateral, 43, 45, 51, 57, 59, 72, 80, 92, 153, 164, 187, 188, 192, 194, 195, 196, 211, 222
perceptual, 50, 74, 89, 156, 166
reentrant, 43
pattern completion, 91, 102
Pavlov, Petrovich, 37, 38, 39, 44, 47
Penfield, Wilder, 95, 153n5, 161
perception
active, 79, 96, 101, 171, 176, 185
color, 56, 64, 68, 73
form, 56, 60, 63, 64
visual, 50, 51, 53, 56, 64, 73, 74
persistence memory, 228–9, 258
personality, 21, 29, 84, 141, 159, 160, 161
photoelectric effect, 237
photon, 65, 235, 245, 259
photoreceptor, 2, 51, 56, 63, 65, 66, 67, 68, 80
photosynthesis, 243
phrenology, 25, 29
phylogenetic cutoff, 232
Pick's disease, 122
pineal gland, 8
pinwheels, 190
planaria, 178, 179, 180, 181
Planck, Max, 212
plasticity, 27, 215
pleasure center, 114, 116
pleasure molecule, 117
point neuron model, 172–3, 197
pontifical cell, 186
pooled response code, 219
postsynaptic potential (PSP), 200
potentialities, 240
prefrontal cortex (PFC)
dorsolateral (DL-PFC), 154, 157, 163, 188
dorsomedial (DM-PFC), 154, 155, 157, 163
orbitofrontal (OFC), 113, 114, 118, 120, 154, 156, 157, 159, 164, 166
polar (PO-PFC), 154, 155, 157, 166
ventrolateral (VL-PFC), 154, 155, 157, 159, 161, 162, 163, 165, 166, 167, 169, 189, 195, 197, 217, 218, 223, 231, 243, 248, 258
principle of continuity, 34, 35
pseudosentience, 247, 248, 249, 259
psychic blindness, 121
psychophysical parallelism, 13
Puccetti, Rolando, 148, 148n52
pyramidal neuron, 193, 195, 196, 197, 202, 210–13, 218, 221, 222, 223, 224, 228, 231, 243, 248, 258, 259

Q

qualia, 251
quantized behavior, 239
quantum coherence, 243

quantum events, 240, 241, 242, 245, 246–8, 253, 254, 257, 259
quantum mechanics, 8, 9, 236–7, 238, 239, 240, 243, 253, 260

R

Ramon y Cajal, Santiago, 170, 176, 202
rate code, 205
realism
  direct, 77, 78
  indirect (representationalism), 77, 78
receptive field, 56–61, 68, 183–5, 186, 192, 193, 196, 228, 230
receptor
  NMDA (*see* N-methyl-D-aspartate (NMDA))
  olfactory, 76
  opioid, 118
  photo, 2, 51, 56, 63, 65–8, 80, 235, 237, 243, 245, 246, 259
  taste, 76
reflex principle, 24, 31–6, 39, 47
refrigerator light analogy, 166
rehearsal
  auditory/verbal, 89
  mental, 89
representation
  coarse coded, 186
  combinative, 185
  compact, 185
  dense, 184
  dispersed, 185
  distribution, 185–6
  explicit, 73, 78, 231
  holographic, 186
  neural, 231
  neuronal, 183–9, 258
  perceptual, 185, 186
  sparse, 184, 185
resting potential, 206, 207
reticular theory, 170, 171
retina, 2, 51–2, 54, 56, 57, 60, 63–6, 68, 70, 71, 74, 75, 79, 80, 158, 187, 189, 190
retrograde amnesia. *See* amnesia
Ribot's law, 99
RNA, 181
rods, 63, 65, 73, 75
route
  phonological, 54, 55
  semantic, 54, 55
routine quantum events, 246–8
Russian doll phenomenon, 229

S

schizophrenia, 95
Schroedinger, Erwin, 238
Schroedinger's equation, 237–40, 254, 260
Seager, William, 15, 241
Searle, John, 210, 243
Seashore Tonal Memory Test, 86
seizure, 62, 84, 124–8, 161
sensation, 1, 7, 12, 21, 25, 64, 112, 118, 119, 205, 223
sentience, 6, 14, 15, 17–19, 22, 33, 48, 217–18, 230–3, 236, 242, 249, 254, 256, 259
sentient events, 242
Shannon, Claude, 224, 225
short-term memory (STM), 86–9, 92, 97, 106, 108, 155

shunting, 229
Siewart, Charles,
single-neuron sentience, 217–18, 230
single-neuron theory, 217–30, 246, 253–7, 259
Skinner, Burrhus Frederick, 39, 40
slave modules, 88–93
social contagion, 101
soma (cell body), 172, 200
soul, 7, 35, 124
spatial encoding model, 221
specious present, 256
Sperry, Roger, 126–30, 135, 137, 138n22, 139n25, 140n32, 141, 142, 143n43, 145, 147, 187, 188n33
spike
  axonal, 208, 213
  back-propagating (BAP), 212
  dendritic, 213–15, 229, 258
  initiation, 212, 214
  NMDA (*see* N-methyl-D-aspartate (NMDA))
  non-propagating, 212
  propagating, 208, 212
spinal cord, 19, 20, 24, 33, 34, 35, 154
spine problem, 203
Spinoza, Benedict de, 13
split-brain
  paradigm, 123–9
  procedure, 123–8
  syndrome, 128, 134, 136, 141, 143
split-brain surgery, 147
spontaneity, 46, 47
stellate neuron, 193–6, 211
stimuli
  auditory, 94, 191, 192
  gustatory, 94, 156
  olfactory, 156
  tactile, 87, 155, 194
  visual, 52, 54, 56, 57, 60, 87
stimulus
  conditioned, 38
  external, 175
  punishing, 110
  rewarding, 110
  unconditioned, 38
string theory, 256, 257
stripe, 71, 73, 191
stroke, 28, 55, 122, 163
subcortical structures (subcortical brain regions), 107, 151, 195, 259
subjectivity, 6, 15, 232, 253
subjectivity barrier, 253
subject/object duality, 15, 231, 235, 236, 241
substance dualism, 7–9, 13
summed-population code, 219
superconductivity, 244, 245
superfluidity, 245
supervenience, 223
supralinear summation, 214, 215, 245–7, 258
sympathy model, 31, 32, 201
synapse
  cannabinoid, 202
  dopamine, 202
  norepinephrine, 202
  opiate, 202
  serotonin, 202
synaptic activation patterns, 218, 221–4, 228, 243, 245, 258
synaptic gap, 176, 200, 209
syncytium, 170, 171, 209

T

T-duality, 256
tic douloureux, 119
tip-of-the tongue phenomenon, 95, 110
top-down, 43, 106, 213
topographic mapping
  functional topographic maps, 188, 190
  structural topographic maps, 187, 188, 189

U

ultraviolet catastrophe, 237
unidirectional pathway, 31
unique hue, 72

V

vacuous elements, 233
valence, 109, 110, 118
vegetative state, 20, 163, 232
ventral pallidum, 116, 118
ventral stream, 52, 53, 55, 56, 62, 63, 71, 73, 92, 113, 120, 121, 155, 156, 157
  and conscious experience, 60, 68, 69, 72, 152–7
  TE, 55, 60, 63, 70, 73, 74, 190
  TEO, 55, 60, 63, 70, 73, 74, 190
  V1, 41, 42, 55, 56, 57, 59, 60, 63, 64, 70, 71, 72, 73, 74, 183, 189, 190, 191, 192
  V2, 41, 42, 55, 56, 59, 60, 63, 70, 71, 72, 73, 191
  V4, 41, 42, 55, 60, 63, 70, 71, 72, 73, 74, 191
ventral striatum, 114, 116, 118
visible spectrum, 65
visual agnosia, 121
visual field, 57, 58, 59, 63, 80, 128, 129, 130, 131, 132, 138, 143, 144
visual word-form area (VWFA), 54
VL-PFC, 155, 156, 157, 158, 159, 161, 162, 163, 165, 166, 167, 169, 189, 195, 197, 217, 218, 223, 231, 243, 248, 258
voltage-gated ion channels
  K^+, 206, 207, 208, 209
  Na^+, 200, 206, 207, 208, 209
vr-conscious experience. *See* conscious experience
vr-NCC. *See* consciousness

W

wanting, 116, 117
the war of the ghosts, 100
Watson, John Broadus, 38, 39
wavefunction, 238, 239, 240, 260
wavelength, 1, 2, 5, 64, 65, 66, 67, 68, 72, 75, 245
  discriminating ability, 66
  of light, 2, 64
  of sound, 75
waves
  electromagnetic, 68
  gamma, 16
  light, 2, 75
  micro, 68
  radio, 67
  sound, 75
  terahertz, 67
  x-ray, 27, 67
Wechsler adult intelligence scale, 135

Wernicke, Carl, 35, 41, 89, 103
Wernicke's area, 35, 89
Whitehead, Alfred North, 234, 235, 236, 240, 241
Whitehead/Heisenberg picture, 240–1
white matter tract, 37, 124
Wigan, Arthur Ladbroke, 147, 148
willfulness, of right hemisphere, 136
Willis, Thomas, 23
wire length, 30–1, 192
Wisconsin card sort, 46
working memory, 88–92
    central executive, 88, 89
    slave modules, 88–92

Z

zombie, 6

The manufacturer's authorised representative in the EU is Springer Nature Customer Service Centre GmbH, Europaplatz 3, 69115 Heidelberg, Germany. If you have any concerns regarding our products, please contact ProductSafety@springernature.com

Printed and bound by CPI Group (UK) Ltd, Croydon, CR0 4YY
30/09/2026
02225656-0012